The Holocaust and its Contexts

Series Editors

Olaf Jensen
University of Leicester, UK

Claus-Christian W. Szejnmann
Loughborough University, UK

Aim of the Series

More than sixty years on, the Holocaust remains a subject of intense debate with ever-widening ramifications. This series aims to demonstrate the continuing relevance of the Holocaust and related issues in contemporary society, politics and culture; studying the Holocaust and its history broadens our understanding not only of the events themselves but also of their present-day significance. The series acknowledges and responds to the continuing gaps in our knowledge about the events that constituted the Holocaust, the various forms in which the Holocaust has been remembered, interpreted and discussed, and the increasing importance of the Holocaust today to many individuals and communities.

More information about this series at
http://www.springer.com/series/14433

Istvan Pal Adam

Budapest Building Managers and the Holocaust in Hungary

palgrave
macmillan

Istvan Pal Adam
Budapest, Hungary

The Holocaust and its Contexts
ISBN 978-3-319-81613-5   ISBN 978-3-319-33831-6   (eBook)
DOI 10.1007/978-3-319-33831-6

Cover illustration: © Agencja Fotograficzna Caro / Alamy Stock Photo

Printed on acid-free paper

This Palgrave Macmillan imprint is published by Springer Nature
The registered company is Springer International Publishing AG Switzerland

Acknowledgements

There are a couple of people without whom this book would never have come into being. First of all, I dedicate this work to Magda, without whom I would be an unhappy clerk in public administration, or a mediocre lawyer in a criminal law office. My special thanks go to my PhD supervisors at the University of Bristol: Tim Cole and Josie McLellan, who for years directed my research with professional advice and provided me with dozens of reference letters. I am beholden to my mentor, teacher and good friend, Michael L. Miller, who encouraged me to pursue a career in academia after he supervised my MA studies at the Central European University. I have to mention another friend from Budapest, Maté Rigó, who first introduced me to the archival material concerning the building managers. I am indebted to Ben Evans and Jesintha Susaimani, who corrected my language slips, and to the archivists of the Budapest City Archive (BFL), who tirelessly dealt with my annoying requests for thousands of research documents.

My research was made possible (in part) thanks to my tenure as a Tziporah Wiesel Fellow at the Jack, Joseph and Morton Mandel Centre for Advanced Holocaust Studies, United States Holocaust Memorial Museum. Here I benefitted greatly from the discussions and seminars with other fellows and many employees of the Centre: so many talented people among whom I am especially glad for Paul Morrow's valuable suggestions. I am also grateful to the Emerging Scholars Program at the Mandel Centre for Advanced Holocaust Studies, and personally to Steven Feldman for the support in the preparation of the manuscript and of the book proposal. This book also incorporates research conducted as a fellow at the Vienna Wiesenthal Institute. I would like to acknowledge the support of the Claims Conference, whose generosity allowed me to fully concentrate on researching and writing while I was a Claims Conference Saul Kagan Fellow in Advanced Shoah Studies. I have received further support from the European Holocaust Research Infrastructure (EHRI), from Yad Vashem, from the Prague Jewish Museum, from the late Ian Keil and from the J. & O. Winter Fund. Finally, I have completed the manuscript of this book during my tenure at the CEFRES, French Research Centre in Humanities & Social Sciences, benefitting from the support of the Charles University in Prague. This book was supported within the framework of the project "Homo Sociologicus Revisited" (No. 15-14478S) of the Czech Science Foundation GAČR. Although these institutions and persons contributed to the book, the statements made and views expressed, however, are solely my responsibility.

I would also like to thank my family for their support: my father, András, my mother, Julianna, my brother Zoltán and his wife, Anikó, my aunts, uncles, cousins, nephew and niece. I have to mention furthermore my late great-aunt, Stefka, the sister of my maternal grandmother, on whose lower arm I first saw the blue numbers tattooed in a German concentration camp, and whose books I always adored. I dedicate this book to her memory, and also to the memory of those relatives who were murdered during the Hungarian Holocaust: to my paternal grandfather, my great-grandmother, aunts and uncles.

CONTENTS

LIST OF FIGURES

INTRODUCTION

In the apartment building in downtown Budapest where I am living, there is an apartment on the ground floor, which is offered for tourists on the popular lodging website Airbnb, and also on Booking.com. I see here sometimes Chinese families, sometimes Europeans, who park their car next to the building, and their registration number tells me from which country they are coming. Usually I do not have much interaction with them, but the other day an American asked me for directions. Americans tend to be curious, so he asked me also about the yellow Star of David sign on the façade. When he got to know that it is there because seventy years ago the building belonged to the ghetto, it was a so-called "Yellow Star house" during the Holocaust, he got interested. He asked me whether Jews had suffered a lot in the apartment which he had just rented. "No"—I responded to him—"this was where the non-Jewish building manager lived." He sighed deeply with relief and went on to see the attractions of the city. If we had had more time to talk, or if I had not been worried about him spending sleepless nights in the apartment, I could probably have told him about how critical role these building managers or—using the French expression—concierges played in the ghetto period.

This book—through a history of the Budapest building managers or concierges—in Hungarian: the *házmester*—asks to what degree agency mattered among a group of ordinary Hungarians, who are commonly perceived as bystanders to the Holocaust? The novelty of my work is that I analyse the actions of a group of ordinary citizens in a much longer timeframe than Holocaust scholars usually do. Thus, I can situate the building managers' activity during the war against the background of how the profession originated and developed since the forming of Budapest as a by-product of the development of residential buildings. Therefore, this is not a classical Holocaust book: in certain respects it is more than that, but it is also less than that. It is much more because it searches for the origins of wartime behaviour in the pre-war times, and it is less, because there are no concentration camps in it. Instead, I analyse the building managers' wartime acts in the light of their decades-long struggle for a higher salary, social appreciation and their aspiration to authority. Instead of focusing on solely the usual pre-war antisemitism, I take into consideration other factors from the interwar times, such as for instance the tipping culture. Throughout the book, I argue that the empowerment of the building managers happened as a side-effect of the anti-Jewish legislation.

In Budapest, during World War II, the Jewish Hungarian residents were separated not into a single closed ghetto area, as happened for example in Warsaw or in other major cities of the region, but by the authorities assigning dispersed apartment buildings as "Jewish ghetto houses".[1] The almost 2,000 buildings were spread through the entire city and were marked on the façade by a yellow Star of David. The non-Jewish concierges serving in these houses represented the link between the outside and the inside world, and—to some extent—they enforced the anti-Jewish laws on the ghettoized people. In this book, I use sociological theory to show that these concierges, thanks to their social networks and focal position, became intermediaries between the authorities and the Jewish Hungarian citizens, which gave them much wider latitude than other so-called bystanders. In other words, an average Budapest building manager could bridge the structural holes between the ghettoized Jewish Hungarians and other elements of 1944 Hungarian society as a result of their social network.

Although Hungary formally joined the Axis only in 1940, the country implemented anti-Jewish laws as early as 1938.[2] In the middle of 1942, the Hungarian government forbade the employment of Jewish Hungarians as building managers or using the Hungarian term, *házmester*.[3] This was a well-thought-out order, as these concierges controlled very important aspects of everyday life: they kept a registry book of residents with all their personal data, they distributed food ration cards, they were responsible for the maintenance of air-raid shelters and they controlled the entrance of the apartment buildings by closing and opening the gate. All these were crucial, especially from March 1944 until February 1945, when some 200–220,000 Jewish Hungarians tried to survive the Holocaust in Budapest, a city already occupied by the German army.[4] However, building managers somehow slipped out of historical consciousness. Nobody has studied them in depth and they do not appear in contemporary Holocaust discourse, except in some survivors' memoirs and oral history interviews.[5] I encountered one of these memoirs in the April 2011 issue of *Szombat*, a political and cultural periodical, which published an interview with the late Dr Péter Popper, the influential psychiatrist.[6] In this, Popper talked about his father's communist friends who helped his family hide in a house in Apponyi Street [in Hungarian: *utca*] in October 1944, when the Hungarian Nazi movement, the Arrow Cross [*Nyilas*], came to power. I was particularly struck by the following anecdote which Popper recalled in the article:

> ...this building manager was also a communist. He was called András Szabó. He hid a bunch of people here: in a small apartment we were stuffed with twenty-odd other persons. ... And this was terrible, you wouldn't even think about this: there was no water, no toilet. Our luck was that there were plenty of old newspapers. Everybody did the "number two" on these papers. When someone was done, they wrapped it in the newspaper and put it in a wooden chest that was outside on the terrace. And there these things froze, and the chest slowly became full. When in January ... the Russians came in, they ran through the buildings looking for Germans and Arrow Cross fighters. Two of them with machine guns broke in to our place and saw that there were only twenty-odd wretched guys who were mere skin and bone. But they still suspected something, and when they looked around they found the chest on the terrace. ... They knew immediately that this was where the treasure was hidden. They lined everyone up next to the wall and started to open the papers whilst we watched, petrified. They opened the first one, the second one, the third one but, finding only turds, concluded that we must be the trickiest company. The diamonds were surely hidden at the bottom. They opened all the packages, one by one ... once they had opened the last and it became clear that there was no treasure they became so angry that they shot through the ceiling—but fortunately, not us.[7]

What is important for me from this story is, firstly, that building managers did have a significant influence on who survived World War II, as the man in Popper's case for example could hide more than twenty people. Secondly, Popper's story is an excellent example of how rich autobiographical sources can be. In fact, they often can tell much more than the official documentation of an event. Therefore in this book oral histories and memoires will balance and supplement the referred archival files and retribution documents. One example of this is my interview with Nissan Hirschman, who grew up in Budapest as the son of a building owner.[8] Talking about the interwar years, Nissan could precisely recall the specific odour of the building managers' apartment, which he described as very similar to that of typical Hungarian food, the smell of stuffed cabbage. Most of the lodges in which these concierges lived were one-room studios, thus the smell of food was present everywhere. Being the friend of the boys whose parents worked as building managers, Nissan learnt a lot about their family background and about the expectations they faced as children. His impression was that these concierges strongly sought an immediate rise on the social scale, and that was what they prepared their offspring for. This desire became especially significant during World War II.

My conclusion is that the actions of so-called bystanders, and the relationship between Budapest building managers and Jewish Hungarians, can only be understood by placing them in a longer durée. Furthermore, with this book I want to suggest that it is impossible—and unhelpful—to allocate building managers to a single category such as "bystander" or "perpetrator". Individual building managers both helped and hindered Jewish Hungarians, depending on circumstances, pre-existing relationships and the particular point in time. In the fast-changing, fluid and complex environment of Budapest in 1944, categories such as "perpetrator", "bystander" and "rescuer" were blurred and difficult to distinguish. Through an examination of this environment at the micro-level of the apartment building, this book brings the complexity of the Holocaust sharply into focus."

NOTES

1. Whenever it is possible I try to avoid naming the persecuted Hungarians as Jews, as this term is ambiguous in the sense that it is in accordance with the categorization of the interwar and wartime anti-semitic systems. In addition to this, as Tim Cole notes (Tim Cole, "Constructing the 'Jew', Writing the Holocaust: Hungary 1920–1945", *Patterns of Prejudice*, vol. 33, no. 3, 1999), the usage of this term could also often contradict the self-definition of these people. As Gábor Gyáni puts it, most victims of the Hungarian Holocaust were assimilated Jews, thus, they had at least a hybrid Jewish-Hungarian or Hungarian-Jewish identity as a result of the assimilation. (See this in Gábor Gyáni, *Múlt és Jövő* 2011/1 p. 35.) That is why, rather than

the simplistic use of the word Jew, I prefer to write about Jewish Hungarians, which expression includes both of the victims' possible (or hyphenated) identities.

2. In fact Act XXV of 1920, the Numerus Clausus Law, was the first interwar anti-Jewish regulation. This act targeted the limiting of the enrolment of Jewish Hungarians into Hungarian universities.

3. Throughout the book I will use the terms "building manager", "*házmester*" and "concierge" interchangeably, although it is worth noting that the official Hungarian term was "*házfelügyelő*". This is how the referred government order, the 3.530/1942. B. M. Decree (B. M. means Interior Ministry.), called them. See it in *Belügyi Közlöny*, vol. 47, no. 25 (1942), pp. 1082–1084.

4. Gábor Kádár and Zoltán Vági, *Self-financing Genocide: The Gold Train, the Becher Case and the Wealth of Hungarian Jews* (Budapest: CEU Press, 2004), p. 19.

5. One important exception is Máté Rigó's article, the "Ordinary Women and Men: Superintendents and Jews in the Budapest Yellow-Star Houses in 1944–1945", *Urban History*, vol. 40, no. 1, 2013, pp. 71–91. However, Rigó only writes about the second half of World War II, while my book presents a much broader picture, where the growing wartime importance of the building managers is contrasted in a historical prospective to their profession's earlier development.

6. This part of Péter Popper's memoir was published in *Szombat*, vol. 23, no. 4, 2011, p. 16.

7. Ibid.

8. Oral history interview with Nissan Hirschman, conducted by the author on 1 November 2010, in Budapest.

CHAPTER 1

Building Managers Caught in the Middle: The Social History of Budapest Concierges Until 1943

This [reform] would be necessary, even if the building managers were the best characters, even if they were ministers or university professors. But they are none of these. They are simply building managers as God created them. And God created this type badly: to be rough, rude and unpleasant, who are keen on getting more and more power.[1] (Andor Gábor, 1911/12)

1 THE EMERGENCE OF A METROPOLIS AND THE RISING NUMBER OF BUILDING MANAGERS

Budapest was formed as late as in November 1873 from three settlements: Pest, which had at that time 200,000 inhabitants, Buda with 54,000 residents and the much smaller Óbuda with 16,000 persons. In this newly created city the number of buildings doubled within 25 years. In the year 1895 alone, 595 tenement houses were built, with 12,783 rooms in them.[2] Hardly any of these buildings were higher than five stories, and almost all of them were constructed around a square courtyard, in an open-corridor system.[3] This meant that corridors were open on the courtyard side, allowing anyone walking or standing on these corridors to be seen from any other point of the building. This form of construction was a fast and cheap way of building, but its downside was that poorer tenants—factory workers and other labourers—shared the common space, the courtyard, with the bourgeoisie.[4] The richest lived on the first floor, the upper middle classes on the second and sometimes on the third, while

© The Author(s) 2016
I.P. Adam, *Budapest Building Managers and the Holocaust in Hungary,*
The Holocaust and its Contexts, DOI 10.1007/978-3-319-33831-6_1

the poorest inhabited the top of the apartment buildings. The concierge lived on the ground floor, and this was the location of various shops and workshops as well. The clearest indication of poorer social status was the shrinking size of apartments and rooms on the upper floors, where the top-floor room-and-kitchen apartments lacked the space designed for maids, and often even toilets and bathrooms.[5] This intimacy of the shared courtyard, where the tenants could observe the differences in their wealth, and the open-corridor system, is something which later gained importance during the war years, and especially in the yellow-star house period.

At the turn of the century Budapest was the most rapidly developing metropolis of the world with its population growing by 78 percent between 1890 and 1910, up to 880,000 inhabitants.[6] This was largely the result of internal migration, which is even more obvious if we take into consideration that in the same timeframe the overall Hungarian population grew only by 20 percent. This process changed the ethnic composition of the city too, resulting in a rapid Hungarianization. Whereas in 1880 only 51.7 percent of the inhabitants were Hungarian speakers—many of the residents had German or Slovak origins—by 1910 eight out of ten Budapest workers had Hungarian as their mother tongue.[7] The influx of rural Hungarians made accommodation prices skyrocket, a situation which only worsened after World War I, when millions of ethnic Hungarians found themselves outside the country's borders thanks to the Paris Peace Treaties.[8] In addition, as a result of the war, building construction slowed down dramatically. While in 1900 670 new tenement houses were finished, in 1917 only 37 were under construction, a number which fell to seven in 1919.[9] In 1921, overcrowding reached a new peak, with an average of six people per room in Budapest.[10] This process further increased the level of rental fees, which around 1910 were the highest in the entire continent.[11] The only restriction which limited this process was that rental fees could not be raised more often than once per year, but no cap was imposed on the rate of these fees.[12] When World War II broke out there were 26,988 buildings in the Hungarian capital, with almost the same number of building managers serving in them.[13]

Holding an apartment, a room or at least a bed was the key in establishing an urban life for those freshly arrived from the countryside and also for those locals who started a new life. The mother of a newly married Budapest woman, for instance, was so desperate that she offered duvets as an incentive to anyone able to get an apartment for the couple.[14]

Building managers were in a better position than an average newcomer in the city, since they were provided with free lodging by the landlord. Therefore, this position served as a springboard for thousands who otherwise were left short of the financial means or opportunities necessary for renting an apartment. Usually the building manager lived in a lodge next to the entrance gate, from where he or she could keep an eye on everyone exiting or entering the building. They had to keep the entrance of the apartment building closed between 10 p.m. and 6 a.m., to prevent robberies. This spatial control was the most important part of the concierge's role. Additionally, concierges were also responsible for cleaning the inside of the building and the pavement just in front of it. They also dealt with the postman and with other officials. In the early years of the city successful candidates for the concierge post were usually handymen whom the landlords could entrust with minor repairs.[15] In these days, being a concierge represented only a part-time post, where the holder of this post received his major income from other professional activities, such as running a workshop, being a security guard and so on.[16] In the 1920s and 1930s, with the emergence of large apartment buildings, this changed, and a growing number of *házmester* started to live solely from earnings received from landlords and tenants (Figure 1.1).

Building managers gained a reputation for being unkind and often hostile, an attitude that was probably due to the fact that they needed to keep order without formal authority.[17] In any case, the building managers were concerned about their negative image from very early on. In July 1905, their journal complained that concierges had gained notoriety for being rude. The article also warned that if a building manager was found guilty of professional misconduct, then this affected the reputation of all the 10,000 *házmester* working at that time in Budapest.[18] A resident of Almássy tér 8 for instance described the *házmester* as a wild and surly person, who once went as far as slapping a tenant.[19] Interestingly, despite the incident he kept his job, as the landlord appreciated his ability to maintain stability in the building.[20] Thus brutality was to some extent tolerated, if not encouraged by the building owners. However, the tenants—being on the receiving end of this anger—suffered because of the hostility. Furthermore, the negative effects of urbanization, and especially a break in their social ties, could play a part in the concierges' potential aggression. It was Zygmunt Bauman who pointed to the dismantling of traditional rural communities as one of the factors that allowed the Holocaust to happen.[21]

Figure 1.1   The location of a building manager's lodge in a modern Budapest apartment building built in 1937. The window of the lodge provides a view onto the entrance lobby (Photo taken by the author, 2014)

2   En route from Poverty to the Middle Classes

Written at the time when being a building manager was only a part-time job, László Németh's account of the contemporary Hungarian school system is a sociographical study which gives us an insight into the nature of the concierges' post as a transitional social position. Németh later made a name for himself as a writer, but at this time he was primarily a medical practitioner in various schools, among others the Medve utca civic school.[22] Because of his employment he had access to the social milieu studies the school prepared about the parents it dealt with.[23] Using these files, Németh gave a precise description of the parental backgrounds of the pupils attending the Medve utca civic school between 1873 and 1934, but especially in the 1920s and 1930s. Civic school was a step between the elementary school and the grammar school.[24] It was a place where tuition fees were affordable for the lower middle classes too, and from where a talented and hardworking student could even reach the baccalaureate with some luck.[25] Therefore, this was an important step for those wanting to acculturate into the bourgeoisie, and at the same time it represented a necessary but painful step down for those children, whose families had suffered significant financial losses.[26]

The children of building managers—according to Németh—were absolutely overrepresented in this school. He stressed that every fourth Medve utca school child's parent was a concierge.[27] Regarding the broader Hungarian society of the early 1930s, he observed, "the most important channel of the middle class' rejuvenation is the building manager trade."[28] He added that three-fifths of the building managers came to Budapest after World War I, where "they bow and scrape for one or two decades, until their sons with the baccalaureate in hand occupy their place in the sunny part of the society."[29] However, Németh explained that there were huge differences among families belonging to this vast group, which at some point he deemed purgatory. On the one hand, there were the poorest concierges serving in villa buildings. These were inhabited only by the landlord and his family, consequently these *házmester* could not count on tips from other tenants. Moreover, they were also left without income from operating the elevator, collecting the rubbish, and so on.[30] Their most important benefit was free accommodation, but even this was often in the cellar.[31] On the other hand, in the late 1930s the richest building managers already lived in two-bedroom apartments with 140–200 pengő salaries per month.[32] There were also those who moved in the opposite direction on the social scale, for example the train officer, who according to Németh had to apply for a concierge job as a result of his growing number of children (seven). It says a lot about the shame this step meant that all their relatives stopped keeping in touch with them once the father started to work in his new position. Similarly, a war veteran lost his well-paid job as a ticket conductor due to the injuries collected as an army man, which is why he became a concierge and gardener for a richer family, where his wife did the cleaning. Their earnings were no more than 80 pengő per month and the free use of an apartment.[33]

In between the two extremes—small villas versus large and modern apartment buildings—lived most of the building managers, with still significant differences in their circumstances. Németh mentions two fathers who belonged to the second poorest parental group within the concierges' heterogeneous pool. The first was a roofer, who earned 5–20 pengő per week, and who—together with his family—also served as concierge in an *older* building. In this case the age of the apartment building served as an indication of the rather limited earnings. Their apartment is described as a basement under street level. They had lived there for 11 years in poverty and dirt.[34] The second one was a carpenter's assistant and at the same time building manager, with 18–20 pengő weekly income. This family lived also in the basement in a damp apartment, where, nevertheless, the employee of the school noted the bright clean and new furniture.[35] But the vast majority of concierges lived in ground-floor studios or room-and-kitchen lodges. Once their position became a full-time job, they spent day and night here, sharing the quickly multiplying tasks with their family members.[36] From these tiny apartments the building managers sent their offspring to the civic schools, and pushed them to climb up with hard work to the rank of the bourgeoisie. This transitional social character is important to keep in mind when considering why so many sons of building managers joined the Arrow Cross party and militia in 1944, which might have also seemed like an opportunity for a radical jump on the social ladder.

3   EN ROUTE FROM PART-TIME POST TO FULL-TIME EMPLOYMENT AND THE ACCULTURATION OF THE BUILDING MANAGERS

Although being a concierge in Budapest at the beginning of the twentieth century meant no more than a part-time job with a very modest income, nevertheless, technical developments—for example, the introduction of elevators, central heating, both manually operated—created a need for continuous involvement in the life of an apartment house. Changes in social life also pointed towards the direction of full-time employment as the emerging nightlife of the city attracted more and more tenants, and since the tenants at that time did not have a key to the main gate of the building, they had to wake up the *házmester* if they arrived home late at night.[37] A third factor to consider is the high unemployment rate, especially following the Wall Street Crash of 1929, which had a twofold effect. On the one hand, there were fewer available jobs, on the other hand, the landlords could set stricter conditions of employment. For instance, this is how a job announcement looked like in 1933: "*házmester* wanted in a four-storey corner building. ... Ideal candidates should be responsible, reliable and intelligent. *No supplementary work allowed.* Retired policemen or gendarmes go to the front of the line."[38] The last sentence of the advert is significant, because the transformation of this post from a part-time into a full-time job, and especially the constant presence in the apartment building, made the building manager appropriate also for the close surveillance required by the secret police. This sort of need was present particularly since the 1919 Hungarian Bolshevik revolution, and the concierges' post was ideal for spying on the residents. They saw who exited or entered the building and when, and they could also observe the life of the tenants from close range. The Budapest municipal decrees on housing matters listed the multiplying obligations of the building managers.[39] In 1936, this included regular cleaning of the staircases, the fence, the courtyard and the pavement; operating the elevator and the central heating; collecting the tenants' rubbish; maintaining the internal building order and checking the building's fire protection status after gate closure.[40] Concierges were also obliged to keep the pavement next to the building and the gateway tidy.[41] As a result, they were busy all day; they hardly left the building, and they saw everything that was going on there. Therefore, their originally limited role tended to evolve over the interwar period to be far more of a full-time role. Obviously, multitasking had its limits, and in larger tenement houses only the well-organized cooperation of an entire family unit could deal with all the required jobs. Hence, if we want to draw the profile of an average Budapest building manager in the 1930s, we need to think of a married person, who was born in the countryside, and put most hopes into their children's potential social progression.

Reading about their heavy workloads, it is little surprise that the concierges formed trade union-like associations to represent their interests. These organizations played an important part also in the acculturation of the newcomers. They taught the existing social rules of city life, a set of behavioural patterns to their members, plus they also provided courses on practical issues such as dealing with the electricity, hot water and so on. This was all the more crucial as many of the building managers arrived in Budapest from the provinces to take up the job without knowing the city, as did for example the newly married Mr and Mrs Pusztai. Their wartime efforts in saving Jewish Hungarians were recognized in the Hungarian Holocaust Memorial Centre, in 2012 (Figure 1.2).[42]

Figure 1.2   Lajos Pusztai and his wife, Gizella Skultéti, the building managers of Falk Miksa utca 6 (A photo from László Pusztai's collection)

According to their son, "[m]y father came from Simontornya, my mother from Tapolca, both came from the provinces. But when they got married they started their life in Budapest, because we had some relatives already living here who arranged for them to get the building manager post in Falk Miksa utca 6. And that was a big thing, because it came with an apartment, a sure thing."[43]

Newcomers like the Pusztais were unfamiliar with the type of behaviour expected from the *házmester*, and thus, it needed to be learned. Social norms are rules of conduct followed by individuals within a particular group. Such norms work alongside existing legal and moral rules.[44] Social norms are a type of learned-behaviour, conduct that circulates within a specific group, in this case among the Budapest building managers. Newcomers like the Pusztais joined either the *Házfelügyelők Országos Nemzeti Szövetsége* [Building Managers' National Alliance] or the so-called *Házfelügyelők Nemzeti és Gazdasági Egyesülete* [Building Managers' Nationwide and Economic Association], where they became aware of the most important rules quickly. The difference between the two organizations was primarily in their territorial focus: the former represented almost exclusively Budapest concierges, while the latter recruited most of its members from provincial towns. Both of these organizations ran a series of social events including excursions and dinners, where sometimes popular folk songs were performed. In 1925, the Building Managers' National Alliance's library was open Mondays and Tuesdays from 6 p.m. to 8 p.m., and in the same period members could also play billiard in the club room. Perhaps the members could benefit the most from the courses organized by these organizations on the basic duties of the concierges. The Building Managers' Association's advertisement for their 1942 course gives an insight into how the complexity of the *házmester*'s tasks further increased: "the topics of the course include everything that a good building manager has to know … for example, operating the elevator, heating, protection against frost, against electric shocks, in general about electricity and gas, how to save coal, all about the bells, about sewage systems, about chimney, about fire, about air-raids…"[45] As a Budapest concierge sadly concluded, his day looked like this: "from 10 p.m. till 5 a.m. gate duty, from 5 a.m. cleaning of the pavement, after which, around 5.30 the garbage truck arrives. Then, I have to quickly clean the staircases, because from 8 a.m. various enquirers start, such as postman, policeman, chimney sweep, etc. After lunch all building managers rest for a while (if the residents let them), and in the evening their job restarts with collecting the garbage from the apartments."[46] The tenants could sense the frustration of the concierges. A telling episode that captures how the lowly ranked *házmester* sent a message of his negative feelings to the residents appears in the autobiography of Tivadar Szinnai, who describes their building manager's morning routine with the following words: "It is the first streak of dawn. Pekarek, the building manager is clattering things, fumbling around in the courtyard. In the daybreak he always comes out to wake up the tenants. And in the back of the building a thrush starts singing."[47] Naturally, the constant service was so exhausting that the building manager could only manage this if some part of his burden was taken on by his wife.[48] Often there was a gender division of labour among couples who jointly fulfilled the tasks of a building manager. At the Pusztais, for example, it was the husband who slept in his clothes in order to be able to react quickly to the late arrivals' calls in the night, while his wife dealt with all the paperwork.[49]

The periodicals of the building managers' organizations appeared to be particularly effective educational tools.[50] For instance, the *Házfelügyelők Lapja*, [Journal of Building Managers] published a regular column entitled "How we should not act?", with everyday examples in it of improperly behaving concierges.[51] The editor of the same journal published an article on why he did not feel like giving a big tip to a *házmester*, because in the middle of the night she had simply opened the gate for him without saying a word. His conclusion is that the building managers have to approach the tenants and their visitors urbanely, because "the more politely we behave the more we are going to be appreciated, and what is the most important, we are going to earn more money as well."[52] Thus, a clear direction had been given to the readers about how a good *házmester* should act. As we shall see in the final chapter of this book, remarkably, Jewish Hungarian tenants sometimes tended to complain during and after the war just because their concierges did not follow these basic rules of conduct.[53]

4   BUILDING MANAGERS UNITED AND THE ANACHRONISTIC NATURE OF THE GATE-MONEY SYSTEM

Building managers felt scattered and powerless, which is why their first association in Budapest was formed as early as 1896. This was when the first issue of the building managers' journal was published in a bilingual, German-Hungarian form, which gives an idea of the multicultural melting pot nature of the city at this time.[54] This first building manager association aimed to represent approximately 10,000 concierges, and requested proper accommodation, a yearly fixed salary, a three-months' notice period in case of dismissal, a retirement fund to which landlords would pay monthly subsidies, and finally, higher gate-money [*kapupénz*]. I find it significant that their journal's very first issue deals extensively with the question of the gate-money, a phenomenon that was a good indicator of how social development stuck and could not keep pace with the urban development. Thinkers and writers bemoaned the general social backwardness of Hungary, which seemed anachronistic compared to the fast industrial modernization and urbanization of Budapest, and which created frustrated masses in various segments of early twentieth-century Hungarian society. Sándor Márai, in his *Memoir of Hungary*, blamed the political and financial elite, and the nobility for not contributing proportionately to the cost of the society:

> And this was the crux of the problem, for the inhabitants of Castle Hill in Buda and then the nation's wealthy living elsewhere, these cultured ladies and gentleman with the refined tastes, forgot to pay their taxes. ... The aristocrats survived the cataclysm unscathed, and in their absent-mindedness they forgot about what the privileged in France, England and then America had already been compelled to accept with gnashing teeth in this century: they did not pay progressive real inheritance tax ... they did not pay the full income tax ... and, most of all, they did not pay progressive real wages.[55]

Márai's words apply neatly to the Budapest building managers' bosses, the building owners or landlords, who did not pay real wages for their concierges.[56] Instead, they kept alive a retrograde arrangement, the so-called gate-money [*kapupénz*] system in the apartment buildings up until the post-World War II period. In this set-up, tenants got a key only to their apartment but not to the entrance gate. The landlords' interest in this was that it provided external payments for their employee, as those tenants who arrived home when the gate was already closed had to wake up the building manager and pay him for admitting them. Since the Budapest night offered more and more entertainment, the concierges received more and more of the so-called gate-money, and thus absurdly they were paid by the tenants and not the landlords. As the pre-World War I popular columnist Andor Gábor puts this, "the Budapest resident does not understand his rights. He does not feel that he has a right to enter his apartment even during the night, and that it should be the landlord who pays for the gate-opening, and not him."[57]

The building owners were highly present in the assembly of Budapest and in Hungarian public life, and thereby were able to maintain this arrangement.[58] A governmental decree on housing affairs set the minimum fees rewarding the concierge for opening the gate of an apartment building between 10 p.m. and 6 a.m., and providing the elevator on demand.[59] In 1924, the so-called "*kapupénz*" [gate-money] between 10 p.m. and 12 p.m. was 500 korona, whereas after midnight this sum doubled and went up to 1,000 korona.[60] Later, from 1936 onwards, it was set at 10 fillér before and 20 fillér after midnight.[61] For the elevator the residents only had to pay after 10 p.m. and before 6 a.m., however, anyone else, regardless of the time, paid every occasion 1,000 korona to avoid climbing the stairs.[62] It was possible to close the gate earlier than 10 p.m., however, it was not allowed to require gate-money before this hour.[63] If a building manager requested higher gate-money than the set amount, they could face a legal procedure with a potential six-month-long prison term at the end of it.[64] Representatives of the authorities, such as policemen, were not supposed to pay a fee at all. Until the late-arriving tenant covered the distance from the gate to their apartment, the building manager had to provide necessary light as well.[65] In 1924, the 500 korona basic gate-money was the equivalent of the price of a box of matches. Nevertheless, the assumption was that a polite and well-serving *házmester* received a much higher sum than this. Therefore, what is fascinating here is that these payments were set by a municipal or governmental decree at a minimum level, above which they worked like tips. Yet, Andor Gábor— who lived in a Budapest apartment building, and who had to regularly deal with a building manager like this—felt that the part that exceeded the fixed price was rather a bribe than a tip. Writing in 1911/12, he commented that the richer tenant paid a sort of protection bribe to save himself from the potential harassment of the building manager.[66] Thus from the tenant's point of view the residents did not tip the *házmester*, rather they paid him to buy a better standard of service than the usually offered averagely unpleasant treatment with which the building managers normally approached the residents. These nuances gained real significance in the Holocaust period, when tipping or bribing appeared to be decisive in certain situations where building managers had to choose whom to help. This will be discussed in detail in a chapter about the saviours of Jewish Hungarians.

Although this sort of fixed payment was set for elevator use and also for garbage collection, conflicts between tenants and building managers erupted almost exclusively around the gate-money system.[67] Periodicals, especially the *Házfelügyelők Lapja* [Journal of Building Managers] serve as important sources for reconstructing the pre-World War II life of the concierges. This piece, which is pasted here as illustration, describes how hard it could be to deal with those tenants, who arrived home late at night after heavy drinking, and that several of these incidents ended with fatal injuries on the building manager's side.[68] (Figure 1.3)

Many of the disputes derived from the fact that tenants had to wait rather long until their concierges opened the gate. Andor Gábor, the

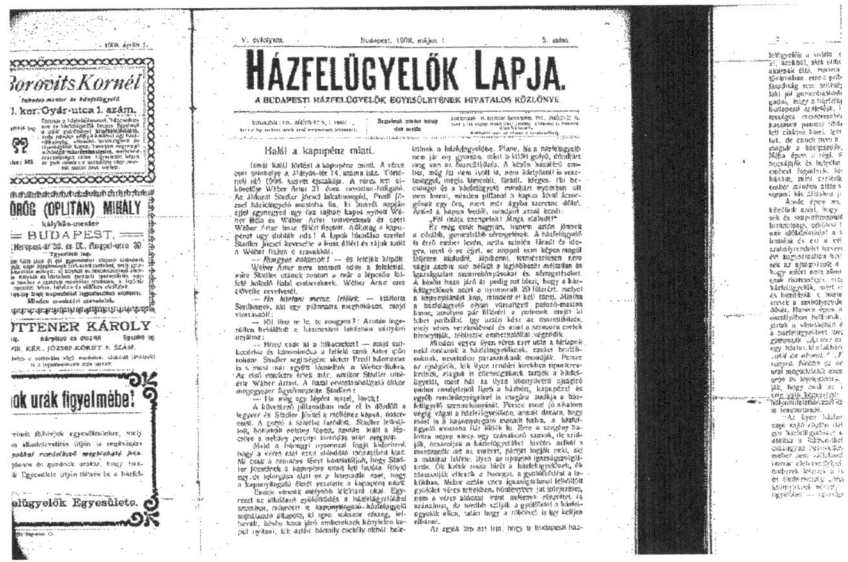

Figure 1.3   The Journal of Building Managers from 1908, a scan from the National Széchenyi Library, OSZK FM3/6497

author of the book *Pesti Sirámok* [Laments from Pest], was often forced to wait literally hours until the building manager reacted to his ringing the bell in the night. The first reaction from the *házmester* was to ring a response bell, which informed the tenant waiting outside the gate that the concierge had received his request, had woken up, and it was only a matter of time until he came and admitted the tenant.[69] At this point— as Andor Gábor writes—"the question is the outfit of the *házmester*: he either dresses up in a good-looking clothing before we meet, which takes him even more time, or I have to face all the secrets of his underwear. Should I say that I am not interested in them?"[70]

The journal of the building managers dealt with the topic of night-time gate-opening with striking frequency. In 1925, it reported that "many tenants complained to the housing authorities because of the torture they had to bear when they wanted to enter into their apartment building after 10 p.m. According to them, if someone happens to arrive to the gate after midnight, he or she often has to wait for hours. When finally—follow-ing several rings of the doorbell, and banging on the gate—the building manager appears, he is obviously angry as he has to get up four-five times per night. This way two suffering and disappointed parties face each other by the time the gate finally opens ... That is why it would be good to introduce the gate-key system, which already works in Vienna, Berlin, Munich and in many other foreign cities."[71] In the following year, in January 1926, the same periodical published an article which collected counter arguments against the gate-key system, asking who would let in those tenants who forget their gate-keys at home, or those non-residents who intend to visit a tenant living in the building[72] The debate reached the assembly of Budapest, and what was decisive was that the police authorities made it clear that giving a key to the tenants would mean a significant risk to public order. They were especially worried about the residents' iceboxes which stood on the corridors, and the merchants' carts parked in the courtyards.[73] The Association of Building Owners also supported keeping the prevailing order, as they were concerned that it would be difficult to make sure that the tenants closed the gate after entering or exiting.[74] These arguments raise a smile today; however, at that time these were serious questions, and a lot depended on them.

After all, the gate-money arguments and most of the building managers' problems were all about one issue, namely that although their tasks increased, the concierges were less and less adequately paid. The pengő replaced the korona as the official currency of Hungary on 1 January 1927 (both of these currencies were subdivided into 100 fillér). The new currency was introduced by Act XXXV of 1925, but building managers were not happy about the changes this act brought. They remembered with nostalgia especially the pre-World War I times, when their gate-money was worth much more. As they wrote, "[t]hat peacetime 10–20 fillérs gate-money meant daily 2 koronas even in a building with only 10 apartments. In an apartment building with 30 apartment units—which was quite common—our income varied between 4–6 koronas. In contrast with this at that time a kilo of bread cost 26 fillérs, a kilo of meat 80 fillérs, and a fat goose was around 6–8 korona. Nowadays, the gate-income of a tenement with 10 apartments is an average 40 fillér, and that of one with 30 apartments varies from 1 pengő 40 fillérs up to 2 pengő, while a kilo of bread cost nowadays 40 fillér, a kilo of meat 3 pengő, a goose 18–20 pengő. While from the peacetime [pre-1914] daily income we could buy a kilo of meat, today it would hardly be enough for a loaf of bread."[75] Reading this quote it is noteworthy that some residents intended to save even on this devalued gate-money. In 1933, for example, a trial took place where the *házmester* sued his employers over years of unpaid gate-money. It was connected to an apartment building located in Nádor utca, in downtown Budapest, a building which was owned by the credit institution *Jelzálogbank*. It appeared that the two directors of this bank got gate-keys and neither them nor their relatives paid gate-money for the building manager, who after his dismissal sued them because of this and, at the end, was awarded 700 pengő as compensation.[76] In 1938, another Budapest concierge took legal actions against a tenant, who lived on the ground floor and avoided paying gate-money by climbing in and out through his window.[77] These legal proceedings were initiated mostly because an average interwar Budapest building manager earned the majority of their income through the gate-money. For instance, Lajos Üst, the concierge of Újpesti rakpart 6 earned 172 pengő monthly, out of which approximately 100 pengő consisted of the gate-payment.[78] Naturally, the exact ratio of gate-money and the fixed salary varied from building to building. Nevertheless, the outbreak of the war put a dramatic end to the profitable night-time gate-opening. When the Allied bombers forced the city into lights-out, the Budapest building managers had to sadly note that "in recent months, our society's nightlife is so much regressed, the gate opening is so much decreased, that from this activity our income is almost equal to zero."[79] Therefore, in the late 1930s and early 1940s the building manager's position represented more and more the combination of an extreme amount of work with low wages.

5   Building Managers Caught in the Middle

The insufficient earnings of the building managers and their growing role in the life of the apartment buildings created tensions. The *házmester* had to work in a socially tense arena, where conflicting interests of tenants, landlords and authorities met. Significantly, none of these groups felt allied enough to the building managers to campaign for their interests, which was mostly due to the awkward structure of their employment. To illustrate this, it is enough to think about the concierges' salary, which was by law defined as 2 percent of the rental fees a tenant paid to the landlord. Tenants gave this sum directly to the *házmester*.[80] This was the so-called "*házmesterpénz*" [*pénz* means money in Hungarian], which the tenants had to pay quarterly in addition to the rental fees.[81] In buildings where the *házmester* needed to deal with central heating and an elevator, their salary could rise up to 3 percent of the rental fees. Nevertheless, it was still far from enough to make ends meet.[82] Thus, the building manager was chosen by the building owner, who, although he employed him, did not really pay him enough salary. In most of the cases the landlord only provided the concierge with free accommodation.[83] Inasmuch as this structure was confirmed by legal means, yet it seemed ridiculous from the tenants' vantage point. Here it is worth turning again to Andor Gábor, who bitterly summed up this ambiguity: "I pay the person who was employed by the building owner for taking care of his building. Since this is clearly the landlord's building, nonetheless, I pay his employee. But this employee is not serving me, even though I pay him."[84] This structure made much more sense for the landlord. From the building owner's point of view it was less about employing someone; rather by choosing a concierge, he opened up a business opportunity for this individual. To take a contemporary example, the best this could be compared to is the owner of a stadium or a theatre, who leases the bar located in the building to an outside entrepreneur, who then can make a profit by running this bar. This explains why the building managers had to pay for cleaning supplies, and why they paid the electricity bill for the elevator.[85] In accordance with this, three members of a building manager's family had to pass an elevator-operator exam, and following this exam they could exclusively enjoy all income the tenants and their visitors paid after using this sort of transportation.[86] Only the concierge possessed a key to the elevator, and they vehemently opposed giving a key to the tenants, saying that this could lead to numerous accidents. In this way, they protected their financial interests.[87] But it was also the building manager who paid for the assistant building manager if he and his family could not deal with everything, and he decided to employ someone.[88]

Due to the specificities of their employment, concierges felt left alone in their struggles with the tenants. First of all, a building manager could find problematic the fact that although it was the landlord who regularly raised the rental fees, the building manager had to collect this money from the tenants, who then targeted him with their negative feelings.[89] Moreover, as the landlord also lived from the tenants' payments, he usually did not stand on the concierge's side when conflicts erupted between the tenants and the concierge, because the tenants provided him a significant monthly income and not the concierge. Every third of the fired concierges, on average, lost their job because the tenants were complaining about them to the landlord.[90] Another set of the *házmester*'s problem came from the obligation that they had to enforce not only the house rules, but also certain regulations of the police and the mayor's office. This is why their journal laments their pitiful situation in 1926, claiming, "the landlords say we are their employees, but they don't give us anything else other than the lodge. The residents say they are giving our income, because they pay the "*házmesterpénz*", just like the gate-money and the rubbish-money. The authorities say that theoretically the regulations have to be implemented by the landlords, but in practice they order us to do this."[91] This quote shows the direction of this profession's evolution: every aspect of society expected something from the concierges, but none of them was willing to fulfil their request for higher salary and higher prestige.

The schizophrenic construction of their position put the building managers into the centre of constant conflicts: battles which forced the *házmester* to stand up for their rights and form union-like organizations. The declared goals of these associations were always twofold: on the one hand they wanted to achieve a radical pay-rise, on the other hand, they demanded the resolution of their employment problems. When writing about any organized movement of Budapest workers in the interwar era, we have to keep in mind that following the early Hungarian Soviet revolution's fall in 1919, there was only a limited space left for any sort of trade union activity. Building managers were attracted by this revolution, which offered a radical change in the social setting. It is worth recalling the cult Hungarian novel, *Anna Édes*, in which one of the main characters is Ficsor the *házmester*. During the short-lived 1919 Soviet Republic this building manager described himself as an old Marxist. He quickly became the building warden, and as such "he enforced the decrees of the Soviet government, warned the members of the bourgeoisie not to even attempt any conspiracy, he was beating his chest and tended to point to his legs that were worn out because of climbing the stairs for years."[92] Although this is only a novel, Budapest building managers in fact did have to explain their actions to criminal investigators once Miklós Horthy took over governing in 1920. Some documentations of these enquiries survived in the post-World War II Communist Party's archive. This is how it is known that in 1919, during Béla Kun's reign, the building managers wanted vengeance against the class-based dictatorship [*"bosszút esküszünk az osztályuralom ellen"*], by which they meant that they revolted against the deadbeat, lazy building owners' rule.[93] Understandably, during the consolidation of the Horthy system Budapest concierges became much more modest; however, from 1924 onwards they restarted to publish their periodicals regularly. In 1927, several dailies reported that the Alliance of the Budapest Building

Managers had prepared a memorandum for the mayor of Budapest, Dr Jenő Sipőcz, outlining the wishes of the concierges.[94] In 1934, Boldizsár Friedrich, the Alliance's new president even visited the interior ministry to protest the maltreatment of the *házmester*.[95]

In 1932, the Alliance of the Budapest Building Managers (*Házfelügyelők Szövetsége*) united with the Craftsmen Concierges' Organization (*Iparos Házfelügyelők*), and in February 1933 this joint organization elected Boldizsár Friedrich as its president.[96] From this moment Mr Friedrich directed the united Budapest building managers until the second half of 1944, and he appeared to be a very successful leader. When he took over, the Alliance had approximately 600 members, but some ten years later as many as 5,000 concierges belonged to it. From 1937 this organization was called the Building Managers' National Alliance, and it provided not only free legal aid, library and funeral support, but it also worked as a job agency.[97] It was registered at Semmelweis utca 4, and interestingly the same address appears on the official documents of the post-World War II, pro-communist Building Managers' Free Trade Union, which arranged the denazification of the wartime concierges.[98] Although in the 1930s Friedrich turned the Building Managers' Alliance into a nationwide organization, most of its members resided and worked in the Hungarian capital. In contrast, the majority of the rival Building Managers' Nationwide and Economic Association's 3,000 members were employed in Hungarian towns, like Szeged or Kolozsvár/Cluj.[99] There was a constant animosity between these two organizations; for example, the Budapest *házmester*'s Alliance mocked the Building Managers' Nationwide and Economic Association as the Budapest agency of countryside concierges.[100] Beside the geographical distribution of their memberships, there were slight differences in the political orientation of the building managers' two main organizations. Friedrich's Alliance declared its clear non-political attitude from the very beginning.[101] Later, this centrist stance meant that the Alliance sought political support solely in the governing mass party of the 1930s and 1940s, the so-called National Unity Party [*Nemzeti Egység Párt*, after 1939 it was named *Magyar Élet Párt*].[102] On the contrary, the rival Building Managers' Nationwide and Economic Association gave more space in its periodical to articles written in a more nationalistic manner. This included topics like the territorial revision of the Trianon Treaty or the defence against the threat of communism, but starting from 1942 even anti-Jewish slogans appeared occasionally in this magazine.[103]

What is interesting is that the building managers regularly compared their work conditions to concierges working in other European metropolises. They noted that in Paris the concierges delivered the letters addressed to the tenants, as the postmen left them all unsorted at the lodge.[104] The Budapest *házmester* kept especially good contact with the building managers of Vienna, the *Christlicher Hausbesorger- und Portier Verein in Wien*. They knew that their Viennese colleagues only registered the main tenants, while in Budapest the subtenants had to be registered too.[105] In 1929, they learned that the gate-money was abolished in Vienna, all the tenants had their own key, and the gates of the apartment buildings had to be kept closed by these keys from 9 P.M. onwards.[106] Therefore they were aware of European social developments, but they chose to walk on a different path. What they wanted to achieve was a quasi-official role, or a semi-authority status, because they felt powerless. As one of them put this, "for all our problems it would be good if the building manager was not employed by the building owner, but one of the municipality's authorities."[107]

6   BUILDING MANAGERS AND THE ATTRACTION OF POWER

The Budapest building managers attempted to break out from their pitiful situation, and were looking for authority. Here the interwar house rules [*Házirend*] of an apartment building at Hársfa utca 10/a are illuminating, as they can help to understand why exactly concierges needed more power.[108] The owners of this tenement forbade the tenants to do their washing in their apartment units. Instead, the landlords asked the tenants to go up to the specially prepared washing room on the top floor. To ensure the observance of this rule—the house rule says—the owners ordered the building manager to enter the apartments and check whether the people renting them were or were not washing their clothes there. This inspection was obviously an action that interfered significantly into the private life of the residents, and it is also obvious that the concierge did not have a right to do that. To counteract this ambiguity, the house rules as a principle called all the tenants to cooperate with the building manager in following the rules of the apartment building. What might be behind this call was the awareness of the owners about the fact that they were asking the concierge to exceed his powers. The *házmester* was clearly not allowed to carry out a check like this: he had responsibility, but not power, and this is key to understanding why the building managers wanted an official or at least a semi-official status for themselves. Historically the concierges were short of the means with which to do a proper job, thus, they evidently craved authority. Apart from its necessity, authority could also bring social appreciation, which consideration seems to lay behind the fact that the Budapest *házmester*'s association asked the police to give them regularly a list of those individuals against whom arrest warrants were issued.[109] The way the Budapest concierges describe themselves (in 1925) is also worthy of note: "the building manager is like the eye of Budapest. He sees everything that is going on in the apartment building. His role is not only keeping the building tidy, delivering the official documents, etc., but he is also obliged to notice and report every little irregularity. This is essential, as this is how we can prevent serious tragedies. Thus, the building manager is not only the representative of the building owner, but he is more or less an official person…"[110] Therefore, the Budapest concierges wanted the recognition of their significance in the form of an official or at least a semi-official status, and in this sense their moment arrived with the outbreak of World War II.

As Hungary prepared for the war, in 1937 the government made the building managers responsible for the maintenance and supervision of the air-raid shelters.[111] Later, the Ministry of Defence assigned the check of the lights-out regulations also to the Budapest concierges. The constant presence in the apartment building, the frequent contacts with the police, and the knowledge of the residents' habits made the building manager suitable also for the tighter surveillance of the wartime society. Some regulations actually mirrored their semi-official role already in the interwar times, such as the compulsory address registration, which ordered each building managers to keep a "registry book of residents". This included the tenant's date and place of birth, religion, the name of their spouse, name and age of children, name of the tenant's parents, and even the temporary place of residence if they left the building for a longer period.[112] If the police found someone in the building not registered in this book, the concierge could be subject to heavy fines; yet, this threat does not explain all the sufferings the building managers caused. For example, I. D. recalled an incident from Stáhly utca 1, where non-registered persons resided in a building, which caught the concierge's eyes.[113] Mr D. and his parents lived here in relative comfort, until his maternal grandparents—along with five other relatives—arrived in 1942 from Nazi-occupied Slovakia. By this time in Slovakia deportations to Auschwitz were already on the agenda, and the seven escapees from the area of Körmöcbánya/Kremnica and Pozsony/ Bratislava sought a hiding place in Budapest. They were smuggled into the apartment, and by not leaving it at all, they tried to stay invisible. But one day, two of the younger refugees lost their patience and left the building, a move seen by the concierge. When they returned, the 50-year-old building manager notified the police. All seven were arrested and transferred to the detention centre, from where most of them were sent to concentration camps. Only three of them survived the Holocaust.

It was also the *házmester* who had to sign the registration form which the new inhabitants of any Budapest apartment building submitted to the police as a part of their address registration. In the late 1930s, with the introduction of anti-Jewish laws, in a city where most Jewish Hungarians lived an assimilated life and dressed like anyone else, the information kept in the "registry book of residents" could become crucial. Since Jewish Hungarians did not have to wear the yellow-star badge until April 1944, prior to this date mostly Hungarian concierges were aware of this personal data as they led the "registry book" and they signed the registration form.[114] For example, the so-called Third Jewish Law (Act XV of 1941) forbade Jewish Hungarians from marrying non-Jews, and it also penalized extra-marital sexual relations between Jews and "good Christians". Obviously, in these racial defilement or miscegenation cases it had significance if the *házmester* knew about a tenant's Jewish origin thanks to the registration process. The concierge had to also note among the first ones a sexual partner's regularity in visiting; therefore the building managers featured often in these trials as key witnesses.[115] There were occasions where their tasks led the building managers to witness intimate situations, which was the case in the Krausz trial. Here the concierge of Szinyei Merse utca 25 had seen light spreading through an open window on a night in early August 1942.[116] When she went up to enforce the lights-out regulations, through the open window, she saw the later defendant and the "victim" (meaning by this a Christian female tenant) lying next to each other in their underwear.[117] The building manager warned the "victim" that it was illegal to have sexual relations with a Jewish male. Despite this warning, she did not break ties with the defendant, which subsequently resulted in the incarceration of the man, thanks to the *házmester*'s declaration in the court room.[118] The building manager offered the information she gathered during her work for law-enforcing purposes without any hesitation.

As their influence grew, but also as Hungary's war efforts intensified, it became easier to find political supporters for the Budapest building managers. On 22 February 1942, at 9.30 a.m., the Building Managers' Nationwide and National Alliance celebrated the raising of its flag in the main hall of the Pesti Vigadó, perhaps the most attractive hall at that time in the city.[119] Beside the president, Boldizsár Friedrich, there was on the podium among other nobilities the wife of interior minister Ferenc Keresztes-Fischer, and Miklós Bonczos, who later became the head of the interior ministry in the Sztójay government.[120] They were watched by an audience of 2,500 Budapest building managers. Mrs Keresztes-Fischer used a simile in her speech which reflects the growing significance of the concierges: "as the Hungarian soldier defends the borders of the country, so too does the *házmester* defend the home, especially in terms of air-raid defence.'[121] (Figure 1.4)

Mrs Keresztes-Fischer was right: as the war progressed the importance of the concierges grew. In a couple of weeks her husband signed the 3.530/1942 B.M. decree, which from the middle of 1942 forbade the employment of Jewish Hungarians as building managers.[122] This was a well-thought-out order, not only because the first and second anti-Jewish laws had not restricted the number of Jews in this profession, unlike in other segments of the labour market, but also because by this time—went the argument—concierges controlled very important aspects of wartime everyday life.[123] In these months a new task was added to the building managers' to-do-list: they picked up the food ration cards at the police headquarters and had to distribute them to the tenants within 24 hours. That this was not an easy assignment is shown by a commentary entitled "Notes on the food ration cards" from July 1943. The author, an average Budapest *házmester*, suggests that either the concierges should get these cards earlier, or alternatively, they should have more time to distribute them, because "there is big responsibility on the building managers, since they have to suffer gravely after all mistakes. The authorities do not replace any lost or miscounted cards, and these cards can easily adhere to each other... It happened with several of our colleagues and happens continuously that they are left without a sugar ticket, fat ticket, or bread ticket, because they mistakenly gave two tickets to someone..."[124] In addition, the coal ration also depended on the concierges, who had to monitor which tenant had coal reserves in the cellar.[125]

In 1942, the interior ministry with its 3.530/1942 B.M. decree set up a restriction in terms of who (the so-called Jew) could not become *házmester* anymore. Prior to this, interwar legislation had set very basic requirements for building managers: anyone could hold this position if

A Szövetség zászlóavatási ünnepélyéről

Az elnöki asztalnál jobbról-balra, *vitéz Bonczos Miklós* állar. titkár, a kormányképviselője, mellette *Frigyich Boldizsár* országos elnök, az ünnepély elnöke, tőle balra *vitéz dr. Keresztes-Fischer Ferencné*, a belügyminiszter neje, a zászlóanya, utána *dr. Cselényi Pál* országgyűlési képv. a Szövetség díszelnöke.

Figure 1.4 A photo taken at the flag-raising ceremony of the building managers *Házfelügyelők Lapja*, vol. 19, no. 5, May 1942, p. 1. OSZK FM3/11448

they had Hungarian citizenship, were registered in Budapest, were able to speak, read and write properly in Hungarian, had a clean criminal record, and were not involved into the communist or socialist movements.[126] It was rather the building managers' organization that tried to add further limitations, for instance, they wanted to exclude anyone with an alcohol problem, because the *házmester* were concerned about their reputation.[127] Even when the 3.530/1942 B.M. decree was announced, the Building Managers' Nationwide and National Alliance's first reaction was to start worrying about who was going to take up the positions of those Jewish Hungarian concierges, who would be dismissed when the decree came into effect.[128] They estimated that this decree was going to result in the dismissal of approximately 1,500 Jewish Hungarians from their building manager posts. However, the authorities surprisingly made sure that the fired building managers and their families got shelter somewhere, as the decree made it compulsory for the successor of the Jewish building manager to offer an apartment in exchange.[129] The *Házfelügyelők Lapja* journal reported this change under the title "Changing of the guard", and this article made it clear how difficult it was to replace this number of concierges, especially since the new openings related almost without exception to the biggest apartment blocks of Budapest. It says,

> ...for these positions no applicant would be suitable who does not have a license to some crafts (plumber, locksmith, mason, etc.) ...Hence, it cannot be someone with a profession like confectioner, hairdresser or waiter. Even if this kind of applicant would have the sufficient apartment for exchange, it would be in vain: we would have difficulty finding a job for this applicant, since the building owners clearly want above all a good specialist. But the problem is that we hardly have any specialists, as most of those who are skilled enough already work as building managers, and as these people do not have any apartment to offer as exchange, we [as a job agency] cannot pave the way for a healthy promotion from the smaller buildings to the bigger ones.[130]

A much more radical account welcomed the decree excluding Jews from the *házmester* craft in *Nemzeti Házfelügyelő*, the periodical of the more revolutionary Building Managers' Nationwide and Economic Association. According to them,

> [t]his order was evoked by the practice of Jewish building owners, who, in 60 percent of the cases, employed Jewish building managers in the last two-three years. We regretted the fact that old Christian concierges, who

worked honestly and faultlessly for decades were fired, and instead mostly Jewish *házmester* appeared. This only could happen as the first and second anti-Jewish laws did not have any effect on the building managers. We, as a nationwide union, felt it necessary to call the attention of the competent authorities to this all the time. We reported our impressions, but carefully: we had to represent circumspectly the interest of the Christian building managers' society in this matter, otherwise many Christian concierges could lose their jobs and apartments subsequently. ... If todays' building manager did not fill such an important post, if he or she did not complete the authorities' work as he or she does, then it would not be that important who can become a building manager. But exactly because all the authorities know that in these times the building manager fills a responsible and essential guarding position, the change of the guard had to happen, even if it appeared abruptly for some people.[131]

Even if the anti-semitic logic of the above quoted excerpt is unacceptable, its author is right at least in the sense that the anti-Jewish legislation targeted less influential positions than that of the *házmester*. The first anti-Jewish law, Act XV of 1938 (usually called the First Jewish Law), aimed to limit the social influence of the so-called Jews by reducing the number of Jewish Hungarians to 20 percent in so-called liberal professions (for example: journalists and actors), and also in small-scale commercial and financial enterprises.[132] This could mean that up to 18,800 Jewish Hungarians would lose their jobs only in Budapest, and with family members the law endangered the livelihoods of some 60,000 people.[133] Despite the government's expectations, this bill did not stop the growing anti-semitic sentiment, which is shown by the extreme right *Hungarista* movement's mass demonstration held on 1 December 1938, and an attack against the Dohány synagogue in February 1939.[134] Events like this paved the way towards the Second Jewish Law (Act IV of 1939), which defined the Jew already on a racial basis rather than religious belonging. It affected everyone who had at least one Jewish parent or two grandparents.[135] It extended the anti-Jewish discrimination to all licensed trades where thousands of permissions for tobacco shops, pharmacies and so on were withdrawn.[136] In other fields of employment, where the First Jewish Law maximized the fraction of Jews in 20 percent, the quotas were further reduced. In intellectual professions the ratio of Jewish professionals was regulated in 6 percent while in finance and commerce in 12 percent; meanwhile, all Jewish civil servants were removed from their jobs.[137] It is estimated that approximately 60,000 Jewish Hungarians lost their work once the Second Jewish Law came into effect, but the legislation did not touch upon the building managers. Moreover, it also has to be noted that the wealthiest Jewish Hungarian entrepreneurs could operate as late as 1944, especially if their production served the Nazi armament programme. This is why, when in 1943 Hitler requested from Horthy, governing regent of Hungary, the radical solving of the Jewish problem, Horthy reminded Hitler that such a step could cause serious damage in the Hungarian armament industry.[138] Many of the Jewish Hungarian entrepreneurs invested their money into apartment buildings.[139] Perhaps there were some who employed Jewish Hungarians as concierges who lost their jobs due to the First and Second Jewish Laws. However, by mid-1942 the authorities realized that the building managers had become crucial players They worked as focal points; they and only they were aware of personal details of the neighbourhood without which the police and the courts were incapable of maintaining the rule of law, they controlled the air-raid shelters and so on. This growing importance explains—went the propaganda of the above quoted journal, the *Nemzeti Házfelügyelő*—why Jewish Hungarians had to be excluded from the *házmester* craft. The next issue of the same periodical gave some background of the freshly introduced anti-Jewish restriction among the building managers. It is entitled "It is also our victory!", because, as the members of the Building Managers' Nationwide and Economic Association in Kolozsvár/Cluj revealed in this text, they had initiated the elimination of Jews from the concierge profession. At the beginning of 1942, the assembly of this particular group of Kolozsvár building managers had suggested to the internal ministry that it should exchange the Jewish *házmester* for more trustworthy non-Jewish Hungarians. Now, when in July the 3.530/1942 B.M. decree was announced, the concierge of Kolozsvár felt that this order was to some extent their special triumph.[140]

On 1 August 1942, the interior minister's 3.530/1942 decree came into effect and the dismissed Jewish building managers' positions and homes were taken up by non-Jews, a change which concerned more than 1,000 Budapest families. One of this book's showcases, which will appear in all the later chapters, is the case of György Papp. In 1942, Papp was a 37-year-old man, the father of two, who in these very days became the building manager of a modern apartment building at Szent István park 10 by replacing a *házmester* who was of Jewish origin.[141] At the same time, Papp also kept his part-time job as an aide at the central food inspection agency, thus most of the concierge's work was done by his wife. Prior to this move the Papps were already building managers, but in a much smaller and poorer building with significantly less income, and had to live in a much worse apartment. They also had a milk stand and when in 1942 they were selected for their new concierge post, they promised to provide Szent István park 10 with milk products—this was a decisive argument when the owners had to choose the right candidate for the *házmester* post.[142] It is known from Imre Papp's People's Court file that he finished only five years of elementary schooling in his hometown, Hajdúdorog, a tiny place in Eastern Hungary, close to the Romanian border. This is where Imre Papp had met his wife, with whom he now found their new home, right next to the fancy Szent István park. Papp well represents those everyday Hungarians who in mid-1942 saw an opportunity in the new anti-Jewish restriction concerning the building managers. Thanks to this, he could now move into a beautiful modern building, in the centre of Budapest. Exceptionally, in this building even the concierge's apartment had two rooms.

The vast majority of the approximately 23,000 Budapest building managers—unlike Imre Papp—were untouched by the 3.530/1942 B.M. decree: most of them had held their positions for years and stayed there for the rest of World War II. These *házmester* at the beginning of the 1940s could be well described as a largely uneducated and frustrated social group with a strong desire for quick social development in the near future. Their frustration was down to the fact that for long decades there was not enough political and social will to significantly strengthen the economic position of the building managers. One could argue that the *házmester* were caught in the middle of a battlefield, where the conflicting interests of tenants, landlords and authorities met every day. Furthermore, from the late 1930s onwards there was a growing tension between the building managers' significant rise in social importance and their persistently poor income. The lack of financial appreciation created the feeling of injustice among the Budapest concierges, especially as their job profile gradually extended; firstly, due to the technical and urban developments, and secondly, thanks to the special circumstances of the war. In addition, they were not given the necessary authority by which they could have done a good job, as they had no formal power over the tenants. It was precisely these tensions that made the concierges aspire to authority, but also because of this many concierges started to support radical movements,

above all the Nazi Arrow Cross movement. The existing Holocaust literature usually focuses exclusively on the war years, by which it sometimes
misses out on deeper reasons behind the Holocaust actors' behaviour. In
the case of the Budapest building managers these circumstances include
the long-standing frustration of these ordinary Hungarians, and their
strong aspiration for a quasi-official role, and to belong to the holders of
power. In many ways these people had control over the wartime public and
semi-public terrain of Budapest, and especially between March 1944 and
February 1945 it often depended on them how many Jewish Hungarians
could survive the Holocaust from those approximately 225,000 persecuted people who still lived in Budapest, a city already occupied by the
Nazi Germans.[143]

Notes

1. Andor Gábor, *Pesti sirámok* [Laments from Pest] (Budapest: Szépirodalmi, 1958), p. 69.
2. Gábor Gyáni, *Identity and the Urban Experience: Fin-de-Siécle Budapest* (New York: Columbia University Press, 2004), pp. 9–11.
3. John Lukacs, *Budapest, 1900: A város és kultúrája* [Budapest, 1900: the city and its culture] (Budapest: Európa, 1991), p. 63.
4. Péter Hanák, *The Garden and the Workshop* (Princeton University Press, 1998), pp. 20–22. As Hanák notes, "this open-corridor pattern of build-ing had far-reaching social consequences. The bourgeois principles of strict privacy and as full a segregation from the 'lower orders'" as possible applied less fully in Budapest than in other big cities of Western or Central Europe."
5. Ibid., pp. 17–18.
6. Lukacs, *Budapest, 1900*, p. 74., Hanák, *The Garden and the Workshop*, p. 12.
7. Gyáni, *Identity and the Urban Experience*, pp. 174–175.
8. László Németh, *A medve utcai polgári* (Budapest, Pannónia, 1988), p. 31.
9. See on this the speech of Mátyás Früwirth in the Hungarian parliament on 7 July 1921, in József Szekeres (ed.) *Források Budapest történetéhez, vol. III* (Budapest: Budapest Főváros Levéltára, 1971), pp. 90–92.
10. Ibid., p. 90.
11. Gábor, *Pesti sirámok*, p. 59. According to an article in *Házfelügyelők Lapja* [Journal of Building Managers] on the reasons for the lack of enough apartments, the average yearly rental fee in 1910 in Budapest was

400 korona, which was deemed as the highest in the world. See this in *Házfelügyelők Lapja*, National Széchényi Library (Hereafter: OSZK) OSZK FM3/6497, vol. 7, issue 9, September 1910, p. 2.

12. Gábor, *Pesti sirámok*, pp. 61–62.
13. This data was mentioned by Ferenc Miklós in the municipal assembly of Budapest, 26 April 1939, in Szekeres, *Források Budapest történetéhez, vol. III*, p. 471.
14. Szilvia Czingel, *Szakácskönyv a túlélésért* [Cookbook for survival] (Budapest: Corvina, 2013), p. 57.
15. Németh, *A medve utcai polgári*, p. 46.
16. See this in an article by Boldizsár Friedrich, "Idegen vélemények" [Strangers' opinions] in *Házfelügyelők Lapja*, OSZK FM3/7340, vol. 19, no. 11, November 1942, pp. 1–2.
17. Gábor, *Pesti sirámok*, p. 69.
18. *Házfelügyelők Lapja* [Journal of Building Managers], older version, OSZK FM3/6497, vol. 2, no. 7, July 1905, p. 3, an article entitled "Udvariasság" [Politeness].
19. Lajos Nagy, *A lázadó ember* [The rebelling human] (Budapest: Szépirodalmi, 1983), pp. 194–195.
20. Ibid.
21. Zygmunt Bauman, *Modernity and the Holocaust* (Ithaca: Cornell University Press, 1989).
22. Németh, *A medve utcai polgári* (Budapest, Pannónia, 1988). The word *polgári* means civic in Hungarian.
23. Ibid., p. 24.
24. In fact the last two years of the elementary school were the equivalents of the first two years in civic schooling.
25. Németh, *A medve utcai polgári*, pp. 22–23.
26. Ibid., pp. 22–23.
27. Ibid., p. 46.
28. Ibid., p. 47.
29. Ibid.
30. Ibid., p. 43. In the 1934–35 academic year, only from the so-called Rózsadomb (nowadays district II) 13 pupils came every day from a family like this to the school in Medve utca.
31. Ibid., pp. 46–47.
32. Ibid., p. 45 and p. 28.
33. Ibid., p. 40.
34. Ibid., p. 27.
35. Ibid., p. 27.
36. Ibid., p. 46.

37. See a short summary of this process in an article by Boldizsár Friedrich, "Idegen vélemények" [Strangers' opinions] in *Házfelügyelők Lapja*, [Journal of Building Managers] vol. 19, no. 11, November 1942, pp. 1–2.

38. *Pesti Hírlap*, vol. 55, 2 July 1933.

39. See the 1936/130 decree of Budapest, and especially section no. 16. But the 3333/1924 M.E. decree also contains a list like this in its third point. (M.E. means Prime Minister).

40. See this also in "Lakbérleti szabályrendelet" [decree on housing issues] *Házfelügyelők Közlönye* [Building Manager's Bulletin], vol. 11, no. 3-4-5, March, April and May 1937 combined issue, p. 2.

41. See this in 3333/1924 M.E. decree, point no. 3.

42. See this in an announcement on the Hungarian government's website: http://www.kormany.hu/hu/emberi-eroforrasok-miniszteriuma/hirek/vissza-kell-utasitani-az-embereket-megalazo-gonoszsagot. Last accessed on 21 February 2013.

43. Oral history interview with László Pusztai, undertaken by the author, on 19 September 2012, in Budapest.

44. For the general concept of social norms, see Cristina Bicchieri, *The Grammar of Society: The Nature and Dynamics of Social Norms* (New York: Cambridge University Press, 2006). For a discussion of the way in which social norms may help guide individual behaviour during large-scale crimes, see Paul Morrow, "Mass Atrocity and Manipulation of Social Norms", *Social Theory and Practice* vol. 40, no. 2 (April 2014), 255–280.

45. *Házfelügyelők Lapja*, vol. 19, no. 7, July 1942, pp. 2–3.

46. *Házfelügyelők Lapja*, vol. 21, no. 1, January 1944, p. 3.

47. Tivadar Szinnai, *Sötét ablakok* [Dark windows] (Budapest: Dante, 1947), p. 50.

48. *Házfelügyelők Lapja*, vol. 21, no. 1, January 1944, p. 3.

49. Interview by the author, 19 September 2012, Budapest.

50. These periodicals were: *Házfelügyelők Közlönye* [Building Manager's Bulletin] (1929), *Házfelügyelők Lapja* [Journal of Building Managers] (1924–44), *Nemzeti Házfelügyelő* [National Building Manager] (1933–44).

51. *Házfelügyelők Lapja*, vol. 19, no. 6, June 1942, pp. 2–3. See also *Házfelügyelők Lapja*, vol. 19, no. 10, October 1942, p. 3.

52. *Házfelügyelők Lapja*, vol. 20, no. 6, July 1943, p. 2.

53. See for example this in Chapter 6, in the case of Dr Béla Lázár.

54. *Házfelügyelők és Házmesterek Lapja/Hausmeisterwesen*, OSZK FM3/8731.

55. Sándor Márai, *Memoir of Hungary, 1944–1948*, (Budapest: Corvina, 1996), pp. 170–171.

56. One example is the Krause vs Zsemba criminal case, where the building owner paid so little and wanted so much from the concierge, András Zsemba, that he finally refused to transport a heater to the apartment building from Teleki tér. The following row resulted in the building manager shooting landlord Krause, who nearly died in the attack. See the details of this incident in *Házfelügyelők Lapja*, vol. 2, no. 3, March 1905, p. 5.
57. Gábor, *Pesti sirámok*, p. 61.
58. Gábor, *Pesti sirámok*, p. 69.
59. This was decree 3333/1924 M.E., however, later this was modified by 5777/1936 M.E. decree.
60. Decree 3333/1924 M.E.
61. Tivadar Dános, *Háztulajdonos, Lakó, Házfelügyelő* (Budapest: Egyetemi Nyomda, 1936), p. 459.
62. Ibid.
63. This was already regulated in a municipal decree in 1904. See it in *Házfelügyelők Lapja*, OSZK FM3/6497, vol. 1, no. 10, December 1904, pp. 5–6.
64. 3333/1924 M.E., section 77, point 7, quoted in *Házfelügyelők Lapja*, OSZK FM3/7340, vol. 1, no. 1, June 1924, p. 5.
65. Ibid.
66. Gábor, *Pesti sirámok*, p. 68.
67. The so-called garbage-money [szemétpénz] was adjusted to the size of the apartments. Everyone paid 1,000 koronas, with an additional 500 for each additional room. See this in: *Házfelügyelők Lapja*, OSZK FM3/7340, vol. 1, no. 1, June 1924, p. 3.
68. *Házfelügyelők Lapja*, older version, OSZK FM3/6497, vol. 5, no. 5, May 1908, pp. 1–2.
69. Gábor, *Pesti sirámok*, p. 67.
70. Gábor, *Pesti sirámok*, p. 69.
71. *Házfelügyelők Lapja*, vol. 2, no. 6, August 1925, p. 2.
72. *Házfelügyelők Lapja*, vol. 3, no. 1, January 1926, p. 2, see an article entitled "Kulcsbér" [Key earnings].
73. *Házfelügyelők Lapja*, vol. 4, no. 4, April 1927, p. 2.
74. Ibid.
75. Boldizsár Friedrich, "A békebeli házfelügyelő" [The peacetime concierge], *Házfelügyelők Közlönye*, OSZK FM3/7713, vol. 2, no. 5, 1 May 1929, p. 2.
76. *Nemzeti Házfelügyelő*, OSZK FM3/5917, vol. 1, no. 8–9, December 1933, p. 3.
77. *Nemzeti Házfelügyelő*, OSZK FM3/5917, vol. 6, no. 9, September 1938, pp. 2–3. "A kapupénz békebeli ellensége az ablakon mászik be a lakásba".

78. Budapest Főváros Levéltára [Budapest City Archives] (hereafter: BFL) BFL XVII/1598. Magyar Házfelügyelők és Segéd-házfelügyelők 291/a. sz. Igazoló Bizottságának iratai. [The 291/a Justificatory Committee Files of the Hungarian Building managers and of the Assistant Building managers], the case of Mr Lajos Üst, a questionnaire filled out by the building manager, p. 1.
79. *Házfelügyelők Lapja*, vol. 19, no. 11, November 1942, p. 3.
80. 67§ of decree 3333/1924 M.E., quoted in *Házfelügyelők Lapja*, vol. 1, no. 1, June 1924, p. 3.
81. The "*házmesterpénz*" was also dubbed "*negyedpénz*", which was a reference to the quarterly timing of the payment. Prior to World War I, it was set as 3 percent of the rental fees.
82. The building managers were paid for operating the central heating only until 1936, when a Budapest municipal decree on housing affairs abolished this earning of theirs. See this in 130/1936 K.GY. and 265/1936 K.GY.
83. See this in 67§ of decree 3333/1924 M.E.
84. Gábor, *Pesti sirámok*, p. 66.
85. As for the cleaning supplies, this was only the custom in the interwar era; before this time, and again after 1942, the building owner was paying the cost. See this in *Házfelügyelők Lapja*, vol. 2, no. 5, May 1925, pp. 1–2, and *Nemzeti Házfelügyelő*, vol. 12, no. 1, January 1943, p. 1.
86. *Nemzeti Házfelügyelő*, vol. 5, no. 2, February 1937, p. 2.
87. *Házfelügyelők Lapja*, vol. 21, no. 3, March 1944, p. 3.
88. This assistant was called "vice", and decree 2222/1931 M.E. regulated their employment. They were entitled to the rubbish-money plus one third of the building manager's 2 percent income after the rental fees. See this also: Gábor, *Pesti sirámok*, p. 67.
89. See this already in the first version of *Házfelügyelők Lapja*, vol. 2, no. 5, May 1905, p. 5.
90. An article entitled "Milyennek nem szabad lenni" mentions this data in *Házfelügyelők Lapja*, vol. 19, no. 6, June 1942, pp. 2–3.
91. *Házfelügyelők Lapja*, vol. 3, no. 3, March 1926, p. 3.
92. Dezső Kosztolányi, *Édes Anna* (Budapest: Szépirodalmi, 1988), p. 33.
93. BFL.VII.18d.1920-13/8198. (The old MSZMP archival fond was 638.1920-IV-13-8198), pp. 2–3.
94. *Házfelügyelők Lapja*, vol. 4, no. 8, August 1927, p. 2. "Building managers at the mayor of Budapest", a summary of articles published in the dailies: *Pesti Napló*, *Pester Lloyd* and *Magyar Hírlap*.
95. *Nemzeti Házfelügyelő*, vol. 2, no. 3, March 1934, p. 3: "Our delegation at the Ministry of Interior".
96. *Házfelügyelők Lapja*, vol. 20, no. 2, February 1943, pp. 2–3.

97. Ibid.
98. *Házfelügyelők Országos Szabad Szakszervezete.* See this denazification process in detail in the last chapter of this book.
99. Their original Hungarian name was *Házfelügyelők Nemzeti és Gazdasági Szövetsége.*
100. *Házfelügyelők Lapja,* vol. 21, no. 5, May 1944, p. 3.
101. See for example this in *Házfelügyelők Lapja,* vol. 3, no. 6, June 1926, p. 2.
102. The Alliance chose, for instance, Dr. Pál Cselényi as its honorary president, a parliamentary member from the National Unity Party.
103. See for example the piece entitled "For the purpose of revision!" in *Nemzeti Házfelügyelő,* OSZK FM3/5917, vol. 5, no. 9, May 1937, p. 3.
104. *Házfelügyelők Lapja,* older version, OSZK FM3/6497, vol. 2, no. 5, May 1905, p. 7.
105. *Házfelügyelők Lapja,* older version, vol. 2, no. 6, June 1905, pp. 4–5.
106. *Házfelügyelők Közlönye,* vol. 2, no. 7. July 1929, p. 2.
107. *Házfelügyelők Lapja,* vol. 19, no. 11, November 1942, pp. 1–2, ("Idegen vélemények").
108. Donated to the author by László Bellér.
109. *Házfelügyelők Lapja,* older version, vol. 2, no. 6, August 1904, p. 6, ("A rendőri körözés és a házfelügyelők").
110. *Házfelügyelők Lapja,* vol. 2, no. 4, June 1925, p. 1, ("Jegyzetek").
111. *Házfelügyelők Lapja,* vol. 14, no. 10–11, October–November 1937. See also: *Nemzeti Házfelügyelő,* vol. 10. October 1942, pp. 1–2.
112. See on this decree 380.000/1941. B.M. (B.M. means Interior Ministry).
113. Oral history interview with I. D., undertaken by the author, on 30 April 2013, in Washington DC.
114. Employers were also aware of one's Jewish origin. For instance, they had to make sure that the ratio of Jews among the intellectual workers was not higher than 15 percent. The ratio of Jewish employees had to be reported to a government commissioner [*Munkanélküliség Ügyeinek Kormánybizottsága*]. See for example the wartime HR policy of the Orion radio factory, in András Forgács, "Egyenruhát nem viselhet", *Népszava, Szép Szó,* 8 March 2014, p. 2.
115. See for example a case where the building manager reported a secret affair in András Lugosi's "Sztalin Főhercege Kohn báró vacsorái a Falk Miksa utcában a fajgyalázási törvény idején" [The Archduke of Stalin: Baron Kohn's dinners at Falk Miksa Street on the course of the race blaspheme law] in *Fons* 17, no. 4, 2010, pp. 527–576.
116. BFL VII.5.c A Budapesti Királyi Büntetőtörvényszék peres iratai. [Criminal cases of the Royal Budapest Court] 3086/1943 the case of Lajos Krausz, p. 22.
117. Ibid. See this also on p. 8.

118. Ibid., p. 6.
119. *Házfelügyelők Lapja*, vol. 19, no. 3, March 1942, pp. 2–3.
120. See on this: László Karsai, "Miklós Horthy, 1868–1957, legends, myths and the reality" in *Beszélő*, vol. 12, no. 3, 12 March 2007.
121. *Házfelügyelők Lapja*, vol. 19, no. 3, March 1942, pp. 2–3.
122. 3.530/1942 B.M. Decree, see it in *Belügyi Közlöny*, XLVII, no. 25 (1942), pp. 1082–1084.
123. The word Jew here is only a classification introduced by the Nazi authorities, and as a Nazi category it involves many more people than the actual Jewish community of Hungary in the 1930s and 1940s. About a debate of Hungarian historians on who should be called a Jew, see the website of the Galamusgroup:http://www.galamuscsoport.hu/tartalom/cikk/151123_a-ger-andras-altal-kezdemenyezett-romsics-vita-irasai
124. *Házfelügyelők Lapja*, vol. 20, no. 7, July 1943, pp. 3–4, ("Észrevételek az élelmiszerjegyekkel kapcsolatban").
125. *Házfelügyelők Lapja*, vol. 20, no. 12, December 1943, p. 3, ("Kötelesség és felelősség").
126. Dános, *Háztulajdonos, Lakó, Házfelügyelő*, pp. 435–6.
127. *Házfelügyelők Lapja*, vol. 2, no. 11, November 1925, p. 1, ("Ki lehet házmester?").
128. *Házfelügyelők Lapja*, vol. 19, no. 6, June 1942, p. 1, ("Őrségváltás").
129. See the full text of the decree in *Nemzeti Házfelügyelő*, vol. 11, no. 7, July 1942, pp. 2–3.
130. *Házfelügyelők Lapja*, vol. 19, no. 6, June 1942, p. 1.
131. *Nemzeti Házfelügyelő*, vol. 11, no. 7, July 1942, p. 1.
132. Loránt Tilkovszky, "A zsidótörvények, mint a Holocaust előzményei" in Randolph L. Braham, Attila Pók (eds.), *The Holocaust in Hungary: Fifty Years Later* (New York: Columbia University Press, 1997), pp. 123–4.
133. Yehuda Don, "Economic implications of the Anti-Jewish legislation in Hungary" in David Cesarani (ed.) *Genocide and Rescue: The Holocaust in Hungary 1944* (Oxford: Berg, 1997) p. 54, pp. 47–76. Braham, in *The Politics of Genocide* (Vol. 1, pp. 128–129.) estimates a lower number, some 15,000, who could become unemployed due to this law. Both Loránt Tilkovszky and Kádár and Vági follow this estimation, which earlier occurs also in Péter Bihari's study in 1990 (Péter Bihari, "A Magyarországi zsidóság helyzete a zsidótörvényektől a deportálásig" in Péter Horváth (ed.), *Hét évtized a hazai zsidóság életében*, Budapest, 1990, vol. II, p. 19. See this also in Kádár & Vági, *Self-financing Genocide*, p. 55).
134. Tilkovszky, "A zsidótörvények, mint a Holocaust előzményei", p. 125.
135. Ibid., p. 127. See this also in Don, "Economic implications of the Anti-Jewish legislation in Hungary", p. 55.

136. Don, "Economic implications of the Anti-Jewish legislation in Hungary", p. 55.
137. Ibid., pp. 56–7.
138. István Deák, "A Fatal Compromise? The Debate over Collaboration and Resistance in Hungary" in István Deák, Jan T. Gross and Tony Judt (eds.), *The Politics of Retribution in Europe* (Princeton University Press, 2000), p. 58.
139. In 1930, allegedly no less than 46 percent of the Budapest apartment buildings' overall value was in the hands of Jewish Hungarians. See this in Alajos Kovács, *Magyarország népe és népesedésének kérdése* (Budapest: Magyar Statisztikai Társaság, 1941), p. 66.
140. *Nemzeti Házfelügyelő*, vol. 11, no. 8, August 1942, pp. 1–2, ("Mi is győztünk!").
141. BFL XXV 1a, Documents of the Budapest People's Court, the case of György Papp, case number 1945/1500, pp. 76–7s7.
142. BFL XVII/1598, Justificatory Committee Files, box no. 6, the case of Mrs Papp; see this in a letter sent by Sándor Ehrlich to the head of the Justificatory Committee, dated 1 October 1945.
143. Kádár and Vági, *Self-financing Genocide*, p. 19. On the number of Jewish Hungarians living in Budapest, see also László Karsai, *Vádirat a nácizmus ellen, vol. 4* (Budapest: Balassi, 2014), p. 12.

CHAPTER 2

The Concierges of the Ghetto Buildings

"The *házmester* came up to our apartment to warn us not to go out on the street"—writes Mrs Anna Dévényi, a pregnant Jewish Hungarian woman in her diary on 21 March 1944, two days after the German troops invaded Budapest.[1] Her building manager was right; the Nazi German occupation was the moment when the situation of Jewish Hungarians declined most sharply. Right after the invasion an SS unit arrested not only the leaders of the Hungarian political opposition, but also hundreds of Jewish Hungarians in Budapest.[2] They used torture and blackmailing to force the wealthier Jews to pass huge savings to the Gestapo in exchange for their survival.[3] On 30 March, Mrs Dévényi switched on the radio to listen to the evening news at 9.40. Her face went red when she heard the announcement of decree 1.240/1944 of the newly appointed Sztójay government, which starting from 5 April ordered all Jews above the age of six to wear yellow-star badges on their outer clothing.[4] Anna Dévényi thought she was not going to be able to walk on the streets with a yellow badge. Many thought the same, no wonder that the aftermath of the Nazi German invasion brought a peak in suicide attempts among Jewish Hungarians. Most of them—like Tivadar Szinnai's physician—took poison, but dozens chose other methods of suicide, such as jumping under a tram.[5] Tram drivers routinely filled accident report forms in these days with texts like "today, around the Zoo, tram number 44 ran over an approx. 70–74 years old Jewess, who jumped under the tram presumably on purpose..."[6] This suicide wave was a reaction to the suddenly worsening situation: despite

© The Author(s) 2016
I.P. Adam, *Budapest Building Managers and the Holocaust in Hungary*,
The Holocaust and its Contexts, DOI 10.1007/978-3-319-33831-6_2

the anti-Jewish laws, most Jewish Hungarians lived in relative safety compared to the surrounding countries' Jewish communities until Hungary's Nazi German occupation on 19 March 1944.[7] From this date on, the new Hungarian government issued decree after decree to increase the pressure on the persecuted people. For example, decree 108.500 K.M. reduced their sugar ration to 0.3 kg per month, and their meat ration to 0.1 kg beef or horse meat per week. As Mrs Dévényi noted in her journal: "[t]he Jew's food ration is decreasing. We are not allowed to consume milk, egg or butter. … They want to starve us gradually."[8]

Once the Sztójay government came into power, it took only a little more than three months to ghettoize and deport to Nazi German concentration camps more than 432,000 people from the Hungarian provinces—the vast majority of them were murdered in Auschwitz. It was exactly this efficiency of concentration and deportation that made the authorities unable to organize properly the expropriation of the Jewish Hungarians' wealth on time.[9] In Budapest, ghettoization was a later and more complicated process than in the countryside. In the capital a dispersed ghetto was established in the early summer of 1944, which in practice meant individual apartment buildings, so-called "Jewish or Yellow Star houses", into which groups of Jewish Hungarians were confined. Therefore, in the capital city the apartment building became the basic unit of the ghetto, and in every building like this the non-Jewish concierge became the most important person, the liaison between the outside and inside world. They represented the bridges over the structural holes of the 1944 Budapest society, which is why the concierges' authority grew rapidly with the forming of these ghetto buildings. This individual importance, combined with the incomplete and inadequate official preparations for seizing the "Jewish assets" created room for everyday opportunism. What makes the group of Budapest concierges and their choices particularly interesting in this precarious situation is that these individuals were not at all prepared for this kind of control over people, especially not over the members of the upper middle classes, who previously had exercised power over the concierges due to their financial and social position. Only a year earlier, for example, the building manager of Pannónia utca 49/b, Gyula Hidegh, was sentenced by the Court of Budapest to pay a 250 pengő fine for verbally insulting a Jewish Hungarian tenant.[10] From late June 1944, however, when the relocation had finished, concierges like Mr Hidegh had jurisdiction over the Jewish Hungarian tenants trapped in the apartment buildings. This sudden power shift within the apartment buildings sums up the drama of the Holocaust in Budapest. Building managers used their newly acquired power in many different ways and for many different purposes. Some helped to improve the situations of the Jewish residents or helped them out when it was needed, whereas others instead found ways to improve their own financial well-being. But very few if any building managers remained passive in these days of May and June 1944. The goal of this chapter is to show that not mere passivity, but activity in a variety of ways, was required of them during the ghettoization process.

1   BUILDING MANAGERS USED AS DATA SOURCE AND THE LAYERS OF HOLOCAUST RESEARCH

When the authorities decided to implement a dispersed ghetto scenario as opposed to the centralized, contiguous ghetto plans, they had to also decide which specific buildings to select for the location of the Jewish Hungarians, and this is when they first had to rely on the contribution of building managers in the ghettoization process. Here, it is worth mentioning that the two scholars who discuss at length the segregation of Jews and non-Jews in Budapest provide significantly different insights. The leading researcher of the Hungarian Holocaust, Randolph Braham, in his early monograph, primarily because of its wide scope but also given its pioneering nature, leaves unmentioned important details of the ghettoization.[11] From the vantage point of the current work it is clear that Braham underestimates the importance of concierges when talking about ghettoization in the capital, which consequently results in a much more administrative and politically driven picture of the process than the way Tim Cole understands the events. While Braham only refers to a 3 May 1944 "order for the identification and registration of apartments and buildings in which Jews lived",[12] he does not tell about the citywide survey undertaken on 1–2 June. During this second survey, building owners, but mostly building managers, gave the relevant data of the buildings' inhabitants, and specifically the numbers of Jewish and non-Jewish tenants.[13] While Braham only notes that Counsellor József Szentmiklóssy led the state officials who identified and registered the "Jewish inhabited apartments and buildings",[14] Cole claims the 1–2 June data survey, completed with the help of the building managers, was key to which building was designated for Jewish and which one for non-Jewish use.[15] Although neither Braham nor Cole note this specifically, it is obvious therefore that it largely depended on the concierges who could stay put and who was obliged to move. As Cole writes, "it was on the basis of this hurriedly collected information that the precise shape of ghettoization in Budapest was determined by city officials."[16]

> And, as he adds later, "... it appears that the practice of city officials was to write the number of 'non-Jewish' and 'Jewish' tenants in the top left-hand corner of the 1–2 June registration form. If 'non-Jewish' tenants were in the majority then the shorthand 'K' (*Keresztény*–'Christian') was pencilled in the top right-hand corner and the property was designated for 'non-Jewish' use. If 'Jewish' tenants were in the majority, then the shorthand 'Zs' (*Zsidó*–'Jewish') was pencilled in the top right-hand corner and the property designated for Jewish use."[17]

It seems that historians excavate the Hungarian Holocaust layer by layer, and the moment of ghettoization is a remarkable example of this top-down direction of the research. In Braham's monumental work there is only space beside the government representatives for the counsellors and leaders of the housing authorities at the Budapest Mayor's Office. Cole steps further and studies the layer of ordinary city officials, while the present book analyses those concierges who provided the necessary data for the work of the city officials. Because the way the Mayor's Office collected data from the apartment buildings through an "*Adatszolgáltatási ív*" [data survey or registration form] was crucial, and those who filled these sheets—mostly building managers, in some cases building owners—became increasingly aware that they could influence who would stay put in their home (Figure 2.1).

In mid-1944, in a correspondence between a city official and the mayor of Budapest, the former reported about the leftover of the data survey sheets. Accordingly, overall 65,000 sheets were printed, out of which 52,700 were distributed in the I-XIV districts of Budapest.[18] Some 71 years later, in 2015, thousands of these filled sheets were found during the renovation of an apartment on Kossuth Lajos tér, close to the Hungarian parliament.[19] On the data survey's first page the address of the building and the owner's name had to be indicated and in a separate cell their Jewish or Christian status. This part was followed by four questions: 1. Overall how many owners own the building? 2. How many of them are obliged to wear Jewish badges? 3. Was the building built before or after 1935? 4. How many apartments are in the building? This page also contained

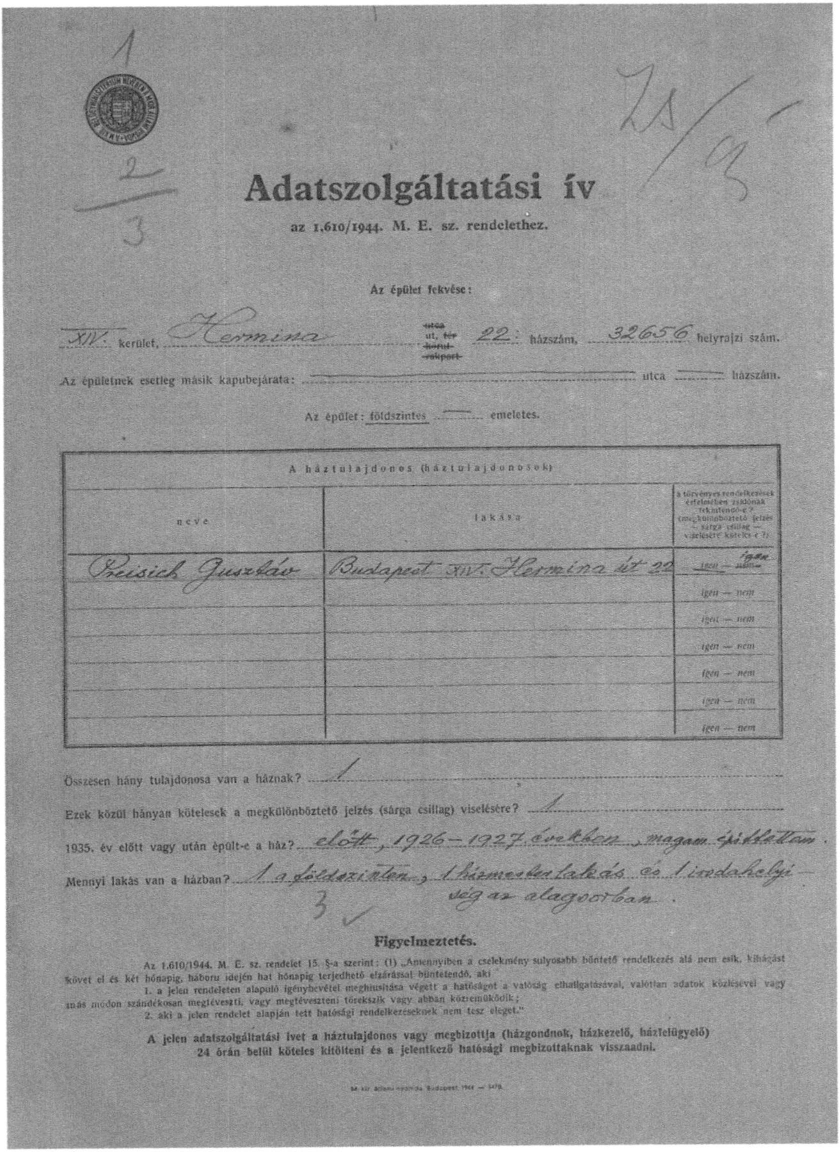

1

2

3

Zs/93

Adatszolgáltatási ív

az 1,610/1944. M. E. sz. rendelethez.

Az épület fekvése:

XIV. kerület, Hermina ~~utca~~ út, ~~tér~~ ~~körut~~ ~~rakpart~~ 22. házszám, 32656 helyrajzi szám.

Az épületnek esetleg másik kapubejárata: ——— utca ——— házszám.

Az épület: földszintes ——— emeletes.

A háztulajdonos (háztulajdonosok)		
neve	lakása	a törvényes rendelkezések értelmében zsidónak tekintendő-e? (megkülönböztető jelzés – sárga csillag – viselésére köteles-e?)
Preisich Gusztáv	Budapest XIV. Hermina út 22	igen — ~~nem~~ igen
		igen — nem
		igen — nem
		igen — nem
		igen — nem
		igen — nem
		igen — nem

Összesen hány tulajdonosa van a háznak? 1

Ezek közül hányan kötelesek a megkülönböztető jelzés (sárga csillag) viselésére? 1

1935. év előtt vagy után épült-e a ház? előtt, 1926–1927. években, magam építtettem.

Mennyi lakás van a házban? 1 a földszinten, 1 házmesterlakás és 1 irodahelyiség az alagsorban.

3 ✓

Figyelmeztetés.

Az 1.610/1944. M. E. sz. rendelet 15. §-a szerint: (1) „Amennyiben a cselekmény sulyosabb büntető rendelkezés alá nem esik, kihágást követ el és két hónapig, háboru idején hat hónapig terjedhető elzárással büntetendő, aki

1. a jelen rendeleten alapuló igénybevétel meghiusítása végett a hatóságot a valóság elhallgatásával, valótlan adatok közlésével vagy más módon szándékosan megtéveszti, vagy megtéveszteni törekszik vagy abban közreműködik;

2. aki a jelen rendelet alapján tett hatósági rendelkezéseknek nem tesz eleget."

A jelen adatszolgáltatási ívet a háztulajdonos vagy megbizottja (házgondnok, házkezelő, házfelügyelő) 24 órán belül köteles kitölteni és a jelentkező hatósági megbizottaknak visszaadni.

M. kir. állami nyomda Budapest 1944 — 1478.

Figure 2.1 An "*Adatszolgáltatási ív*" [data survey], with the shorthand "*Zs*" in its top corner (Source: BFL/IV.1420r, data survey for the 1610/1944 M.E. order, Budapest XIV, Hermina út 22) a warning that those who entered false data on this form could be sentenced to up to six months' imprisonment. On the other side of the form were listed the so-called main tenants [*főbérlők*], with their classification in terms of the anti-Jewish regulations: Jew who was obliged to wear the yellow star, Christian or exempted Jew (meaning exempted from the effects of the anti-Jewish laws). This part also contained information on an apartment's situation within the building, the number of rooms, the rental fees, as well as the apartment's direction: facing the street or the courtyard. To conclude, the authorities sought information primarily on the Jewish and non-Jewish ratio among the owners and among the tenants. Furthermore, they were curious to know the building's age and the quality of apartments because they wanted to assess whether it was a modern or an older house. Finally, they also considered the rental fees compared to an average standard while designating a building. The ultimate idea was to provide the city's non-Jews with modern and cheap apartments, but to some extent respect the already existing residential situation, especially where a clear majority of non-Jews or Jews were detected within one apartment building.[20]

In the end, what really mattered for the designators, the clerks of the Mayor's Office, was the ratio of Jews and non-Jews residing in a building, and it had to feel empowering when a building manager filling out the data survey realized how much depended on their work in this respect. Many concierges were actually accused of manipulating the all-important Jewish–Christian ratio, a fraud through which these concierges appeared to be powerful enough to challenge the rules of ghettoization in the locality by simply filling out the data surveys. It is thereby little surprise that they are highly represented in the dozens of letters and telegrams that were submitted by ordinary Budapest citizens as petitions to the city mayor once the first list of ghetto buildings or—as they were mostly called because of their mark on the façade—"yellow-star houses" was published, on 16 June 1944.[21] On this day, Mrs Dévényi—who was already in the eighth month of her pregnancy—wrote this in her journal: "after all I have to move. Until the last moment I hoped that our building was going to be designated as a Yellow Star house, but it was not. Where can we go now, we don't know yet. ... I am afraid of these days, I am afraid of packing, placing our things somewhere, I am afraid of the coming blows. But I vowed that I am going to take care of myself, because I want to give birth to a healthy child."[22]

2   INFLUENCING WHO SHOULD STAY AND WHO SHOULD GO

As the petitions submitted to the city mayor reveal, there were several concierges who helped the Jewish Hungarian building owners by misleadingly giving the impression on the data survey that the ratio of Jewish tenants was higher than 50 percent of the overall population in a specific building. This is exactly what happened at Jósika utca 10 in the city's VII district, where the building warden reported the *házmester*'s misconduct in a letter to the mayor of Budapest. Building wardens were trusted persons—often retired army officers—who were appointed in each and every apartment building to decide on any war-related issues and to make sure that no residents could commit any sabotage.[23] The warden of Jósika utca 10 reported that "János Pados, building manager, confessed how he misrepresented a higher number of Jewish tenants than Christians for the sake of the owner, Mrs Adolf H., and this is how she managed to achieve her building's Jewish designation."[24] The warden's letter continues with a suggestion from the non-Jewish residents' side: "we Christian inhabitants, who are in the majority within the house, share the opinion that it would be the easiest if the Jews should be the ones who move away; since they are in a better financial situation they can obviously better afford the cost of moving."[25]

According to other petitions, some concierges went so far as to seize control over an entire apartment building by ousting from there the Jewish building owner. In order to achieve this, occasionally it was enough to arrange non-Jewish designation for the property. One landlady who suffered an attack like this was Mrs Jutasi, the owner of Podmanicky utca 31. According to her letter sent to the Mayor's Office, the *házmester* maliciously indicated on the predesignation data survey only those inhabitants who actually paid rental fees, therefore the building owner was not mentioned among them, nor was a forced labourer who had not yet returned for a while from the Eastern front.[26] Moreover, the Garai and Fehér families were listed as Christians although they were obliged to wear yellow stars, whilst instead of the Jewish Mr Gedeon, Z. the building manager put his wife, the non-Jewish Mrs Z. on the list as main tenant. By these seemingly minor factual changes the concierge managed to overturn the ratio of Christians and Jewish Hungarians, and the building owner Mrs Jutasi had to search for a new home. There were other building managers who were more open about making use of the ghettoization process.

For instance, József Horváth, a concierge from XIII district, specifically asked the mayor to designate the building where he worked as a "Jewish house" partly because the "owner of the house is a *Jewess*," but more importantly, "because by this we, Christian labourers with low income, could fulfil our wish to free ourselves from these shabby, poorly maintained and dump apartments and get instead of them healthier living spaces as replacements."[27] Thus this building manager regarded ghettoization as an opportunity for poorer Christian groups, practically by swapping their low quality apartments for better ones seized from Jewish Hungarians.[28] It is likely that by the time he offered his home for "Jewish" designation, he already had in mind an apartment to request in a nicer area of the city. Dozens of swaps like this happened in June 1944: since there was a lack of available space in apartment buildings designated for Jews, it was obvious that Jewish Hungarians accepted lower quality living spaces in return for their better standard apartments situated in "non-Jewish buildings". As these examples can reveal, the building managers had a significant impact on the designation of "Yellow Star houses", and by this they could influence many Jewish Hungarians' fate. This is because those Jewish residents, who had to move away from their homes had stopped having access to their accumulated reserves of food and clothes. And those building managers who were involved in these manipulations were not at all passive bystanders during ghettoization, but active agents, who often used their influential positions for improving their own financial status, or their living circumstances, while some found ways to provide help for the Jewish Hungarians.

During the second phase of ghettoization, which represents a very short period between 16 June and 22 June 1944, reflecting especially the outpouring of non-Jewish complaints, the city leaders agreed to change their plan to designate 2639 "Yellow Star houses" for Jewish use, approximately 10–12 percent of the apartment buildings of Budapest. They reduced the list to 1951 addresses, and this second, definite list of ghetto houses was finally issued on 22 June 1944.[29] There is compelling evidence that manipulative attempts happened during this short phase too, for example at Pacsirtamező utca 22/B. Here on 21 June 1944 a group of Christian residents sent an express telegram to the Mayor's Office clarifying the situation. They reported that "during yesterday's supervision the *házmesterné* [a female building manager] again has given false data. We request the urgent inspection of the case. 12 families with 35 persons are Christians, while 9 families with 21 persons are Jews, this is the exact ratio. Sincerely: the Christian inhabitants of Pacsirtamező utca 22/B."[30]

Petitions against the original 16 June designation arrived both from the Jewish Hungarians' and from the non-Jews' side, however, non-Jews had obviously many more successes in terms of the outcome of their appeals. For instance, Lendvay utca 15 in the VI district was on the first list of ghetto houses, which is why the Christian inhabitants requested a review of the case.[31] During this check the building manager allegedly cheated to the extent that he put on the list of main tenants his Christian relative who had come to Budapest only for a short family visit.[32] On the contrary, Erzsébet körút 39 was originally designated as a building for non-Jewish use, despite the fact that out of 12 apartments only four were inhabited by Christians. Here the Jewish Hungarian tenants' appeal revealed that both the building manager and his assistant were wrongly indicated on the list of main tenants, just as was a Christian subtenant. This petition arrived at the Mayor's Office on 19 June 1944, and the employee who dealt with it wrote on the back of the sheet a sole word: "Rejection".[33]

3   DESIGNATING SZENT ISTVÁN PARK 10

The above examples can tell us about how and why the Budapest concierges influenced who had to move on due to the ghettoization orders, and who could stay put; the latter thus continued to have access to their food and clothes stock, and consequently had more chance of surviving. The sources suggest that building managers sometimes got involved in the designation process and used their influential position only because they wanted to attract the admiration of the tenants. Szent István park 10 was a relatively new, modern building in 1944. Two years earlier, in the summer of 1942, the concierge, Jenő Rózsa, had to leave his post because of the regulations forbidding the employment of Jewish Hungarians as *házmester*.[34] This is when György Papp and his wife took over and moved into the building and were employed as concierges. In June 1944, after the first phase of ghettoization data gathering, Szent István park 10 originally was not on the list of designated buildings for Jews, despite the fact that 15 out of 18 apartments in the building were freehold apartments, inhabited by their owners, who were regarded as Jews.[35] In this situation the concierge Mrs Papp started to use her connections, the so-called social capital, to change this designation.[36] Mrs Papp reminded the residents that both she and her husband came from Hajdúdorog, the same town as Ákos Doroghi Farkas, who in June 1944, as the newly appointed mayor of Budapest, obviously had direct influence on the designation of the ghetto houses.[37] Once the first list of ghetto buildings was published, the building warden, Vilmos Hajdú, approached Mrs Papp to do something about the designation through her link with the mayor. A couple of days later, when she returned from the Mayor's Office, the *házmesterné* was proud to note that—thanks to her connections—if one more house was going to be designated in the city then it was Szent István park 10.[38] In fact, the address is among those listed on the second list of Yellow Star houses.[39] Given that the post-war investigations concerning the tragic events of 1944 in this specific building are well documented, Szent István park 10 will feature in all of the coming chapters of this book, and the actions of Mr and Mrs Papp will be further explained.

4   The Moving Out: Moving In Procedure, and the Building Managers' Role

Despite the involvement of ordinary Hungarians, ghettoization in Budapest is mostly remembered as a political decision of the governing elite and the occupying Nazi German leaders.[40] It is all the more surprising because, for example, the implementing orders of ghettoization had given many practical duties to ordinary Hungarians, among them the concierges: tasks through which these building managers took part directly in the actual moving out, moving in and the sealing or closing process. Following the war, in April 1945, the new communist mayor of Budapest, Zoltán Vas, ordered the individual investigation of each and every concierge's wartime acts. The mayor entrusted the Building Managers' Free Trade Union to conduct the investigation, which formed a special Justificatory Committee [*Igazoló Bizottság*] for this task. The Committee's membership included representatives of the five political parties that made up the Soviet-backed new interim government, plus lawyers and trade union leaders.[41] In the summer and autumn of 1945, it posted a call for each building's residents to write letters to the Committee if they had seen "anything morally or politically questionable in the building manager's activity".[42] The Committee also required the concierges to fill out a questionnaire inquiring about their wartime acts and habits. For example, question number 18 specifically asked about the concierges' compliance: "What kind of actual role you had in connection of executing the anti-Jewish regulations?" The answers to this question reflect how much the concierges were aware of being part of a system which targeted the robbing and marginalization of a previously powerful social group. Some simply answered "I was a building manager"[43] or they had done "only those things which were required from a concierge".[44] These sorts of responses suggest either that the *házmester* saw it as self-evident that they took part in the ghettoization of Budapest Jewry, or, it is also possible that some respondents wanted to give the impression that the *házmester*'s role was rather passive. When someone observes the events passively, they often do not regard themselves as responsible for the outcome. However, in these days of June 1944 the Budapest building managers had been acting on behalf of the ghettoizing authorities, and after the war several of them recalled actual tasks that they had performed. For instance, Mária Sztankó from Andrássy út 13 answered on the investigators' questionnaire honestly: "as a building manager I had to list and hold the Jewish assets left in the house".[45] Similarly, István Konrád confessed that he "helped to write inventories of the Jewish valuables" in Szondy utca 18.[46] Some even tried to formulate their answers in a way that could leave a more positive impression on the post-war Justificatory Committee. Győrffy Istvánné from VII, Csányi utca 4 answered that "as a building manager I listed and safeguarded the Jewish furniture and other things."[47] Contrary to Mrs Győrffy's answer, in June 1944 the concierges were primarily entrusted to hold control of these "Jewish assets", not by the expelled Jewish Hungarians but by a government that was interested in financially benefitting from the anti-Jewish measures.[48] The decree of the Interior Ministry ordered those so-called Jews who had to move out from their apartments to write an inventory of their furniture, personal belongings and clothes. It had to be indicated what was going to be taken to the Yellow Star house. Everything else had to be closed up in one of the rooms of the emptied apartment. This list was to be signed by the building manager as well as the building warden.[49] Many non-Jewish Budapest citizens requested [*kiigényelték*] pieces of the ghettoized Jewish Hungarians' furniture in the second half of 1944. The *Magyar Szó* daily reported this, quoting commissioner Túrvölgyi on the issue: "As for the furniture left in the former Jewish apartments, we receive very many requests. Obviously, the bomb victims are going to get the necessary furniture [first]. They can pick it up at the competent branch of the Mayor's Office finance department, which is located at Szent István körút 15."[50] Mrs Dévényi's diary reflects this problem from those Jewish Hungarians' vantage point, who had to move into the designated ghetto buildings. She was particularly disappointed to leave her living room furniture. "I am so sorry to leave all this here"—she laments—"I loved this furniture so much. How long and how hard I worked for this room [to look like this]. I had to get all the furniture piece by piece, and once I got them, how much I took care of them."[51]

Writing inventories aimed at preventing Jewish Hungarians from selling, gifting or hiding their valuables.[52] In line with this, Tivadar Szinnai cited in his autobiography a rumour about the coming police raids in the Yellow Star houses: "there will be frequent raids of apartments when they check whether the Jews possess only those things that are mentioned on the list, and any kind of difference can cause internment."[53] Significantly, the safekeeping and storing of the assets left behind officially belonged to the Finance Ministry's responsibilities.[54] However, in practice everything had to be done by ordinary Hungarians, for example by the building warden of Király utca 90, who, in a report written to the Mayor's Office, complained because the building manager let a Jewish Hungarian tenant move out without taking a proper inventory of the assets he took with him and those he left behind.[55] This building warden wanted to make it clear that he was not at all responsible for the financial loss the concierge's negligence could cause for the state.[56] (Figure 2.2)

In the summer of 1944, possessing a list of assets left in an emptied "Jewish apartment" also presented a certain temptation for the building managers. Decree 147.662/1944-IX of the Budapest mayor on the *Compulsory inventory writing about the Jewish assets* specifically named the building managers as the holders of these inventories. As they also held keys to each and every apartment, many concierges were accused of robbing the tenants' valuables before the former tenants could return after the war in 1945.[57] Ágnes Gergely in her memoir published in 2013 only recalls that when she and her mother had to move out from their

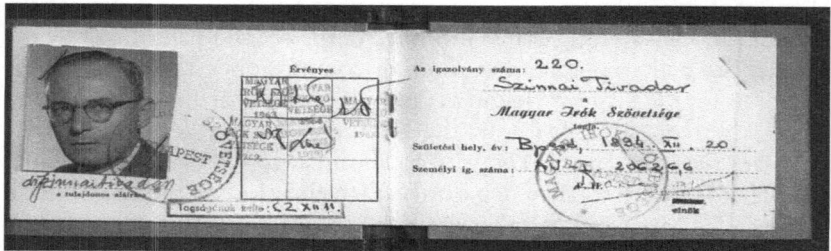

Figure 2.2 Tivadar Szinnai's post-war member card at the Hungarian Writers' Association (from the private collection of Ádám Tábor, Budapest)

apartment located in Visegrádi utca—in an apartment building designated solely for non-Jews—they had to leave their keys with the concierge in June 1944.[58] Although Gergely does not say openly that she accuses the building manager of stealing, she suggests this by writing in the same sentence about the lack of their bedroom furniture by the time they arrived back immediately after the end of the war.[59] In 1945, concierges were sometimes seen dressed in the clothes stolen from the Jewish Hungarian tenants' emptied apartments. In fact, stealing was among the most common reasons for denouncing the concierges at the post-war Justificatory Committee, and in some cases the surviving inventory was attached as proof of the existence of those things that were no longer to be found in their June 1944 location.[60] In certain cases the concierges handed these inventories to the Arrow Cross fighters or to other looters. For example, one of the strongest post-war charges against Mr Mikes, a building manager from Zsitvay Leó utca, came from a Jewish doctor practising there until 1944, who blamed the *házmester* for delivering the list of his assets left behind to a right-wing physician.[61] Hence, it can be fairly concluded that possessing the inventories of Jewish assets further increased the concierges' power over the property of the relocated middle classes, and opened new ways of enrichment for them. They could take the Jewish Hungarians' objects themselves, or they could simply facilitate other ordinary Hungarians stealing them (Figure 2.3).

5   Renting Out the Expelled Jewish Hungarians' Apartments

In apartment buildings designated for non-Jewish use, renting out of the empty apartments provided additional income for the concierges, and it also gave them opportunities to improve the living conditions of their friends and family members. Braham, in *The Politics of Genocide*, presents a centralized view of the apartment distribution where "[a]fter the departure of the Jewish tenants, the superintendent [meaning by this the building manager] of every affected building was to prepare and post a list of vacancies, specifying the location, number of rooms, and rental cost of the newly free apartment," and it was the authorities who decided who received this kind of apartment.[63] However, theory and practice sometimes differed in these chaotic weeks, and in practice building managers played a more direct role in renting out the formerly "Jewish-inhabited" properties. For example, once the Benedikt family was relocated from their

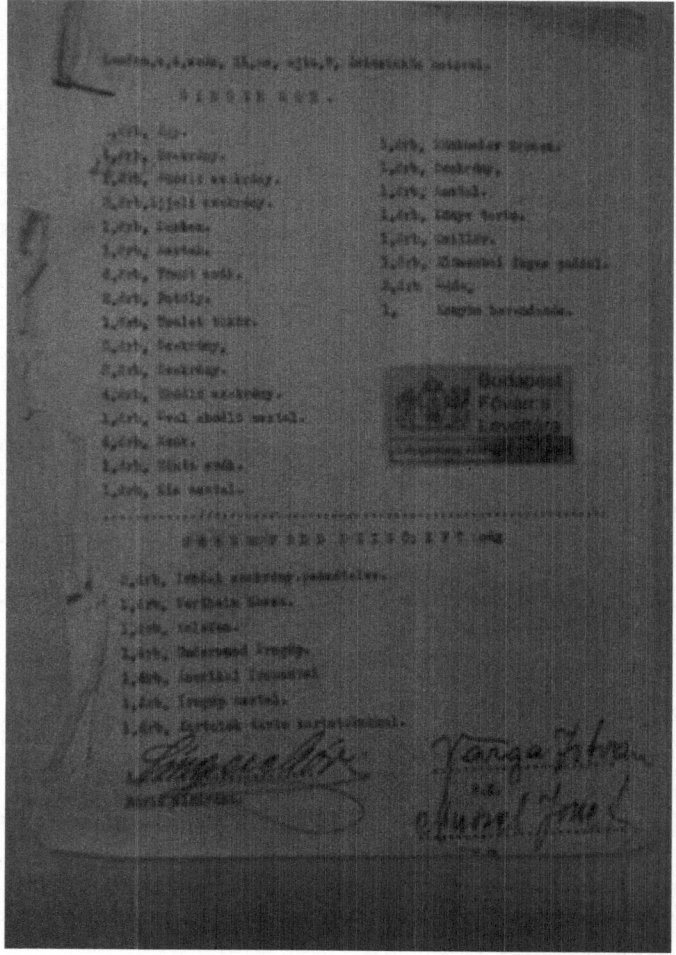

Figure 2.3 An inventory from Laudon utca 4, apartment II/7, where the ownership of the lost belongings was proven precisely by this document[62]

home at Lehel utca 19, the concierge rented their first-floor apartment to a train ticket conductor and his wife. The new tenants until this point were living at Lehel utca 7, only a couple of buildings further from Lehel utca 19, therefore it is likely that the building manager used his social capital when filling this vacancy.[64] Similarly, Imre Patai mentions in his diary that during his time in the Yellow Star house, his previous apartment on Szent István körút was rented by the building manager. He even names the new tenant, a bookbinder who was in fact the son-in-law of this *házmester*.[65] When Patai attempted to call the concierge to account, he answered disrespectfully: "the Budapest Jews should be happy that they weren't deported like the Jews from the provinces." Although it happened only in November 1944, the case of János Dolmányos also belongs here. He was the building manager of a Yellow Star house at Csáky utca 21. In November, concerned about their safety, the Jewish Hungarian Boschán family moved from here to a building protected by the Swiss embassy. [66] They tried to return to their old home right after the liberation, in January 1945, when they found that their apartment was already inhabited by the *házmester*'s brother-in-law.[67]

Contemporaries estimated at least 25,000 vacated apartments as a result of the ghettoization in Budapest, and it was the concierges' direct interest to rent them, otherwise their earnings could decline sharply.[68] Their periodical, the *Nemzeti Házfelügyelő* moaned about this issue in an article entitled "Building manager in the storm of decrees", which starts with a general complaint: "the concentration of Jewish Hungarians brought lots of problems for the building managers, especially for those whose apartment building got Jewish designation. Naturally, there are several of them who are concerned about living together with Jews. ... No surprise that they turned to the authorities because they do not want to clean after Jews and collect their rubbish. ... A serious problem of the concierges of non-Jewish designated buildings that once the Jewish inhabitants were taken from these buildings, there is no one to pay the rent..."[69] Traditionally, if an apartment became available in a building, the concierge placed a note next to the entrance with the relevant information. This sort of notice appeared on the gate of Csengery utca 52 in June 1944, and almost exactly a year later Mrs Irén D., once the supervisor of the building, threw new light upon this advert. Writing to the Justificatory Committee she recalled that she promoted Mrs Lóránt, her cleaning lady to the building manager post, and in return Mrs Lóránt continued cleaning her apartment up until the German occupation, when she suddenly announced the end of her cleaning services in Irén's apartment.[70] The building supervisor, being of Jewish descent, felt the need to strengthen her position, therefore she sublet the majority of her living space, three rooms from her four-room apartment to a Christian subtenant. As she explained to the Justificatory

Committee after the war, "when in June 1944 I had to move to a Yellow Star house, both my subtenant and I asked Mrs Lóránt not to rent out my flat by putting out a note, because in those times a lot depended on the building managers' goodwill." Despite Irén's request, the building manager rented the furnished apartment to a security guard. Sometime later in 1944, when Irén once again tried to exercise her power over the concierge she answered that she had no authority anymore over her or over the building, and if she had tried to come back to Csengery utca she would had been reported to the Gestapo.[71] In these cases it is not only worth noticing how many ways a building manager could benefit from the ghettoization, but it is also interesting to see that very often the lower middle classes took over the rentals of the higher strata. The security guard, the bookbinder and the train ticket conductor all could significantly improve their living standard by taking over the empty apartments of the relocated Jewish Hungarians.

6   FINDING AN EMPTY ROOM

In the summer of 1944 there was clear shortage of living space designated for Jewish use. In addition to the second list of Yellow Star houses reducing the available vacancies considerably on 22 June, several non-Jews also decided to stay in their apartments located in the Jewish designated buildings. This theoretically could be viewed even as progressive counter segregation behaviour, yet, in practice these actions further lowered the available dwellings for the approximately 225,000 Jewish Hungarians living still in Budapest.[72] The ghettoization decree allowed every Jewish family to have only one room, and Jewish Hungarians—being lucky to stay put in a building where they already lived—were encouraged to provide space for their extended family, or for their friends.[73] Those who did not manage to come to an agreement with some "Jewish main tenant" were directed by the Jewish Council's housing department.[74] Being able to choose with whom one needed to share one's apartment suddenly created a special property market driven by trust and interest, and it is telling that Tivadar Szinnai, for example, had not one but two of these kinds of opportunities. On the one hand, he and his wife were invited by a friend to move to their place on Hunyadi tér; on the other hand, they had a mutual agreement with a nearby lawyer as well, according to which if one of them was going to be lucky enough and find his apartment located in a designated building, the other could move in immediately into a spare room.[75]

To make a deal like this official, Szinnai had to take the main tenant's welcoming declaration [*befogadó nyilatkozat*] to the local Jewish Council's housing department, which on the basis of this document issued a formal relocation assignment [*beutalás*].[76] Beside this—at least according to Samu Stern, a one-time president—the Jewish Council contributed to the cost of moving for those who could not afford it, and assisted the relocation of the masses in various ways. Nevertheless, this help did not increase the popularity of those involved, rather the notoriety. Stern claims that "although we provided transporters specialist, we gave all possible help, but all was in vain: those who had to leave their homes kept blaming us."[77]

For the actual relocation Jewish Hungarians were given only a couple of days, since the final list of Yellow Star houses appeared on 22 June 1944, whereas the deadline for completing all relocations fell on the evening of 24 June.[78] Zsuzsanna Ozsváth, who could stay put because their house in Abonyi utca was designated for Jewish use, mentions the disturbance of these days. "[M]y father stayed home and we watched the hurrying masses of people from the window. Some carried their belongings in horse-drawn wagons, others in wheelbarrows, on their backs, in their hands. Marching in endless, chaotic lines, they looked harried, lonely, desperate, and, I even thought, insane."[79] Ozsváth, besides describing these implausible street scenes, also gives a longer account of the occurrences within the building:

> The next few days brought about changes of a magnitude that we could not even have imagined before. First of all, large numbers of people were moving into our building. Some were children, some adults; some were old, some sick, some invalid. The foyer on each floor, as well as the entrance halls of the individual apartments, were filled with groups of men, women, children, old people, furniture, packages and personal belongings. The building looked, as my father said, like a war zone, with large groups of combatants and refugees moving back and forth, both inside and out. It took a few days before the chaos settled.[80]

Obviously, the building managers were heavily involved in restoring order and finding everyone a place. One woman, Mrs L. from Kmetty utca 2, refers to the moment when she had to move out from the building that was designated for non-Jews.[81] She explains that due to her old age and poor health she was unable to arrange the relocation, but the building manager, Mrs Németh offered her a helping hand. According to her letter to the Justificatory Committee, the concierge not only helped in transporting Mrs L.'s belongings to the Yellow Star house, but she also held safe many valuables.[82] But not all concierges were ready to help. For instance, Mrs A., a mother of two, wanted just a little more time before she moved out from Pannónia utca 22, because her children had flu, and she simply did not want to spread the sickness to their new flatmates in the ghetto house. "I had asked the building manager to give me just a little more time for moving out, but he refused, saying, the sickness is not that serious. And when I asked him to help [in moving] I asked him in vain."[83] Perhaps the most helpful were those building managers who assisted already in the creation of the Yellow Star house. For this, the best example comes from Szent István park 10, where the building manager, Mrs Papp, as was mentioned earlier, came from the same place as the city mayor, and with her personal connection was instrumental in the building's Jewish designation. Her husband, Mr György Papp, now helped the 53-year-old Mrs J. to move within the building from one apartment to another, for which she offered him first 50 pengős, and then when he rejected the money, two of her carpets, which he accepted.[84]

7   SEALING THE GHETTO BUILDINGS

The last phase of ghettoization began when the buildings designated for Jews were sealed, and it was 7200/1944 order of the police chief that introduced new rules for the Jewish Hungarians.[85] This order specifically referred to the building managers (in this document as *házfelügyelő*) and gave them specific tasks to fulfil. On the basis of 1240/1944 decree of the government, the building managers or building owners were required to write (together with the building warden) a list of the Jews living in the Yellow Star house. On this list they had to indicate the person's name, age, sex and the apartment in which they were to be found. These lists were produced in triplicate and were signed both by the *házmester* and the building warden.[86] One list was placed on the main entrance of the building, while the others were kept by the building owner or the concierge, and were given to the authorities upon request. According to paragraph 3, it was the concierge's responsibility to check the number of the ghettoized people every day, and to report if any of the Jewish Hungarians went missing.[87] Therefore, these concierges played a critical policing role. Not by accident, even the Gestapo gave a note to the *házmester* of Szent István körút 13, when it arrested Imre Patai, who was registered there.[88] Here the building manager wanted to make sure that he was able to give a satisfactory explanation about the whereabouts of the person missing from the ghettoized Jews' list. Patai survived the Holocaust, and his diary—with many valuable references to the Budapest building managers—is available at the archive of the United States Holocaust Memorial Museum. It will be occasionally quoted in the coming chapters of this book (Figure 2.4).

The creation of a Yellow Star house naturally also meant the physical presence of a yellow star on the façade of the building. When the mayor of Budapest published the first list of Jewish ghetto houses, the appendix of 147.501/1944-IX decree defined the differentiating sign as "a canary-yellow Star of David, 30 centimetres in diameter, on a 51 by 36 cm black background."[89] Theoretically, the landlords were responsible for getting these signs but in practice the concierges picked them up at the taxation departments of the district municipalities. Mrs Tóth, *née* Erzsébet Csőre, a building manager from Vilmos Császár út remembers that it took no less than three days to get a sign like this. To speed up

Figure 2.4   The Photo of Imre Patai, USHMM, ACC. 2000.155

the marking process, this concierge asked one of the tenants, Mr M., to draw a yellow star for this purpose.[90] This tenant gave a different account, stating that the building manager was only hastening the marking process because she wanted to invite her *Nyilas* [Arrow Cross] friends to come and rob the building.[91] Indeed, soon after the ghetto houses were sealed two young men dressed in Arrow Cross uniforms arrived at Vilmos Császár út 19/d. The concierge let them in with unexpected obedience, and on the pretext of searching the premises they entered the apartments and stole several articles of value from there, including Mr M.'s leather gloves.[92] Reading his complaint gives the impression that some of the trapped Jewish Hungarians expected protection from the building managers even after the ghettoization was completed. But from the viewpoint of an authority that ordered the ghettoization of the Jewish Hungarians, the building managers' role was closer to a watchdog's position; they not only controlled the border between Jewish and non-Jewish living space, but also had to keep these people under surveillance. What is interesting here, however, is that the careful reading of the tenants' testimonies reveals how the surveillance worked in reciprocal ways. The following chapters will take a closer look at the Jewish Hungarians' observations of the Budapest building managers' behaviour within the ghetto houses.

In essence, the Budapest building managers appeared to be surprisingly active during the ghettoization of Jewish Hungarians. Instead of simply witnessing it, the concierges took part actively in this process, and many of them tried to influence it at every stage. They had multiple opportunities to exercise power in these critical weeks, given the role of the authorities, but also of the owners and by the requests of the tenants. Hence, through ghettoization the anti-Jewish legislation brought the empowerment of the Budapest *házmester*. This was not at all the Nazi authorities' intention, rather it was a consequence of the implementation of a dispersed ghetto plan. In a way, it was just a side-effect of the anti-Jewish legislation. The authorities delegated crucial tasks to the Budapest building managers, and by this they changed radically the power relations within the apartment building. There are clear references among the post-war retribution files of the concierges' involvement in the preliminary measures of the building designation, just as in the actual moving in and moving out phase. Close to 2,000 apartment buildings were transformed into ghetto houses with a yellow star fixed on their façades, which became the living space of the confined people. Once the relocation was completed, the authorities specifically put the building managers in charge of guarding and controlling the number of ghettoized individuals. From this moment, the Jewish Hungarians were only permitted to leave the Yellow Star houses for a short afternoon period between 2 p.m. and 5 p.m. (1920/1944.M.E. decree, later this was changed to 11 a.m. to 5 p.m.). The entrance gates of these buildings were guarded by the building managers, and for the trapped Jewish Hungarian tenants these ordinary individuals symbolized the connection between the limited and unlimited space. They themselves represented the door for the outside world—an outside world about which Georg Simmel rightly notes that its only outside character derives from the presence of the door itself.[93]

NOTES

1. Huhák, Szécsényi, Szívós (eds.), *Kismama sárga csillaggal* (Budapest: Jaffa, 2015), p. 20.
2. Gábor Kádár and Zoltán Vági, *Aranyvonat* [Gold Train] (Budapest: Osiris, 2001), p. 156.
3. Kádár and Vági, *Self-financing Genocide*, p. 87.
4. *Kismama sárga csillaggal*, pp. 24–25.
5. Szinnai, *Sötét ablakok*, p. 86.
6. A report of the BSZKRT numbered 3312/1944, reference stop: Szépilona.
7. See especially on this Deák, "A Fatal Compromise?", p. 58.
8. *Kismama sárga csillaggal*, p. 44.
9. Kádár and Vági, *Self-financing Genocide*, pp. 77–78.
10. BFL XVII/1598, Magyar Házfelügyelők és Segéd-házfelügyelők 291/a. sz. Igazoló Bizottságának iratai. [The 291/a Justificatory Committee Files of the Hungarian Building managers and of the Assistant Building managers] (Hereafter: Justificatory Committee Files), box no. 4, the case of Mr Hidegh, the letter of Emil N., dated 16 April,1945.
11. Randolph L. Braham, *The Politics of Genocide: The Holocaust in Hungary*, Vol. 2. (New York: Columbia, 1994), pp. 850–861.
12. Braham, *The Politics of Genocide*, vol. 2, p. 851.
13. Cole, *Holocaust City*, pp. 101–103. Scholars rarely note though that this was actually the second data collection in which the Budapest building managers took part in a very short time. In April and at the beginning of May 1944, the Jewish Council collected data through them about the apartments rented by Jewish Hungarians. See on this for example BFL/IV. 1409c, Petitions submitted to the Mayor's Office, IX 2128/1944, a letter dated 2 May, in which the concierge of Hollán Ernő utca 6 corrects the lists of Jewish tenants. On the other side of the letter a note from the city mayor's counsellor tells that the data gathering was initiated by the *Magyarországi Zsidók Szövetsége* [Alliance of the Hungarian Jews].

14. Braham, *The Politics of Genocide*, vol. 2, p. 852. This resonates with a statement from Samu Stern's memoir, in which the former head of the Jewish Council states that they were in contact with Szentmiklóssy who acted with good-will when designating the buildings for Yellow Star houses. See this in Samu Stern, *Emlékirataim: Versenyfutás az idővel* [My memoirs: a race with time] (Budapest: Bábel, 2004) p. 323.
15. Cole, *Holocaust City*, pp. 102–103.
16. Ibid., p. 102.
17. Ibid., p. 103.
18. BFL/IV.1409c, Documents of the Mayor's Office, IX-3075/1944 (box no. 1866).
19. See on this: http://www.bparchiv.hu/id-2259-szenzacios_irategyuttes_kerult_elo_magya.html, last accessed on 6 January, 2016.
20. Cole, *Holocaust City*, p. 102, p. 105, and pp. 112–115. Braham, *The Politics of Genocide*, vol. 2, p. 852.
21. These documents are available at the Budapest City Archive with the reference number BFL/IV.1409c, IX-2781-2791, Documents of the Mayor's Office, Petitions submitted to the Mayor's Office. See on this especially Cole, *Holocaust City*, pp. 131–156.
22. *Kismama sárga csillaggal*, p. 66.
23. See the description of a building warden in Péter Handi, "A ház rétegei" [The layers of a house] in *Remény*, 13, no. 1, 2010.
24. BFL/IV.1409c, Petitions submitted to the Mayor's Office, IX-2789/1944, a petition dated 19 June 1944, p. 3.
25. Ibid.
26. BFL/IV.1409c, Petitions submitted to the Mayor's Office, IX-2784/1944, pp. 31–32.
27. BFL/IV.1409c, Petitions submitted to the Mayor's Office, IX-2789/1944, p. 83.
28. In another petition the inhabitants of Rákóczi út 51 express their will that they do not want to remove the Jewish designation over their building, because the majority of them had already found better quality exchange apartments in non-Jewish buildings, BFL/IV. 1409c, IX-2027/1944. Similar cases are discussed in Cole *Holocaust City*, Chapter 6.
29. 147.501-147.514/1944 decrees of the Mayor of Budapest. About the number of buildings, see Friedrich Born's report published in László Karsai, *Vádirat a nácizmus ellen, vol. 4* (Budapest: Balassi, 2014), p. 88. See it also in Cole, *Holocaust City*, pp. 108–125 and 156–159 on the 22 June designation list.
30. BFL/IV.1409c, Petitions submitted to the Mayor's Office, IX-2789/1944, a document dated 21 June 1944, p. 171.
31. Cole, *Holocaust City*, p. 105 and p. 126.

32. BFL/IV. 1409c, Petitions submitted to the Mayor's Office, IX-2789/1944, pp. 121–123.
33. BFL/IV. 1409c, Petitions submitted to the Mayor's Office, IX-2782/1944, p. 48.
34. BFL XVII/1598, Justificatory Committee Files, box no. 6, the case of Mrs Papp, the minutes of a hearing at the Justificatory Committee on 22 November 1945.
35. Cole, *Holocaust City*, p. 142.
36. BFL XXV 1a, Documents of the Budapest People's Court, the case of György Papp, case number 1945/1500, pp. 76–77.
37. According to the Justificatory Committee's questionnaire filled by Mrs Papp, she came from the Eastern town of Hajdúdorog, while the mayor's middle name "Doroghi" refers to the same place.
38. BFL XXV 1a, Documents of the Budapest People's Court, the case of György Papp, case number 1945/1500, see the testimony of Vilmos Hajdu p. 61.
39. Cole, *Holocaust City*, p. 142.
40. On the memory of the Hungarian Holocaust see Zsófia Frazon and Zsolt K. Horváth, "A megsértett Magyarország. A Terror Háza mint tárgybemutatás, emlékmű és politikai rítus" in *Regio. Kisebbség, Politika, Társadalom*, 2002/4, pp.303–347, Ferenc Laczó, "Between History Politics and Historical Responsibility. The Legacy of the Hungarian Holocaust in Contexts", in *OSTEUROPA*, 12/2011, Péter György, *Apám helyett*, (Budapest: Magvető, 2011).
41. Ágnes Nagy, "Lakóközösség kontra háztulajdonos, házmegbízott kontra házfelügyelő:Osztályharc a bérházban. A budapesti házfelügyelők igazolása 1945-ben" [The tenants' community counter building owner, class struggle in the apartment building: the justificatory process of Budapest building managers in 1945] *Budapesti Negyed*, vol. 17, Spring 2009, p. 164.
42. See an advert of the Justificatory Committee for example in *Népszava*, 13 April 1945, LXXIII: 46, p. 6.
43. See for example: BFL XVII/1598, Justificatory Committee Files, box no. 10, the case of Mr Győző Kovács, see a questionnaire dated 14 June 1945, or see box no. 11, the case of Nehéz Lajosné, VI, Ó utca 3.
44. BFL XVII/1598, Justificatory Committee Files, box no. 11, the case of Mr Mihály Mezei, questionnaire dated 14 June 1945.
45. BFL XVII/1598, Justificatory Committee Files, box no. 12, the case of Ms Mária Sztankó, questionnaire dated 5 July 1945.
46. BFL XVII/1598, Justificatory Committee Files, box no. 10, the case of Mr István Konrád, questionnaire dated 16 June 1945.
47. BFL XVII/1598, Justificatory Committee Files, box no. 13, the case of Mrs Győrffy, questionnaire dated 28 June 1945.

48. Braham notes that the Ministry of Finance got authority over the Jewish assets left in the non-Jewish houses. See this in Braham, *The Politics of Genocide* vol. 2, p. 854.
49. Braham, *The Politics of Genocide*, vol. 2, p. 854.
50. *Magyar Szó*, 23 August 1944.
51. *Kismama sárga csillaggal*, pp. 74–75.
52. Kádár and Vági, *Self-financing Genocide*, p. 79. The authors refer here to decree 1600/1944 M.E., which already ordered the listing of assets owned by *Jews* on 16 April 1944. They also note that "[t]his decree retroactively annulled every sale and purchase as well as donation agreement going back until 22 March, thereby trying to prevent the uncontrolled raining away of Jewish wealth."
53. Szinnai, *Sötét ablakok*, p. 217.
54. Braham, *The Politics of Genocide*, vol. 2 (1994), p. 854.
55. BFL/IV. 1409c, Petitions submitted to the Mayor's Office, IX-2784/1944, p. 18.
56. Ibid.
57. See for example the building warden's report in V, Pannónia utca 18. BFL XVII/1598, Justificatory Committee Files, the case of Antal Szalay.
58. Ágnes Gergely, *Két szimpla a Kedvesben: Memoár* (Budapest: Európa, 2013), p. 73.
59. Ibid.
60. BFL XVII/1598, Justificatory Committee Files, box no. 10, the case of József Mnozik, an inventory from Laudon utca 4, apartment II/7.
61. BFL XXV.2b-1945-9344, Budapesti Népügyészség Büntető Iratok [Criminal Files of the People's Prosecutor Office], case number 9344–1945. See also BFL XVII/1598, Justificatory Committee Files; district V, the case of Mr István Mikes.
62. BFL XVII/1598, Justificatory Committee Files, box no. 10, the case of József Mnozik, an inventory from Laudon utca 4, apartment II/7.
63. Braham, *The Politics of Genocide*, vol. 2, p. 854.
64. BFL XVII/1598 Justificatory Committee Files; box no. 8, the case of Mr Béla Bicsérdy, p. 7.
65. The dairy of Imre Patai, 31 August 1944, United Sates Holocaust Memorial Museum (USHMM) Archive, ACC. 2000.155, box no. 4.
66. BFL XVII/1598 Justificatory Committee Files; box no. 3, the case of Mr Dolmányos. See the minutes of the Justificatory Committee hearing, on 24 June 1945.
67. BFL XVII/1598 Justificatory Committee Files; box no. 3, the case of Mr Dolmányos. See the letter of Klára Boschán, dated 19 June 1945, and see also the minutes of the Justificatory Committee hearing, on 24 June 1945.
68. The 25,000 emptied apartments was an estimation of the Mayor's Office housing department, published in *Pest Hírlap*, 18 June 1944.

69. *Nemzeti Házfelügyelő*, OSZK FM3/5917, vol. 13, no. 7, July 1944, pp. 1–2.
70. BFL XVII/1598, Justificatory Committee Files, box no. 10, the case of Mrs Lajos Loránt.
71. Ibid.
72. Braham, *The Politics of Genocide*, vol. 2, p. 853. Here Braham accepts Lévai's data (from *Zsidósors*, p. 167), according to which approximately 12,000 Christians remained in buildings designated for Jewish use. As for the number of Jewish Hungarians, Karsai quotes the report of the German governor, according to which even at the end of October 1944 there were 200,000 Jews who resided in Budapest. See this in László Karsai, *Vádirat a nácizmus ellen, vol. 4* (Budapest: Balassi, 2014), p. 12.
73. Braham, *The Politics of Genocide*, vol. 2, pp. 853–854. Cole, *Holocaust City*, pp. 126–127. Lévai *Zsidósors*, p. 167.
74. Braham, *The Politics of Genocide*, vol. 2, p. 854.
75. Szinnai, *Sötét ablakok*, pp. 182–183.
76. Szinnai, *Sötét ablakok*, p. 190. The committee's address was VII, Wesselényi utca 7.
77. Samu Stern, *Emlékirataim: Versenyfutás az idővel* [My memoirs: a race with time] (Budapest: Bábel, 2004), p. 324.
78. Cole, *Holocaust City*, pp. 164–165.
79. Zsuzsanna Ozsváth, *When the Danube Ran Red*. (Syracuse, New York: Syracuse University Press, 2010), p. 92.
80. Ibid., pp. 95–96.
81. BFL XVII/1598, Justificatory Committee Files; box no. 11, the case of Mrs Dezső Németh, a letter submitted by Mrs L., dated 12 June 1945.
82. Ibid.
83. BFL XVII/1598, Justificatory Committee Files; box no. 8, the case of Mr István Zseni, the statement of Mrs Zsigmond A., dated 20 June 1945.
84. BFL XXV 1a, Documents of the Budapest People's Court, the case of György Papp, case number 1945/1500, pp. 43–44.
85. BFL/IV. 1409c, IX-2046/1944, box no. 1860.
86. Lévai, *Zsidósors*, [Jewish fate] (Budapest: Magyar Téka, 1948), pp. 170–171.
87. Braham, *The Politics of Genocide*, vol. 2, pp. 855–856.
88. USHMM, ACC. 2000.155, the diary of Imre Patai, a note on 11 August 1944.
89. Braham, *The Politics of Genocide*, vol. 2, p. 853.
90. BFL XVII/1598, Justificatory Committee Files; box no. 12, the case of Mrs Ferenc Tóth, an appeal against the Committee's resolution.
91. Ibid., the letter of Mr Mah., 19 June 1945.
92. Ibid.
93. Georg Simmel, "The bridge and the door" in *Theory, Culture and Society*, February 1994, pp. 5–10.

CHAPTER 3

Building Managers, Bystanders and Perpetrators

This book attempts to show a historically broader view of the Holocaust than is usually shown by scholars, a view that includes the everyday actors and bystanders of the Holocaust. This view is particularly fitting for the Holocaust in Budapest because of this event's several special features. Firstly, the worst part of the Holocaust in Budapest appeared at the very end of the war, and secondly, here the ghettoization, plunder and later the murder of thousands were carried out in the heart of a metropolis. Shops kept their normal opening hours, ordinary people lived their everyday lives while round-ups happened in their proximity. Mrs Dévényi, eight months into her pregnancy, found herself trapped in a ghetto building. She wrote: "we live isolated from the rest of the world. If I look through the window, I can't see the beauty of the Danube as I could see it from home. Here I can only see the dirt on the courtyard, and I can only listen to noises. But life goes on outside of the building. I read the adverts of the holiday resorts. The café houses advertise themselves too … People live their lives and maybe they don't even know what is happening around them. Only we are not allowed to live and only we are not allowed to leave this building."[1] This diary entry shows from the perspective of a ghettoized person that while the segregation and plunder of Jewish Hungarians proceeded smoothly, the bystanders of Budapest lived their lives as if nothing had happened. This chapter will contextualize the book in terms of other works on the everyday actors of the Holocaust,

© The Author(s) 2016

I.P. Adam, *Budapest Building Managers and the Holocaust in Hungary,*
The Holocaust and its Contexts, DOI 10.1007/978-3-319-33831-6_3

with a special emphasis on the *bystander*. One important argument is that the Budapest concierges were not an exception: there were similar groups in other countries as well, whose members from time to time cooperated with the Nazi authorities, yet their actions do not amount to the level of primary perpetrators. Moreover, some of them even saved certain people from persecution. The second part of the chapter will then give a rough idea about the Hungarian society in which building managers had to function. It is crucial to understand their possible options, and to see what a Budapest concierge risked if they considered leaving the position of the bystander.

1   THE BYSTANDERS AND THEIR PLACE WITHIN HOLOCAUST HISTORIOGRAPHY

Although a number of historical works were written about the Holocaust in its immediate aftermath, the significant increase in historiography dealing with the topic emerged only after the trial of Adolf Eichmann, held in Jerusalem in 1961.[2] Since then numerous studies have been written. Nevertheless, throughout the 1970s and 1980s the majority of them dealt almost exclusively with the perpetrators' history, something that characterized already Raul Hilberg's monumental work, *The Destruction of the European Jews*.[3] These studies describe Central European history in the late 1930s and in the first half of the 1940s in an almost exclusive context of perpetrators and victims, within which the acts of the former group represent absolute evil.[4] Hilberg himself presents a homogenous historical picture of the Holocaust with an emphasis on its unique bureaucratic character.[5] And although this homogenous description has been challenged from the 1990s, especially with the occurrence of gender-focused Holocaust research,[6] nevertheless, the categorization of the actors of the Holocaust era introduced by Hilberg as perpetrators, victims and bystanders prevails. While offering a gender viewpoint brought significant publications on the history of victims,[7] there is still a relative lack of bystander-focused Holocaust research. This is in many ways the result of the particularly rich material on the implementation of the persecution. As Christopher R. Browning highlights in the context of the Third Reich: "because the Final Solution was a bureaucratic-administrative process, and so many of the perpetrators, as a matter of a normal procedure, documented their actions at the time, most of what we call perpetrator-history is based on contemporary German documentation."[8] This accessibility of sources on Holocaust administration is one key reason why so many historians focus on the perpetrators. As a result, as Donald L. Niewyk signals, "the reactions by onlookers both inside and outside Nazi-controlled Europe" is one area that remains understudied.[9] This is partly because the sources generally used for assessing the bystanders' attitude and role within the Holocaust are very limited: mostly personal accounts, interviews and memoirs.[10] However, in the case of the Budapest building managers, thanks to a post-war denazification process, several People's Court files, and furthermore, numerous newspaper articles and various other documents are available that describe the concierges from a critical point of view.

A further problem is that the literature on bystanders tends to focus mostly on the bystanders' inactions, which in a sense characterizes for example Gordon J. Horwitz's work about the Austrians who lived nearby the Mauthausen concentration camp.[11] Although according to the prologue, this book's focus is outside of the barbed wire, Horwitz writes mainly about the horror and suffering in the camps and much less about the people living around. Instead of thinking through the bystanders' limited possibilities, or describing how inconceivable breaching the Nazi laws could seem to them, Horwitz lists more and more of the inmates' agony in order to show the horrible things that these Austrian bystanders overlooked. As Michael L. Marrus correctly concludes, this overwhelmingly condemnatory approach does not leave much space for understanding and explanation. Marrus is right when criticizing historians because many of their works describe the bystanders as motivated by disbelief, indifference and unwillingness.[12] Some authors tend to blame the masses without successfully assessing their knowledge and agency over the unfortunate events happening around them, while other historians may adopt the current global value system to social situations culturally completely different from this.[13] Such approaches can easily result in studies lamenting how bystanders failed to help. Instead of this, as Marrus suggests, "we shall go much further in the attempt to comprehend the behaviour and activity (or inactivity) of bystanders by making a painstaking effort to enter into their minds and sensibilities."[14]

Vera Ranki uses the term bystander for the passive population of those countries from where Jews were deported to Nazi concentration camps.[15] I disagree with those scholars, who define the bystander as passive masses, who were neither the victim nor the perpetrator of a mass atrocity. In reality, this category—including in it the building managers—shows a much more diverse picture of people, who got involved in a situation of genocide accidently. It is because of this accidental nature that we sometimes see them as—and why they often want to portray themselves as—neutral peers.[16] Nevertheless, this seemingly accidental involvement does not mean that they were innocent. Victoria J. Barnett sees that "the genocide of the European Jews would have been impossible without the active participation of bystanders to carry it out and the failure of numerous parties to intervene to stop it."[17] Therefore, she continues, these individuals bear some responsibility for what happened around them. This is a good starting point, but in order to avoid being judgmental this book relies on the more nuanced framework of Thomas E. Hill Jr., who thinks that "[w]ithin a system of oppression our responsibility will vary (to some extent) depending on our place in the system."[18] With a reference to the non-intentional participation of the bystander, Hill sees that sometimes one wakes up and finds oneself within an oppressing system. In these moments—argues Hill—there is a moral obligation to counter the wrong-doings of the perpetrators, which he calls a second-order responsibility. I find Hill's words true for the situation of the Budapest building managers. As Chapters 4 and 5 will show, these concierges often failed but sometimes succeeded in countering the Nazi persecution against the Jewish Hungarians. However, among the approximately 25,000 Budapest building managers, that particular group which, in mid-1942, wanted to pick up the positions of the dismissed Jewish concierges deserves a different evaluation. They did not just accidently find themselves in an influential position of an oppressing system, but they deliberately applied for these posts and intended to benefit from them. This makes the case of concierge Imre Papp interesting in particular, and this is why it is worth differentiating between the groups of bystanders in general. Since they intended to profit from the anti-Jewish rules, this group perhaps fits more into the profile of perpetrators. Nevertheless, they saved many Jewish Hungarians, so in this sense they were rescuers too, which makes their profile very ambiguous.

Perhaps the biggest problem of the existing literature originates from referring to the bystander as a more or less homogenous and inactive category. I am using the term bystander rather for those members of the society, who did much more than mere on-looking or bystanding, although most of the time they still did significantly less than those who are usually categorized as primary perpetrators. I agree with László Csősz, who points out, firstly, that even doing nothing influenced the victims' fate, and secondly, there is always an overlap between the perpetrators and the so-called bystanders, especially in the case of Hungary. In this country, a significant part of the society acquired landed property or apartments confiscated from Jewish Hungarians, and thousands—including concierge Papp—took up jobs after the release of the Jewish Hungarian employees as a result of the anti-Jewish legislation.[19] When talking about the Budapest building managers I follow this more active notion of bystanders. Moreover, at times I am questioning even the separation of the bystander's category from the groups of perpetrators and victims.

2   HETEROGENEOUS EUROPEAN MASSES AS THE ACTORS OF THE HOLOCAUST

In Holocaust literature the initial homogeneity of the bystander category was recently stretched by several works, and perhaps the best example of this comes from Frank Bajohr. His thorough analysis of the Aryanization process in Hamburg demonstrates how large segments of German society became accomplices of the Nazi anti-Jewish measures by taking active part in daily auctions of the stolen goods of deported Jews.[20] Bajohr's scope resembles mine when he points to the actual everyday profiteers of the discriminatory legislation, who were nevertheless still far from being primary perpetrators of the Holocaust. A parallel process blurred the borders between perpetrators and bystanders when the definition of the former group broadened beyond ideologically led Nazi leaders to include ordinary men in Christopher Browning's classic work on everyday Germans who became killers during the war.[21] As Browning elsewhere made clear, he wanted to study the choices of the "little men", who stood "at the bottom of the hierarchy of machinery of destruction".[22] The present book aims to contribute to the widening of the definitions of the perpetrator and the bystander. The average Budapest building managers financially benefitted from the anti-Jewish measures, especially by collecting bribes and tips, but also by looting. Nevertheless, these individuals were also helpers, and as we shall see in Chapter 5, often the savours of the Jewish Hungarian residents. Among the more than 20,000 concierges, there was a smaller circle who in June 1944 became the *házmester* of the dispersed ghetto buildings. Although these concierges serving in the Yellow Star houses did not officially belong to any authority, nevertheless on a daily basis they policed the discriminative regulations and acted as intermediaries between the authorities and the ordinary citizens, which gave them much wider latitude than other bystanders. Through the lens of their history one might get a better chance to understand the decision-making of everyday people in crisis situations.

This book about the Budapest building managers is actually not only about the Budapest concierges. In fact building managers held influential positions in other major European cities too. Therefore, instead of offering here an exceptional page of Hungarian history, this book wants to serve as an alternative understanding of mass atrocity, which might be well comparable to the history of other professional groups in other European nations. In this context it is fascinating to learn that in certain Polish cities even giving gate-money to the concierges had been an established tradition, and was called in Polish *szpera*. Writing about Warsaw during World War II, Gunnar S. Paulsson, in his *Secret City* mentions the regular bribing of a concierge, who provided escape routes from the ghetto: "[t]he municipal offices in Długa Street also had entrances on both sides of the wall [meaning the Jewish and the Aryan sides], and, until the Germans got wind of it, the concierge would allow people in and out of the ghetto for 'a few złotys'."[23] Elsewhere Paulsson refers to a porter of a neighbouring building, Kazik, who was in the position of providing hiding space for fugitives.[24] More importantly, the real significance of Paulsson's book is that it introduces the masses of everyday urban rescuers to the Holocaust literature when it tells about the escape routes of Warsaw Jews. According to Paulsson, the hiding Jewish middle class families' "main point of contact with the outside world was through their servants",[25] namely former nannies, cooks, wives or chauffeurs. These pre-persecution employees acted as helping bystanders in Warsaw, just as did the building managers in Budapest in 1944–45. As Paulsson shows, some Polish building managers (in Polish: *dozorca*) were in the position to assist Jews. But from other sources it is known that there were denouncers as well among the Warsaw concierges. For example, Marek Edelman's friend, Abrasz Blum, was arrested when the local building manager locked him up in an apartment and called the Gestapo.[26]

In an important article entitled "Context sociaux de la dénonciation des Juifs sous l'Occupation", the French historian Laurent Joly's focus is on the denunciations of Jews between 1940 and 1944 in occupied Paris.[27] He mentions, for instance, a Parisian concierge from rue de l'Orillon, who in July 1942 had caught a former Jewish tenant's 10-year-old son, when the boy went back to their apartment, and passed him to the police. Joly finds that concierges were overrepresented among those who stood trial after the war for denouncing Jews during the Nazi reign, which he explains with the fact that these people had had more frequent contacts with the Nazi authorities than others. Simply because of their position, the

French concierges were obliged to report about Jewish residents living in their buildings. The cases of Parisian and Warsaw concierges got into this book to prove that the role of these everyday professionals was noticeable in other territories of Nazi-ruled Europe, not only in Budapest. The final part of this chapter will give an overview of the wartime Hungarian society and will present everyday examples of how Budapest building managers reacted to the multiplying anti-Jewish regulations.

3   THE HOLOCAUST HISTORY OF EVERYDAY PEOPLE

This book explores the options and choices of a group of everyday people in the period of the Holocaust. Understanding the masses and their role in the Shoah is all the more important in the current Hungarian context, where, as recently as 2014, the populist government led by Viktor Orbán decided to erect a Holocaust memorial on Szabadság tér, in downtown Budapest, without any kind of consultation with the Holocaust survivors and the offspring of the victims. This memorial—critics argue—gives the one-sided impression that almost all grave acts against Jewish Hungarians were committed by the occupying Germans. This message is conveyed by placing in the centre of the memorial an eagle, the symbol of Hitler's Third Reich. Large parts of the Hungarian political opposition, artists, public figures and Holocaust survivors were all against this statue, and many of them were continuously attempting to block the building of this memorial. In the end, the memorial had to be erected in the middle of the night. As a protest, individual Jewish Hungarians brought objects left behind by their murdered loved ones to create a competing, more human and more realistic memorial called the *Eleven Emlékmű* [living memorial]. The lack of acknowledgement of everyday Hungarians' complicity in the Hungarian Holocaust is something which, in the end, led to the decision of the umbrella organization of the Hungarian Jewish Communities (MAZSIHISZ) to announce that it commemorates the 70th anniversary of the tragic 1944 events separately from the Hungarian government (Figure 3.1).

The memorialization of the Holocaust in the broader Hungarian society remains problematic, just as in other post-communist countries, as these states often struggle to root back their national identities to the historical past, which sometimes includes the maltreatment of their Jewish citizens.[28] At the same time, among the younger generation of research-

Figure 3.1   Construction field in the heart of Budapest: *on the left* are items brought by the relatives of Holocaust victims, *on the right* are columns prepared as part of the new, government-sponsored Holocaust memorial (photo taken by the author, summer 2014)

ers of the Hungarian Holocaust there are several, who recognize the Hungarians' responsibility for the Holocaust in Hungary.[29]

The remaining chapters of this book will investigate the responsibility of the Budapest building managers. The authority of these concierges started to grow especially from the moment Hungary entered World War II. At the beginning of the war the *házmester*'s territorial control was still practised with the same traditional tools as it was during the interwar years: it was based primarily on collecting information and controlling through persuasion. This is in fact a more general characteristic of those individuals who were engaged in this profession all around the world for most of the twentieth century. Not by accident does Bonnie G. Smith depict the Parisian concierge, Madame Lucie, as someone so experienced in command and manipulation.[30] Like their French colleagues, some Budapest building managers had few if any ethical reservations about manipulating their tenants and spying on them. But for those who had some scruples, their periodical, the *Házfelügyelők Lapja* provided patriotic reasoning why they were allowed to enter the residents' privacy particularly in wartime. In its September 1942 issue it published an editorial about the service men's needs: "[o]ur brethren on the battlefield face a harsh winter, while fighting for our Homeland ... [W]e have to make sure that winter clothes are provided for our fighting brothers. We building managers have to take a great deal of this work. As we all stand on a post from where we can see behind the supplies, we know about the things lying forgotten in the attics and in the cellars. These things can have enormous value nowadays. ... But it is not our duty to collect these items; this will be done by authorised persons. Neither is our task to donate, but instead *to make the people donate.* Let us keep in mind these things and urge our tenants to give, let us remind them about their forgotten valuables in the attic or anywhere else..."[31]

Another crucial segment of the building managers' territorial control was connected to the compulsory address registration. In a sense, this registry process was a prominent part of the general control activity of the Hungarian state, and here the information collected was shared between the police authorities and the building manager. The concierge had to approve with a signature the so-called *bejelentő lap* [registry form], before it could be handed in to the police, which was the final stage of a new address registration. Then the concierge also wrote all data in the "registry book of residents". In wartime the urgency of controlling grew immensely, and building managers could feel more and more part of a patrol that made sure that laws—among others the anti-Jewish laws— were obeyed. In 1941, foreign Jews living in Hungary, and those Jewish Hungarians, who could not trace back their family's presence in the country earlier than 1867, were deprived of their citizenship and residence permits. More than 15,000 of them were killed in Kamenets-Podolsk, a deportation that happened some three years prior to Hungary's German occupation.[32] Arthur Saffier, although born in Budapest, had only Polish citizenship when he moved to Csalogány utca 45/b. The local concierge, Mrs Kruger knew this from the registry book of residents, and informed on Arthur to the police as a foreign Jew living in her building.[33] As a result, Arthur was arrested, but he was lucky because his lawyer managed to free him from the internment camp and thus he avoided the mass murder at Kamenets-Podolsk. He kept living in the same building up until the German occupation of Hungary in March 1944, when he then moved to his mother-in-law's. Nevertheless, when he moved out, he had to give his new address, which the concierge entered in the registry book. On the basis of this entry the Gestapo easily found Arthur and took him to the Svábhegy for interrogation. Arthur had survived the war and he testified against the building manager in her post-war trial at the People's Court. In the very same trial there was called as witness a certain person, Mr Világosi. Since he lived in the same building for years, he was able to capture the very essence of concierge Kruger's character in a couple of sentences, which in the minutes of the People's Court read: "Mrs Kruger serves faithfully any kind of government in power. At the time of the Arrow Cross coup she agreed with the extermination of Jews, and truly believed in the *Nyilas* propaganda. However, when the Russians arrived she spread the news about her own Rusyn/Ruthenian [*ruszin*] origin. ... She is perfectly fine with the current situation and expects that as she said 'now we are going to rule' [as a reference to the communists]. Obviously, she does not have any kind of political preferences, she simply thinks about her own benefits." [34] This description is very relevant, because it summarizes the conformity behind the building manager's persistently anti-Jewish behaviour. She had choices, she could leave tenant Saffier in peace, or could just ask him to leave. However, she preferred to notify the police and the Gestapo respectively about the Jewish origin of the tenant.

Since this description seemingly fits to the great majority of the Budapest building managers, and since these people to some extent represent the bulk of the wartime Hungarian society, it is worth looking at the origins of this widespread accommodation of behaviour. Hungarian society gradually got accustomed to the idea of marginalizing the so-called Jewish citizens from the 1920s onwards. On 1 March 1920, Horthy was elected as regent, and three months later the country had to sign the Treaty of Trianon. In this peace treaty the victorious Entente powers set the new Hungarian borders, which meant that Hungary lost more than two thirds of its territory (71.4percent). For the "tragedy of Trianon" the Horthy regime accused the democrats, the liberals, the communists and the Jews. This anti-semitic sentiment was heated further by many of the refugees from the newly lost territories, who did not find available positions in commerce and industry because many of these were already under the control of Jewish Hungarians. This widely shared anti-semitism characterized Horthy's years (1920–44) and the era's public life. As the historian István Deák rightly assesses, openly anti-Jewish measures were not only approved but also demanded by a significant part of the Hungarian population.[35] One such rule was Act XXV of 1920, the Numerus Clausus Law, which limited the enrolment of Jewish Hungarians in the universities.[36] During the 1920s and 1930s, the public administration developed and maintained a racially based discrimination, which was tacitly agreed by successive governments.[37] From 1938 onwards this anti-semitic practice became official and was dubbed "the changing of the guard" [*őrségváltás*]. This was a paraphrase that meant the exclusion of Jewish Hungarians from all important segments of the Hungarian society—including the building managers—and the occupation of their positions by "trustworthy" Christian Hungarians. In line with this, in the spring of 1938 the so-called First Jewish Law was passed, which aimed at reducing the presence of Jews among physicians, lawyers, editors and journalists, and in commercial and financial spheres.[38] Act XV of 1941 banned the marriage of Jews and non-Jews, whilst Law XV of 1942 "obliged Jewish agricultural landowners to *relinquish* their landed property".[39] By this time the Aryanisation already reached the level of shops, pharmacies and workshops, and in the meantime Jewish merchants, lawyers, journalists and newspaper editors all had to give up their professions to provide space for the officially-backed national Christian middle classes. In 1942, the government extended the Aryanisation into the building managers' profession: no Jewish Hungarians were allowed to hold this post anymore after 1 August 1942. By this time, most Budapest concierges, like the above-described Mrs Kruger, and millions of other ordinary Hungarians believed in the inferiority of the Jews. However, this was a sort of functional anti-semitism. Just as Mrs Kruger, who wholeheartedly believed in the *Nyilas* propaganda in 1944, and yet was the supporter of the Soviet occupying troops less than a year later, plenty of everyday Hungarians switched party colours a number of times due to the political circumstances. And this is a general phenomenon: neither the concierges nor the Hungarians were unique in this respect. In the *Homage to Catalonia*, Orwell reports on thousands of Spaniards who joined the Communist party in 1937 "as a way of saving their skins".[40] In the Austrian culture, Helmut Qualtinger's cabaret piece, the *Herr Karl*, became the symbol of those masses who changed their political affiliation like a weathercock between the Nazis and the Social Democrats in the late 1930s. On the one hand, these moves were and are about the wish of belonging to the winners, which could be observed on the European peripheries even in the case of current mass movements. On the other hand, in the 1930s and 1940s both the Nazi and the communist ideologies suited those Budapest concierges, whose primary goal was immediate enrichment through a radical redistribution of wealth. Mrs Anna Dévényi, 11 weeks after giving birth to her daughter, in a diary entry dated as late as 1 October 1944, expressed her amazement at how many ordinary Hungarians still believed passionately in the Nazis. She found this enthusiasm astonishing at a moment when the swift approach of the Red Army on the Eastern front, and Romania's and Bulgaria's withdrawal from Hitler's alliance, made the approaching victory of the Allies inevitable. As she complains, "...it is unbelievable that they are so close [the Soviet troops] and these [local masses] act as if they could still win the war. I can't even read the dailies. They are full of lies and misinformation. And how many people still believe in them, they can't even imagine that it could be otherwise. ... Part of them is indifferent, others wish to keep these times forever..."[41]

Especially after the Nazi German occupation of Hungary in March 1944, obviously the vast majority of the Budapest building managers accepted the Nazi ideology, and within this the marginalization of Jewish Hungarians. Since they did not question the morality of the stricter and stricter anti-Jewish decrees published day after day, in this period it became part of normality that concierges reported about Jews trying to evade the regulations. It is enough to mention here two cases from the so-called DEGOB database, which means testimonies given by returning concentration camp inmates. These stories were recorded by the National Committee for Attending Deportees in 1945–46, and although the interviewees are identified only by their initials, their testimonies are available online nowadays.[42] In one such interview Ms M. Á. explains how her building manager denounced her because this concierge got to know that she obtained fake Christian documents for herself and for her family. As a result, on 24 June 1944, M. Á. was arrested and deported from Budapest first to Sárvár, and then from there to Auschwitz.[43] In another case, the *házmester* noted L. R., a fugitive Jewish forced labourer hiding in a Budapest building, and asked him for his registry documents. Since he could not provide the concierge with relevant papers, L. R. ended up in Dachau.[44] But one can easily find similar cases among the People's Court files as well. János Monostori was the building manager of Benczúr utca 1, where, at the beginning of December 1944, two young ladies moved in. When they tried to register themselves, the concierge told them that their Christian documents looked false. A couple of days later concierge Monostori threatened the young women with denouncing them to the Arrow Cross, shouting "I am not going to hide two Jewish girls..."[45] These women might have posed a danger for the *házmester*, as he could have been arrested for harbouring Jews. Therefore, they meant a source of stress for him, which is why he tried to force them out from the territory he controlled. Finally, the building manager succeeded, the two ladies searched for another hiding place, but when a week later they came back for their belongings, concierge Monostori closed the gate and phoned the Arrow Cross, who took them to one of their head offices at the Hotel Royal. Why was this building manager so much afraid of letting the fugitives stay? Prior to the Arrow Cross takeover, those who helped the Jewish Hungarians risked up to six months' internment, but after 15 October 1944 anyone who assisted the escapees could even be sentenced to death, or just badly beaten by the *Nyilas* militia members without any legal procedure. Nevertheless, by rescuing Jews the Budapest building managers in certain cases risked even their jobs, and losing their job also meant losing their homes, therefore there was a lot at stake for them. The deputy president of the post-war Building Managers' Free Trade Union claimed that there were no less than 94 Budapest concierges who were killed by Arrow Cross militiamen for sabotaging the Nazi regulations.[46] However, historical sources do not support this claim; on the contrary, there are thousands of retribution documents and testimonies which prove the Budapest building managers' collaboration with the Nazi rulers.

Thus, it is fair to say that in the last year of World War II, Budapest building managers informing on Jewish Hungarians was business as usual, so much so that if a concierge did not inform on hiding people to the police, it could seem to be an irregularity. The photo of Mr and Mrs Pusztai is placed in Chapter 1 because this couple received the Hungarian version of the *Righteous Among the Nations* award for saving their Jewish tenants during the war.[47] In November 1944, concierge Mrs Pusztai was summoned to the local Arrow Cross headquarters at Szent István körút 2, because of her unwillingness to report Jews.[48] Although there were several people hiding in her building in Falk Miksa utca 6, instead of denouncing them, Mrs Pusztai took three of her kids with her to the Arrow Cross headquarters. With her children—one of them was still a baby—she managed to evoke the feeling of solidarity from her interrogators and she was let free. Therefore, as the example of Mrs Pusztai shows, some Budapest building managers indeed had options, and they could decide whether or not to hand in Jewish Hungarians to the Nazis, although this sort of sabotaging of anti-Jewish laws put the concierges into considerable danger. Mrs Pusztai, just like Mrs Kruger and Mr Monostori, served as a building manager in a non-Jewish building. However, the power relations were somewhat different in the Yellow Star houses, where the *házmester* had significantly more freedom to act. The next chapter will follow the footsteps of those concierges who served in the designated ghetto buildings, and will also discuss the creation of the so-called international ghetto in Budapest.

NOTES

1. Huhák, Szécsényi, Szívós (eds.), *Kismama sárga csillaggal*, p. 79.
2. Michael L. Marrus, *The Holocaust in History* (London: University Press of New England, 1987), pp. 4–5. See on this also: Tim Cole, *Selling the Holocaust* (New York: Routledge, 2000), p. 8.
3. Raul Hilberg, *The Destruction of the European Jews* (New York: Holmes and Meier, 1961).
4. See on this Jürgen Habermas, *A posztnemzeti állapot. Politikai esszék.* [The Post-national state. Essays about politics] (Budapest: L`Harmattan, 2006), pp. 45–46. See also Gábor Gyáni, "Emlékezés és felejtés" [Rememberence and forgeting] in *Kritika*, vol. 34, September 2006.
5. See this also in Raul Hilberg, "Two Thousand Years of Jewish Appeasement" in Donald L. Niewyk (ed.), *The Holocaust: Problems and Perspectives of Interpretations* (Boston: Wadsworth Cengage Learning, 2011), pp. 144–149.
6. See on this, Joan Ringelheim's speech at Stern College, New York in March 1993, cited in Tim Cole "The Return of György András M.: Writing Exceptional Stories of the Holocaust" in *Journal of Jewish Identities*, 1, no. 2, 2008, p. 31.
7. See for example: Katalin Pécsi, *Salty Coffee: Untold Stories by Jewish Women* (Budapest: Novella Kiadó, 2007); Laura Palosuo, *Yellow Stars and Trouser Inspections: Jewish Testimonies from Hungary, 1920–1945* (Uppsala: Uppsala Universitet, 2008); Louise O. Vasvári, "Emigrée Central European Jewish women's Holocaust Life Writings" in *Comparative Literature and Culture* Vol. 11, March 2009. Andrea Pető, "Women and Victims and Perpetrators in World War II: The Case of Hungary" in Rogen M., Leiserowitz R. (eds.), *Women and Men at War* (Osnabruck: Fibre, 2012), pp. 81–97.
8. Christopher R. Browning, *Collected Memories. Holocaust History and Postwar Testimony* (Madison: The University of Wisconsin Press, 2003), p. 39.
9. Niewyk, *The Holocaust*, p. 7.
10. Cole, *Holocaust City*, p. 135.
11. Gordon J. Horwitz, *In the Shadow of the Death: Living Outside the Gates of Mauthausen* (New York: Maxwell Macmillan, 1990). See on this problem

also: Tim Cole, "Writing 'Bystanders' into Holocaust History in More Active Ways: 'Non-Jewish' Engagement with Ghettoization, Hungary 1944" in *Holocaust Studies*, 2, no. 1, 2005, pp. 55–74.

12. Marrus, *The Holocaust in History*, pp. 156–157.

13. See for example: Bela Vago, "The Hungarians and the Destruction of the Hungarian Jews" in Braham and Raphael Vago (eds.), *The Holocaust in Hungary: Forty Years Later* (New York: Columbia University Press 1985), pp. 93–105. This is also a popular argument for example against Jan T. Gross' *Neighbours: The Destruction of the Jewish Community in Jedwabne* (London: Arrow Books, 2003).

14. Marrus, *The Holocaust in History*, p. 157.

15. Vera Ranki, *The Politics of Inclusion and Exclusion. Jews and Nationalism in Hungary* (New York: Holmes and Meier, 1999), p. 135.

16. Victoria J. Barnett, *Bystanders: Conscience and Complicity during the Holocaust* (Westport: Greenwood, 1999), pp. 9–10.

17. Ibid., pp. 11–12.

18. Thomas E. Hill Jr., "Moral Responsibilities of Bystanders", *Journal of Social Philosophy*, vol. 41, no. 1, 2010, p. 29.

19. László Csősz, *Tettesek, Szemtanúk, Áldozatok. A Vészkorszak Jász-Nagykun-Szolnok megyében* [Perpetrators, Witnesses, Victims: the Holocaust in Jász-Nagykun-Szolnok County] (PhD Thesis, University of Szeged, 2010), pp. 111–113. See this also in Kádár and Vági, *Self-financing Genocide*, p. XXV.

20. Frank Bajohr, *Aryanization in Hamburg: The Economic Exclusion of Jews and the Confiscation of their Property in Nazi Germany* (Oxford: Berghahn Books, 2002).

21. Christopher R. Browning, *Ordinary Men, Reserve Police Battalion 101 and the Final Solution in Poland* (New York: Harper, 1998).

22. Christopher R. Browning, "German Memory, Judicial Interrogation, and Historical Reconstruction: Writing Perpetrator History from Postwar Testimony", in Saul Friedlander (ed.), *Probing the Limits of Representation: Nazism and the "Final Solution"* (Cambridge: Harvard University Press, 1992), p. 27.

23. Gunnar S. Paulsson, *Secret City: The Hidden Jews of Warsaw 1940–1945* (New Haven: Yale University Press, 2002), p. 63.

24. Ibid., p. 50.

25. Ibid., p. 52.

26. Hanna Krall, *The subtenant: To outwit God* (Evanston, Ill. : Northwestern University Press, 1992), pp. 245–247.

27. Laurent Joly, "Context sociaux de la dénonciation des Juifs sous l'Occupation" in *Archives Juives*, vol. 46, no. 1/2013, pp. 12–34.

28. Jeffrey Blutinger, "An Inconvenient Past: Post-Communist Holocaust Memorialization" in *Shofar*, vol. 29, No. 1, 2010. p. 74.

29. See on this for example, Ferenc Laczó, "Caught Between Historical Responsibility and the New Politics of History: on Patterns of Hungarian Holocaust Remembrance" in Simona Mitroiu (ed.) *Life Writing and Politics of Memory in Eastern Europe* (London: Palgrave, 2015), pp. 185–201.
30. Bonnie G. Smith, *Confessions of a Concierge: Madame Lucie's History of Twentieth-Century France* (New Haven: Yale, 1985), p. 142. See also this on p. 89.
31. *Házfelügyelők Lapja*, vol. 19, no. 4, September 1942, p. 4.
32. Ibid., p. 32.
33. BFL XXV.1.a - 779/1945, the case of Mrs. János B. and Arisztid S., pp. 11–12. In this section, the original name of the concierge, Mrs. János B. was changed to Mrs Kruger to protect her privacy.
34. BFL XXV.1.a - 779/1945, the case of Mrs. János B. and Arisztid S., p. 36, the testimony of József Világosi.
35. Ibid., pp. 45–48, p. 57. See also on this: István Deák, "The Peculiarities of Hungarian Fascism" in Randolph L. Braham and Raphael Vago (eds.), *The Holocaust in Hungary: Forty Years Later* (New York: Columbia University Press 1985), pp. 43–51.
36. See on this: Mária M. Kovács and Viktor Karády (eds.) *The Hungarian numerus clausus law and academic anti-Semitism in interwar Central Europe* (Budapest: CEU Press, 2011).
37. Ágnes Ságvári, *Studies on the History of Hungarian Holocaust* (Budapest: Napvilág, 2002), p. 83.
38. Ibid.
39. Ibid., p. 16.
40. George Orwell, *Homage to Catalonia* (Boston: Mariner, 2015), p. 98.
41. *Kismama sárga csillaggal*, p. 116.
42. See this on www.degob.org
43. http://www.degob.hu/index.php?showjk=1807
44. http://www.degob.hu/index.php?showjk=2420
45. BFL XXV.1.a - 171/1945, the case of János Monostori, pp. 8–10.
46. See this in an article entitled "Kerületi taggyűlések" in *Házfelügyelő*, vol. 1, no. 2, September 1945, p. 4.
47. The award the Pusztais received is called *Igaz Emberek Társasága*.
48. Oral history interview with László Pusztai, undertaken by the author, on 19 September 2012, in Budapest.

CHAPTER 4

Turning the Yellow Star Houses
into Protected Houses

Creating Yellow Star houses meant radical changes in the power structure of the apartment buildings. Concierges rose through the ranks quickly, and they became more and more indispensable. As the authorities did not show too much interest in regulating the inner life of the ghetto buildings, it remained largely unclear what was allowed and what was not inside the Yellow Star house. In the autumn of 1944, towards the end of the war the Hungarian state administration started to fall apart, and this had implications both inside and outside of the Budapest apartment buildings. Outside, in the broader national context, it brought a German-backed coup of the extreme-right *Nyilas* or Arrow Cross movement, while inside its effect varied from building to building. Within the Arrow Cross the different factions had different goals; one of these was to gain international recognition for Ferenc Szálasi's government.[1] This goal indirectly led to the appearance of a modified version of the ghetto house, the so-called "Protected house" in November 1944. This protection in theory meant that a certain neutral country got authority over a specific group of Jewish Hungarian people, who were connected to this state by family or business relations. Then these people could move into buildings placed under the supervision of the certain state. In the autumn of 1944, the expectation of the new Arrow Cross rulers was that if they allowed the establishment of "Protected houses", then those neutral countries that set up these sheltering buildings were going to recognize Ferenc Szálasi as the legitimate leader of Hungary.[2]

© The Author(s) 2016

I.P. Adam, *Budapest Building Managers and the Holocaust in Hungary*,
The Holocaust and its Contexts, DOI 10.1007/978-3-319-33831-6_4

In practice, however, the "Protected house" primarily meant utter chaos in massively overcrowded buildings, where—on the pretext of checking the validity of the protective documents—Arrow Cross militia members regularly robbed and rounded up Jewish Hungarians; many of them were killed on the shore of the river Danube. The nature of this complete disorder within the apartment house was complex. On the one hand, it gave a growing freedom of action to the *házmester*, but on the other hand, it was also a challenge for them. By the summer of 1944, the concierges were already struggling to maintain order in the Yellow Star houses, and the same task became more and more difficult in the later period, when the number of ghettoized Jewish Hungarians multiplied in the decreasing number of ghetto buildings. It was a stressful time for being a *házmester*, but also a time that brought opportunities. The creation of the "Protected house", and this sort of imaginary extraterritoriality, resulted in new freedom for them, and some of those serving in the ghetto buildings managed to fill this power vacuum with their own rules, and forced these rules upon the trapped Jewish Hungarians. Thus in the period after 15 October, certain building managers introduced new control techniques and assumed an even greater control than before over the ghettoized people.

1   THE AUTHORITIES' DECREASING CONTROL OVER THE GHETTO HOUSES: JEWISH HUNGARIAN CHILDREN AND THE OFFSPRING OF THE *HÁZMESTER*

In June 1944, the Hungarian authorities constructed a dispersed ghetto from 1,951 Budapest apartment buildings, which are known as *Csillagos Házak* or Yellow Star houses. The June ghetto orders confined the Jewish Hungarians to Yellow Star houses, and they introduced a narrow timeframe—from 2 p.m. to 5 p.m.—when one person per Jewish family could leave these buildings to do the food shopping. By putting this shopping period in the afternoon, the authorities made sure that non-Jews could buy up most foodstuffs before the Jewish Hungarians could reach the shops and marketplaces. Nevertheless, the authorities did not provide internal rules for the ghetto buildings. In this situation it was the Jewish community leaders who tried to regulate ghetto life. However, since they did not have formal authority to do this, they could only set a recommended framework of everyday life. Once the moving out and moving in process was completed, the journal of the Jewish community published its suggestions, which were supposed to ease the conflicts over the tragically limited living spaces. It started with the assumption that "…due to the circumstances, from now on three or four families have to share the home of a single family. To make this situation bearable, we suggest collecting all the food ration cards in every apartment, and cooking together."[3] The leadership of the community also advised the harmonization of bathroom needs. In each and every apartment a so-called unit supervisor [*lakásfelügyelő*] was elected, who was in charge to decide over the tenants' daily matters. For the solving of deeper conflicts the Jewish Council's Housing Department formed a conciliation committee.

The setting up of the dispersed ghetto in June 1944 meant that the Budapest concierges' power in apartment buildings assigned for Jewish use grew immensely, yet it did not become limitless. Until the forming of the "Protected houses", in late summer and early autumn 1944, the authorities felt that they were still in a position to regulate life within the apartment buildings. They were even willing to side with the Jewish Hungarians against the concierge in order to keep the rule of law. This is exactly what happened at Szervita tér 5, where the Budapest Mayor's Office interfered in a dispute over who was allowed to move into a certain apartment of the ghetto house. On 22 September it issued a resolution addressed to the owner of the building and copied to the *házmester*, saying that the Mayor's Office authorized the Jewish Council to decide who could reside in which apartment.[4] Accordingly, the building owners and building managers had to accept and obey these decisions; otherwise they would be carried out by the police authorities. It is noteworthy that this resolution was formulated as a template: the address of the building was left blank and presumably it was used on several occasions. In this specific case the Jewish Council reported to the Mayor's Office that the building manager of Szervita tér 5 had not allowed someone to move into apartment no.2 on the fourth floor of the building.[5] In other instances one can find traces of meddling from as high as the Internal Ministry, which contacted the Mayor's Office to force the owners and concierges of certain buildings to let the people sent by the Jewish Council move in.[6]

But while the governmental and local administration was only able to operate with these indirect actions, the building managers had more direct tools at hand to regulate the everyday operation of the ghetto building, and these tools were first tested against the weakest inhabitants, the confined children. At the beginning of the period, the internal rules of the ghetto houses were vague. In most cases the inner territory, the courtyard [in Hungarian slang: the *gang*] and the staircases were the land of freedom, until the building manager started to limit this anarchy. Especially for schoolboys and girls, ghetto life could even seem beneficial at first sight. Laura Palosuo has noted this with reference to Peter Tarjan, who as a child enjoyed the crowdedness of the Yellow Star house, because "there were always other children to play with".[7] Zsuzsanna Ozsváth describes similar positive feelings: "...for the moment, all rules and regulations had lost their meaning and urgency to most parents of the ghetto house. We did not have to sit down for our meals each time we ate; and nobody watched whether or not we chewed our food as we should. Neither did we have to do homework every day, nor learn French, German or Latin words regularly as we had had to at first when we stopped going to school in March. Now the adults were involved in things other than our training."[8] There was one particular adult, though, who was specifically concerned with the children's misbehaviour, and this was the building manager.

Obviously, children presented a serious threat to the order of the ghetto house: imprisoned in the crowded apartments, they naturally tended to invade the common areas for their play and caused disorder and constant noise. Eszter Lázár explains that all the kids wore sandals made with wooden soles, which clashed loudly on the floors as she and her friends were running around the corridors.[9] Eszter was happy to find many Jewish children in the ghetto house: in the pre-ghettoization weeks it made her frustrated that several non-Jews refused to play with her once she had had to start wearing the yellow-star mark. This is where the classic terms of spatial control, such as exclusion and purification, have to be introduced in this book.[10] János Gross was remembered both as a rigid building manager and as a strict father, who had forbidden his offspring from playing with Jewish children; by this action purifying their living space and protecting his offspring from the alleged threat of negative Jewish influence.[11] Another father mentioned in the Justificatory Committee's files was Alajos Bankovszky, the building manager of a Yellow Star house at VI Podmaniczky utca 29. His case is unique because the post-war investigators based their decision on a child-survivor's account.[12] This child was the eight-year-old Gyuri L., who until he was taken by an Arrow Cross militia, lived here with his mother. Both of them were shot into the Danube, but while the mother died on the spot, Gyuri escaped with an arm injury, swam out from the water and gave his testimony in a hearing of the Justificatory Committee, on 26 July 1945. Gyuri remembered that concierge Bankovszky yelled at the Jewish Hungarian children when he "kicked them out" (excluded them) from the courtyard of the Yellow Star house, and the building manager only allowed his own son to play here ["*s csak az ő fiának engedte meg az udvaron játszást.*"][13] He also recalled how the building manager's son (aged ten) threatened that the Arrow Cross might take him in a chest to Nazi Germany. According to him, this son of the concierge cut dozens of the four-angled Arrow Cross symbols out of paper, and spread them through the entire courtyard of Podmaniczky utca 29.[14] The testimony of Gyuri not only sheds light on what serious implications the building manager's spatial control had on the children's lives, but also shows that the offspring of the building managers were sometimes raised according to the norms of the new *Nyilas* social system. For instance, János Hofgart, a concierge from Barát utca regularly took his son to *Nyilas* party events.[15]

This sort of political affiliation was connected to the concierges' expectations for their children: traditionally the most important goal they set for them was to exceed their parents' lower social position. And this is also why the building managers often used their social connections to get proper schooling for their children.[16] Nissan Hirschman belonged to a group of children growing up in Buda, around Szilágyi Dezső tér and Batthyány tér, in the interwar years.[17] Among his friends, there were several sons of the building managers, and they were without exception the only child of their parents.[18] According to Nissan, parents who came from the countryside put considerable pressure on their children to reach the final exam of the secondary school. As Nissan remembers, "…with a baccalaureate one could become an army officer, or a clerk in a bank. The tuition fee was rather high, but the building managers worked hard to be able to afford to send the youngsters to the gymnasium. They said to them: you are not going to be servants like us; you are going to achieve more!"[19] This parental expectation explains partly why many of these children joined the *Nyilas* Arrow Cross movement, as its populist propaganda advertised a shortcut to social mobility.

The same parental expectation can be seen embodied in scenes recalled by tenants witnessing, for instance, 13–14-year-old teenagers—the sons of building managers—with Arrow Cross armbands and pistols in their hands.[20] But some of these stories ended very bitterly. It is enough to recall what happened with the young László Turi, who was arrested in April 1945. His mother, Mrs Turi was the concierge in Sziget utca 43 (nowadays Radnóti utca), where in the last months of the war the son often appeared wearing an Arrow Cross badge and armband. He informed the tenants that he had joined the so-called Prónai unit, one of the most infamous Arrow Cross militias. Born on 1 October 1928, László Turi was just 16 years old, armed with a revolver, with which he reportedly often terrorized the residents of the ghetto building. The post-war police found several witnesses to this, and they learnt also that the son of the concierge had robbed the emptied Jewish apartments in November 1944, after the Jewish Hungarians had been taken from here by the Arrow Cross. Following the war, in May 1945, the older Turi, in a letter written in dramatic style and addressed to the minister of internal affairs, requested the freeing of his son from the most feared prison in Budapest.[21] He described how a young life was getting gradually broken in the cellar of Andrássy út 60, a building where so many were tortured both during and after the war. In the court file of the young Turi, one can find a description of his family environment, which explains that the parents wanted their son to finish secondary schooling and become a merchant. According to the probation supervisor officer, when in the autumn of 1944 László Turi threatened the Jewish Hungarian residents with the Arrow Cross, "it was only an act of emphasising his self-importance rather than the expression of ill-will."[22] The officer depicted László Turi as a normal teenager, who liked to visit cinemas in his free time and was an amateur philatelist.

Unlike this post-war probation officer's attitude towards László Turi, many of the wartime building managers were less solicitous towards the ghettoized children: in fact, after the war, residents recalled scenes when the *házmester* physically assaulted Jewish Hungarian children in 1944. The historian Máté Rigó in an article refers to a building manager, Mrs Dobozy, who was seen by several tenants beating the children of the ghetto house with a cane.[23] This sort of brutal treatment of children was remembered by the survivors as sickening. However, it was not just about the sadistic nature of the concierge, but rather due to the fact that the inner courtyard was the only available space for play. The children appeared more frequently in the concierge's sight, which is why they became more often the target of physical abuse.[24] To have a full picture, it is worth citing those personal recollections as well where Jewish Hungarians remember how nice some building managers were to them as wartime children. Gábor Kálmán, for instance, remembers one episode, when he was in the air raid shelter, and he badly needed to urinate, but he was not allowed to come up to street level to use the common toilet. He recalls how Kajtár *bácsi*, the building manager, resolved this situation, leading him to the other part of the cellar, where the coal was kept, saying "you can do it here, just don't tell anyone".[25]

Certain adults posed just as much of a threat to the order of the ghetto houses as the children. In Cserhát utca 19 a mentally disabled Jewish Hungarian had problems in silently accepting the crowdedness and radical reduction of living space. It is known from her relatives' post-war testimony, that her presence caused a headache for the concierge: "she [the building manager] was all the time hunting my disabled sister-in-law, threatening that if she did not move away from the Yellow Star house she was going to bring the *Nyilas* to drag her away. At the end, we had to find a shelter for her elsewhere."[26] Other adults occupying the courtyards and corridors were also targeted by the rigid control efforts of the building managers. In a case discussed by the Justificatory Committee, Mrs Rosenthal explained that in the hot summer of 1944, the Jewish Hungarian tenants tended to sit out in the evenings in the corridors of Podmaniczky utca 63. After a certain time, the concierge repeatedly threatened to report them to the Gestapo if they did not go into their apartments. Mrs Reiner suffered similar threats, although according to her, the concierge only fought against those who had been speaking loudly outside, hence the building manager's goal was here to maintain silence and exclude those who disrespected this wish.[27] It is possible that certain residents complained about noisy neighbors, and the concierge only tried to manage the consequences of overcrowding. Nevertheless, other building managers were rather motivated by anti-Jewish sentiment, like Gyula Tóth, a *házmester* from Váci út 28. He reportedly used threats and anti-semitic speeches to silence those talking loudly in the common areas of the Yellow Star house. He said for instance that "this is not a synagogue, you dirty people", when two Jewish Hungarians conversed in his proximity, and he shepherded the individuals into their apartments.[28] All in all, these examples illustrate that the unregulated internal life of Yellow Star houses left considerable space for the concierges to exert control, many of them taking actions first against louder adults and children in the commonly shared areas. It was these building managers who erected new boundaries to the social life of these trapped people, their main goal in doing so being to maintain the internal order. And it was the mixture of these primitive and exclusive rules introduced by the building managers, plus the suggestions of the Jewish Council and the centrally ordered regulations of the Nazi authorities concerning exiting and entering, through which the micro-state of the ghetto building first came into existence.

2   THE PROTECTED HOUSE AS A POWER VACUUM

This international rescue effort became world-famous primarily because of Raoul Wallenberg's heroic life, but the initiative of protecting Jewish Hungarians connected to the neutral states through family lives and business activities goes back to late July 1944, when the Hungarian government approved the emigration of a smaller group to Sweden (300–400), and a larger group with Swiss help to Palestine (7,000).[29] This decision was a reaction to the mounting international protest that followed the deportation of 437,402 Jewish Hungarians from the provinces and the re-annexed pre-Trianon territories, mostly to Auschwitz.[30] The only sizeable Jewish community remained in Budapest, and for saving its members the Swedish, Swiss, Portuguese, Papal and Spanish embassies in Budapest all started to issue protective papers [first *schutzbrief*, later *schutzpass*]. These documents certified that the holder of the pass was either eligible for the issuer country's citizenship, or at least would help them to migrate to these countries in the near future.[31] Consequently, this person fell under the protection of the given state, could live in the apartment building supervised by the state's embassy, and was theoretically exempt from some of the Hungarian anti-Jewish regulations. Mrs Dévényi, for instance, acquired Swedish papers for herself, and she was allowed to walk without a yellow-star badge.[32] She put her thoughts on this in her diary, finding it painful that "the Swedish strangers" had to save her from the hands of the Hungarians.[33] On 23 August, the Jewish Council started to arrange the relocation of those privileged ones who were under Swedish protection to the modern apartment buildings of Pozsonyi út, nowadays the heart of Újlipótváros district.[34] Interestingly, this time the project was hijacked by some of the Jewish Council members, who were concerned about the flip side of the safe conduct, as it also meant the forced moving in the opposite direction of those unfortunates who had to make space for the "protected Jews".[35] Finally, it was the *Nyilas* coup that created the circumstances for the "Protected houses" to come into being, and the network of these buildings was called the "international ghetto". As Tim Cole claims, originally "the 'Protected houses' were to be a preliminary gathering points on the journey from Yellow Star house to transit camp, awaiting the necessary travel permits for emigration."[36] However, by the time the international ghetto started to function, it was clear to all actors that the planned emigration and the "protected status" were no more than a fiction temporarily respected by the Arrow Cross government, which hoped for international recognition by permitting the humanitarian action of these foreign states.[37] To quote László Karsai's ironic words on this, "the diplomats of the neutral states, like Sweden, hurried to act as if they would really organize the transport of the protected Jews, while the Hungarian authorities acted as if they would take these preparations seriously. However, both parties knew very well that without the approval of the Germans no train could leave the territory of Hungary."[38]

From a spatial point of view, the ghetto building—both in its Yellow Star and Protected house forms—was a set space for social interaction, even though it had certain special characteristics compared to normal spaces of everyday life. Dan Michman collected a couple of important definitions of the ghetto, such as Michael Alberti's view, according to which the process of ghettoization served a double goal: getting total control over Jewish population and exploiting it.[39] Michman also quotes Hilberg's classic book from 1961, *The Destruction of the European Jews*, which differentiates three preliminary steps of ghettoization: marking, movement restriction and the creation of Jewish control organs.[40] Nevertheless, for this book, a more useful description of a concentration camp was given in 2005 by Diken and Laustsen, who generally understand the concentration camp as a "temporary site", a "product of order" with a "particular form of life" in it.[41] Elsewhere, they add to this a fourth characteristic, namely that the functioning camp represents a "state of exception", something which is also mentioned by W.A. Douglas Jackson.[42] These features are in most cases valid for the Budapest ghetto buildings as well, with the exception that these apartment buildings were pre-existing sites with established social relations and rules. However, in 1944, radical changes in the broader, outside context had significant effects inside of these buildings. When the so-called international ghetto came into existence, these four characteristics kept functioning, but the particular form of life was less and less defined and controlled by the traditional means of power (such as ministries, police, the Mayor's Office or the Jewish Council), and the building managers found themselves in a power vacuum, where many of them started to act as autonomous agents. In this sense, the "Protected house" is a proof of Christopher Browning's theory about the sealed ghetto being the failure of the centrally led Nazi expulsion policy, where the local authorities were left to improvise.[43]

In most micro-histories written about the Holocaust, one finds examples of how the will of the nationwide authorities is received and employed by local individuals. The protected ghetto building of Budapest, however, tells a different story, where authority at the national level reluctantly closes its eyes and leaves space for the neutral embassies and the local building managers to improvise new rules or to try to maintain a fragile status quo. Of course, towards the end of the war the Hungarian state administration started to fall apart, but it was also the unclear legal background that gave almost full control to certain building managers in the Protected houses. While in the case of the Yellow Star houses one can find examples of external law enforcement concerning the inner territory of the apartment building, this is not the case in the Swedish, Spanish, Papal and Portuguese houses, except for the random raids carried out by the Arrow Cross militias. From the point of view of the *Nyilas* government, these were just gathering spots for all those Jewish Hungarians who possessed protective papers, and thus had certain exemptions from the anti-Jewish rules. However, from the vantage point of the concierge, this was the same apartment building where they worked before, with hundreds of problematic Jewish Hungarians herded into it. The concierge might feel abandoned by the authorities, but it was also a perfect occasion for earning bigger sums at the expense of the trapped people. As the following examples will show, it varied from building to building how much the *házmester* made use of this potentially full control. Yet, significantly there were certain aspects of ghetto life that the concierges generally intended to control more than others. Their decisions and choices in this relative freedom, paired with crisis and chaos, can tell much about how the original idea of racial exclusion was modified by everyday interests, experiences and expectations.

3   THE ARROW CROSS TAKEOVER AND THE CLOSURE OF THE GHETTO HOUSES

By the autumn of 1944 it became clear to the Regent of Hungary that Germany was going to lose World War II. On 15 October, Horthy's attempt to withdraw from the Axis alliance was aborted shortly after the radio announcement of this plan. The Regent was held by the Gestapo, and on the next day the extreme right Arrow Cross or *Nyilas* movement's leader, Ferenc Szálasi, formed a government with the support of the occupying Nazi German forces. Shortly after this, Adolf Eichmann arrived in Hungary and requested the "loaning" of 50,000 able-bodied Jewish Hungarians from Budapest to the Third Reich. These political changes went ahead swiftly in the Castle of Buda, but for the purpose of this book it is more important to see what was going on in the ghetto houses of the Pest side, which is best described in diaries like Imre Patai's wartime journal. Patai spent the day of 15 October in a Yellow Star house on Szent István körút, downtown Budapest. In the evening he walked down to the building manager's lodge, and talked to the inhabitants gathered there.[44] He reports that the tenants were surprisingly confident despite the news of the *Nyilas* coup: they placed a barricade next to the entrance and they even managed to organize an armed patrol. However, at this point the building manager, Istvánffy, slowly started to move away from his initially collaborative approach with the defenders of the building. First of all, when they listened to the news, he did not let Patai switch from the Hungarian radio station to a foreign one to get somewhat more balanced news. A little later the same concierge recommended demolishing the barricade, and Patai's account makes clear his personal disappointment: "I had seen that Istvánffy [building manager] already accepted the rule of Szálasi, in such a moment when the coup's success was not yet at all certain."[45] The concierge failed to match Patai's expectations: despite all potential tips, he took the side of the *Nyilas* conquerors vis-à-vis the tenants. On the next day, as one of its first decisions, the Arrow Cross government ordered the sealing of the ghetto buildings for ten days. Patai knew that he needed to react quickly: "the buildings were closed around 10 a.m., and we [Patai and his wife] went down immediately to the gate, but Karcsi, the son-in-law of the *házmester* did not want to let us go. I went straight to Istvánffy and complained because of the violation of my rights of free movement. Karcsi referred to a policeman, who had advised him not to let out anyone. I told him that a single policeman does not rule the world. Finally, Istvánffy decided that since we are perceived as *exempted*, we were not Jews, hence he could let us out."[46] The way Patai communicated with the concierge is noteworthy: his experience told him that building managers and ordinary police officers were supposed to approach him with respect and obey his decisions. Although he was registered in a ghetto building, he dared to complain over the violation of his rights of free movement. In the end his will was accepted, Patai was free to go, but this was a rather narrow escape.

There were a handful of people as lucky as Patai, but most Jewish Hungarians were locked in Yellow Star houses, and some of these apartment buildings, like Gyulai Pál utca 6, were besieged by Arrow Cross fighters. Just as in Patai's ghetto house, here as well a defence unit was formed from the ghettoized men on 15 October. In attempting to place the building under their own control, these individuals went as far as to intercept the concierge wanting to open the gate. When a *Nyilas* unit was already shooting at the building, somebody took the key from the building manager by force and ran towards the upper floors.[47] Finally, the Jewish Hungarians were forced to yield to the Arrow Cross commando, but during the time between the outbreak of the turmoil and the opening of the gate, several tenants found hiding spots due to their intimate knowledge of the space. As one of them, Mrs H., told the post-war investigators, "six of us hid in a small chamber opening from the biggest room of the cellar, where 55 cubic metres of coal was stored. The door of this spot was behind the coal, and for a stranger it was absolutely impossible to discover this place, unless betrayed by someone."[48] Sometime later the hidden Jewish Hungarians heard steps and the voice of the concierge, Mr Lippárt, saying "they have to be here!"[49] Thus, in this incident the *házmester* offered his knowledge of the space to the new representatives of power, who then beat and robbed the Jewish Hungarians. The same siege appears in a letter sent to the Building Managers' Free Trade Union's leader, Mr Boldis after the war. The author of this letter was inside the apartment building which was surrounded by the Arrow Cross unit located in the nearby Centrum printing house in October 1944.[50] They attacked on the pretext that somebody was shooting from the apartment building, while the pretended reason for beating up one of the Jewish Hungarian guards was that he allegedly assaulted the wife of the building manager. "How did you dare to raise your hand to a Christian Hungarian woman?"—they shouted while beating this man, pretending that the *Nyilas* only acted out of self-defence. The letter mentions the building manager's role in discovering the group hidden in the cellar, whereas others who escaped to the roof of the building were thrown down the stairs by the Arrow Cross men. In the end, everyone was lined up in the courtyard, the *Nyilas* searched through their clothing and robbed them, and finally marched them to the Tattersaal, an assembly point, from where most of them could return to their homes.[51]

From several other ghetto houses, residents reported that the worst harassments committed by the Budapest concierges fell on these days immediately following the *Nyilas* coup, when the defencelessness of the Jewish Hungarians was at its greatest. An outstanding illustration of this can be found in a letter signed by six residents of Király utca 67, which arrived at the Justificatory Committee in the second half of July 1945. They plausibly explain how the Jewish tenants were ordered into the air-raid shelter of the building on 16 October 1944, where they were kept for more than 24 hours.[52] Since the walls of the cellar were shared with a popular bakery situated on the ground floor of the building, an "unimaginable heat built up behind the closed doors ... The people closed in here undressed themselves as they would do on the beach, and they had to deal with their physical necessities in front of other tenants."[53] In this situation, Antal Herzl, the concierge and his nephew offered the roasting tenants the occasional opening of the cellar door for a couple of minutes for a skyrocketing price. Blackmailing was not at all a novelty in the building, as since the beginning of the ghettoization the concierge collected weekly tax-like payments from the wealthy tenants.[54] But the interesting aspect of the scene in the cellar is that it involved the act of opening the door, which could be easily placed in the interwar tradition of services where tenants had to pay for opening the entrance gate in the night. Similar scenes were recalled by the former tenants of Erzsébet körút 54, where Ágnes Zádor remembered that they were closed in a dark and stinking cellar. When she got thirsty, the female concierge brought her water and bread for which Ágnes' mother paid.[55] These instances show firstly how the *házmester* became the ruler of space, and, secondly, they also reveal how the centrally ordered territorial restrictions took a financial character at the micro-level. In some cases the impatient desire for enrichment made use of these severe anti-Jewish measures in which building managers appeared to be critical players.

An episode in Magda Denes' memoir from these days suggests that some of the concierges deserved high tips because of their assistance in this dangerous situation. An Arrow Cross militia was rounding up the Jewish Hungarians in the ghetto building where Denes lived with her mother and grandparents.[56] The Denes family hid for the period of this raid, and later they tried to escape the building with their friends. Some of them succeeded, but when Magda and her mother reached the iron entrance gate, the concierge stopped them, saying that if they left the building the newly arriving Arrow Cross guards could catch them; instead it was better to stay and wait for the right moment. In a way, this building manager showed that he cared about the Denes and he wanted them to survive. In spite of this expression of good will, the next day Magda's mother approached him with a lot of money in her hands and asked for his assistance in leaving the ghetto building. "My mother went to see the super [meaning by this the concierge] with a few hundred pengős.... She returned with the news: 'They are not budging in front of the gate. When they do, the super will let us know. But it will be difficult." Then the Denes had to wait: as

Magda explains in short sentences, they had to wait rather long. The short length of the sentences reflects the limited options of the trapped people: they had to wait and rely on the help of the bribed or rather well-tipped building manager. "We sat. Two hours passed. Four hours passed. We ate jam. More hours passed. The super knocked. 'Time for you to go.' It was mid-afternoon, close to early-winter dark. We raced down the stairway to exit." The Denes escaped and went into hiding.

4   The Arrow Cross Takeover and the Concierges

A couple of days later the Arrow Cross government ended the blockade of the Yellow Star houses. On 19 October 1944, the Defence Ministry ordered all Jewish males between 16 and 60 years of age, and all Jewish females between 16 and 40 years of age to take part in the national defence actions by forced labour work. This order specifically commissioned the Budapest building managers to urge those Jewish residents who fell into the corresponding age group to be ready by 6.30 a.m. and to line up in the courtyard of every building.[57] Moreover, the concierges were also made responsible to report directly to the police any forced labourers returning to their homes. This contribution shows to what extent the concierges became part of the law enforcement, functioning in these cases as the police's right-hand men. In many ways the building managers' longstanding craving for authority was finally fulfilled, and naturally many concierges saw an opportunity in the rise of the Arrow Cross movement.

It is undeniable that many *házmester* welcomed the Arrow Cross movement, although there were various expectations behind this sentiment. Perhaps the most common reason was everyday opportunism that might lead to *Nyilas* party membership, as with the case of Mrs Ványi from Klébelsberg utca 4. The answer this concierge gave for the post-war question why had she joined the Arrow Cross party was short and straightforward: "I joined, because it offered a job for my children."[58] Mrs Ványi's words mirror the seemingly once-in-a-lifetime opportunity the Arrow Cross political movement brought to these families, who had had an extremely low standard of living for decades. The next type worth mentioning here is the *activist* building manager. The Hofgart family undoubtedly belonged to this group. Mr and Mrs Hofgart were the concierges of Barát utca 9, and as such they tried to persuade all other building managers serving in the same street to collectively join the Arrow Cross party.[59] They were present at the dinners and at the Christmas party of the *Nyilas* movement, and they regularly took their 10-year-old son to these get-togethers for educational purposes.[60] The testimonies reveal that Mrs Hofgart stopped doing her meat shopping at the nearby butcher, just because this person did not follow her advice to join the Arrow Cross party, or Alliance MAROK, an organization of the rightist suppliers.[61] Once the butcher rejected this recommendation, the *házmester* started to buy meat elsewhere, which suggests that these individuals selected their contacts in accordance with their political beliefs.[62] The extreme right MAROK alliance even published its own Yellow Pages for conscious rightist customers. Furthermore, there was a so-called Gruber-list, which listed all the *Nyilas* butchers. Building managers did not have a list like this, but for example concierge István Halmai from Szív utca 17 expressed his belonging to the *Nyilas* movement by following the dress code of the Arrow Cross sympathizers: he wore a green shirt with the *Nyilas* badge on it, day in, day out.[63] He also fixed an Arrow Cross flag on his motorbike and kept a portrait of the "nation leader" [*nemzetvezető/führer*] Szálasi on the wall of his lodge.[64] Halmai also tried to pass his affiliation to his children as well, who allegedly finished their daily prayer with the standard Arrow Cross acclamation: "*Kitartás Éljen Szálasi!*" [Don't give up! Hurrah for Szálasi!].[65] Thus it seems that some of these concierges expected to be part of the new elite created by the Arrow Cross *Nyilas* movement, making their belonging clear even in their appearance. Finally, there were undercover building managers as well among those joining the Arrow Cross ranks. In Hunyadi tér 12, for instance, it was not the concierge, but rather the Jewish Hungarian tenants' expectation that made *házmester* József Hamar join the *Nyilas* movement in April 1944.[66] Reportedly, shortly after the Nazi German invasion, the Jewish residents explicitly requested him to become a member of this organization, because they thought that as an insider he could protect the tenants and their wealth more effectively.[67] Practically, Hamar was a secret agent of the Jewish Hungarian inhabitants, and as such he was an exception among those dozens of concierges who became *Nyilas* party members.

5   MOVING INTO THE PROTECTED HOUSE

"Sanyi comes with the news: the Jews are again going to be relocated. They are setting up a main ghetto and a separate ghetto for the protected ones. Everyone who has protection must go to live in the designated protected houses around Pozsonyi út, otherwise you lose protection.

And who doesn't have the protected status must move to the main ghetto."[68] Sanyi was Mrs Dévényi's husband, and he was hurrying to tell this sensational news to his wife about the emptying of the dispersed Yellow Star houses and the setting up of the internationally protected ghetto buildings. On 12 November 1944, the concierges of the Yellow Star houses were given a new police decree, which ordered them to allow those Jewish Hungarians to leave who possessed a temporary passport or a protective document issued and stamped by a neutral state. These persons were free to move between 8 a.m. and 3.30 p.m. for three days (13–15 November), in order to move into the protected buildings around Pozsonyi út and Szent István Park.[69] Apart from what the decree listed as necessary documents for leaving the Yellow Star house, another document was needed to enter the Protected house: a relocation certificate issued by the Jewish Council's housing department, and signed by those who were evicted from the building that had the "protected" status, and also signed by those who were the beneficiaries of the "protection" and were moving into the newly vacated apartment.[70]

It is not easy to assess how many Jewish Hungarians were living in the protected buildings, but the official sources of the *Nyilas* authorities, and those published by the neutral embassies, can give us a rough idea. When on 17 November *führer* Szálasi outlined his plan to solve the issue he called the "Jewish question", he talked about six distinct categories of Jewish Hungarians, the second being that of the "protected Jews", whose number he put at 15,000 souls.[71] To break down this number it is worth summarizing the different type of "protection" that were available in 1944 Budapest. The number of Jewish Hungarians officially holding a Swedish schutzpass reached 7,000 after the *Nyilas* coup.[72] Although the *Nyilas* authorities only approved 4,500 Swedish schutzpass on 31 October 1944, Braham estimates that in November the overall number of Swedish protective pass holders (fake and real ones all together) was way above 10,000, and he reports that these people were placed in no more than 32 Swedish protected apartment houses.[73] Besides them, the biggest group was formed by about 7,800 "Swiss Jews", furthermore, there were 2,500 protected papers issued by the Papal Nunciature, and approximately 700 people held Portuguese schutzpasses. In addition, there was also a small group of Jewish Hungarians, approximately 100, under Spanish protection, and a couple of Turkish protective papers were issued as well.[74] All of this data originates from the books written by Jenő Lévai, a survivor who in the second half of the 1940s produced numerous books on the

Holocaust in Budapest, such as the *Fekete könyv*. However, historians sometimes modified these numbers slightly. For example Lévai's figure of 2,500 was the summary of the Papal protected Jewish Hungarians and those who were placed under the protection of Regent Horthy.[75] However, when using these numbers one has to think of cases that neither Lévai nor Braham consider, such as cases where, firstly, the same person could potentially possess several types of protective papers from various neutral legations. Secondly, cases such as that of Imre Patai, who had Swedish protective papers, but by late November had still not moved into the protected building because, as he explains, the circumstances there were quite challenging, with more than ten people sharing a single room. Still, Patai kept himself registered in a room like that, making sure to have a place in case it appeared to be safer to be in the Protected house than in hiding in buildings designated solely for non-Jews. As a consequence, it is close to impossible to estimate in reality how many people lived in the protected buildings. Instead, we have to work with dynamic numbers, which perhaps peaked in December 1944. For example, in this month there were no less than 540 people living at Szent István park 10, in a building which was normally inhabited by around 60 people.[76] When Mrs Szinnai moved to a "Swiss house" on 15 November 1944, she had to share a two-room apartment with 51 individuals.[77] A week later 42 people lived only in the bigger room and in the lobby.[78] Mrs Dévényi documented the moment when she arrived at a "Swedish house" with her four-month-old baby girl: "We got quite a nice room. A lot of people are living here with us, at least 30 of us in this apartment. Our room is full of stuff left by the previous inhabitant, and I want to keep these things safe. I put everything together, the fragile things into the wardrobe, the rest I put into the bin under the bed. There are all kinds of stuff here: shoes, photos, embroidered pieces. I clean the room, and it starts to become friendly. My only wish is to be able to stay here till the end."[79] The crowdedness in the so-called international ghetto grew continuously. The representative of the International Red Cross, Friedrich Born, at the end of November visited the "Swiss" building at Pozsonyi út 54, and he estimated seeing there no less than 1,800 Jewish Hungarians.[80] He was unable to walk on the staircase because of the masses sitting on the stairs. Nissan Hirschman moved to Újpest rakpart 7 as late as on 24 December 1944. This building was also designated for people holding Swiss protective papers, and the kitchen where Nissan was ordered to stay already had three residents, so Nissan could only set up a sleeping spot for himself under the kitchen table.[81]

It is difficult to tell the number of people living in the international ghetto, but what is certain is that a sizable amount of upper class Jewish Hungarians fell under the almost complete control of the building managers, which was exercised over the boundaries of the Protected house. Still, in the story of each and every protected building there was another key person besides the building manager. Already by the end of August, when the relocations were first on the table, a new housing office was established within the Jewish Council, which acted as a focal point for the setting up of the Protected houses. They appointed to every building an individual as 'house supervisor', who kept tabs on when and how many places became available in that particular property.[82] Dr István Kemény worked at this housing office as the supervisor of the four buildings that fell under Portuguese protection. In the summer of 1945, he sent a short letter to Oszkár Büchler, who led the post-war denazifying process against the Budapest building managers, because he had something to share with him about Antal Szalay, the building manager of the so-called Phoenix house.

Phoenix house is an impressive apartment building, which occupies until the present day an entire block between Pannónia, Katona and Tátra streets. Based on the testimonies of the tenants and the information given by Dr Kemény, a representative of the Jewish Council appointed to supervise the Portuguese building, it is possible to outline the directions of spatial control exercised here by Antal Szalay, the building manager. Dr Kemény explained how Phoenix house was chosen for Portuguese safe conduct in October 1944. He also remembered sending Jewish Hungarians there for whom he assigned rooms in the building, only to see them coming back to his office complaining over the almost physically tangible tension between the building manager and the ghettoized people living there.[83] Szalay, like most concierges, came from the provinces: he was born on 12 January 1892 in Veszprém, and became building manager of Phoenix House on 1 August 1930.[84] In autumn 1944, he repeatedly used anti-semitic curses, questioned the authority of the Jewish Council's Portuguese representative, and maintained an atmosphere of terror in the building. Creating conflicts and using offensive language was a control technique retrospectively legitimized by the post-war People's Court in the Papp case: the above mentioned Szent István park 10 with its 540 inhabitants was an apartment building under Swiss protection. Although several tenants complained about concierge György Papp's verbal and physical abuse, the People's Court understood that the building manager's anti-Jewish outbursts and threats "served exclusively the saving of the Jewish residents", and added that Papp did very well to hide his real "Jew-friendly attitude".[85] Furthermore, even an inhabitant underlined in his statement at the court that it would have been impossible to keep any kind of order without verbal brutality and threats in a building with more than 500 people in it.[86] Thus this last testimony in a way expressed sympathy towards the building manager. Papp was a concierge who took over this post in mid-1942 when his predecessor was dismissed because of his Jewish origin. The court regarded him as someone who got into a complicated situation accidently—like bystanders usually do—and had to deal with this highly overcrowded building. Surely this sort of crowdedness meant an unusual stress and challenge to these concierges, and the sporadic checks of the Arrow Cross militias only made things even worst.

It is interesting to see that very similar conflicts appeared between the concierge and the Jewish Hungarians with relocation papers issued by the Jewish Council in a "Swedish house" at Pannónia utca 24, which stood only some 50 meters away from the Portuguese Phoenix house.[87] Here, *házmester* Lajos Tőke went as far as to state to the newly arriving protected inhabitants that "here the Swedish embassy has no right to command. Here I am the commander, and if you cause problems to me, I will hand you all to the *Nyilas* units."[88] This concierge, who originally came from the distant village of Túrkeve, received in this period a weekly 400 pengő tax-like payment from the community of tenants, more than double an average concierge's monthly salary.[89] It is worth noting that in Phoenix house it was the representative of the Jewish Council, Dr István Kemény, who advised the people relocated there to pay extra amounts to building manager Szalay. As he later explained, he hoped that these larger tips could improve the atmosphere in the building, which sounds like an attempt from outside to influence the authoritarian control exercised inside the Protected house. This attempt fits well the matching expectations of the wealthy Jewish Hungarians and the poorer *házmester*, whose position suddenly became so important: the former expecting special treatment for money, the latter desiring enrichment.

Another way of earning at the expense of the ghettoized people, and consequently another major direction of spatial control, was related to foodstuff. Even though its timing was discriminatively set, until the *Nyilas* coup Jewish Hungarians could leave the ghetto house for approximately three hours per day for the purpose of food-shopping. On 16 October, Szálasi's government ordered the sealing of all Yellow Star houses, and even after the reintroduction of shopping times, it became much more dangerous for Jewish Hungarians to walk on the streets of Budapest than ever before. It represented considerably less danger for market sellers to approach the ghetto buildings and to try to sell their goods there. But as one can learn from the former Phoenix house tenants' letter, which they sent in 1945 to the Justificatory Committee, in 1944 concierge Szalay regularly forced these market sellers out of the building. Following the expulsion, right outside the gate he bought the food from them, and offered it to the Jewish Hungarians inside the building for a sensationally higher price.[90] The building manager also forbade the tenants from receiving parcels from the outside world. Moreover, the same letter explains occasions when Szalay controlled access to foodstuff in the air-raid shelter. Here, the concierge set up a small kitchen, where only his family members and those tenants who were willing to pay for the use of the stove were allowed to cook. As during the siege of Budapest the residents spent weeks down in these shelters, there was a continuous need for cooking. The post-war building warden confirmed this practice, adding that either money or valuable goods such as paintings or silver cutlery, or even occasionally pieces of clothing, were asked by the *házmesterné* for access to this stove.[91]

6   CONTROLLING ACCESS TO FOOD

Access to food is central in many works written about ghetto life. Some underscore that the Nazi Germans consciously restricted the transport of food to the Warsaw ghetto, in order to cause widespread famine there. A group of Jewish doctors documented the symptoms of hunger in these unique circumstances, noting for example how malnutrition slowed down the victims dramatically, which made it harder for them to resist Nazi orders.[92] "Hunger became the leitmotif of the ghetto existence, accompanying it minute by minute, day after day"—says another account.[93] Nevertheless, what is even more telling is that in the very last days of the Warsaw ghetto, during the uprising, when ghetto fighters wanted to question the authority of their commander, Marek Edelman, they went on hunger strike.[94] Even though this was the most absurd act in a place where food was the biggest scarcity, still they thought there was no better way to wreck Edelman's power than by saying no to the provisions offered by him. And this is exactly why it is crucial to explain the Budapest building managers' aim to gain complete control over access to food in the ghetto buildings, because there was much more at stake here than simply accumulating wealth. Exploiting a situation like this not only works business-wise, but it has implications for power relations too. It seems that the building managers rightly suspected that if they became the exclusive source of foodstuff, then the ghettoized people—among whom they distributed the food—would obey their orders with a much higher probability than if they could get the all-important food by themselves. Moreover, this was a male-dominated society, where fathers were the breadwinners in almost every single family.[95] Thus the building manager, who brought alimentation in a period when food was hardly available, could become also a father figure in a ghetto community.

Budapest building managers were keen to control access to food, even though there was a shopping time introduced by the authorities, when theoretically one Jewish Hungarian per family was permitted to leave the Yellow Star houses. In June 1944 this period was first set between 2 p.m. and 5 p.m., which later was changed to 11 a.m. to 5 p.m., but this still meant that by the time the ghetto inhabitants reached the markets, the non-Jews could have bought up everything.[96] During the Arrow Cross era, when the crowdedness in the ghetto buildings' culminated, controlling access to food became even more important. This is seen at Tátra utca 5/c, a "Swedish house", where Mrs Kálmán Tóth, the concierge was remembered as intentionally hunting for food smugglers. She threatened to denounce a Christian lady who agreed to carry in a parcel addressed to a Jewish resident living there.[97] Someone else recalled that the same building manager asked for 10 pengő per day to admit one litre of milk for a baby living in Tátra utca 5/c.[98] The tenants believed that Mrs Tóth basically ran a small-scale food shop in the concierge's lodge.[99]

In the very same street, only a couple of blocks further from the city centre, in Tátra utca 25, according to the tenants' complaint, the building manager (Mr Kárlecz) always delayed the start of the shopping break a bit. In the autumn period he was supposed to let the Jewish Hungarians out at 1.30 p.m. However, he opened the gate only 10–15 minutes later, which made it extremely difficult for these residents to do the shopping on their own. Having no other choice, in the end they bought what they needed through the building manager's mother-in-law, Mrs Marosi, who of course charged very high prices.[100] This concierge punished a Christian woman who brought food for Jewish Hungarians living there by locking her in the cellar.[101] Similarly, in another tenement in the neighbouring VI district, *házmester* Ferenc Auguszt and his wife allegedly disrespected the centrally allowed narrow shopping time and refused to let out the Jewish

Hungarians. As the newly chosen building warden explained after the war, this was how they had created a situation where their tenants were forced to buy food through them.[102] Occasionally the foreign embassies also sent food to the Protected houses, but these supplies were rare and hardly ever provided enough food for everyone. The Red Cross representative was in Pozsonyi út 54 at the end of November, when a supply like this arrived. According to him all food was taken by those residing in the lower floors, while people on the three upper levels did not get anything.[103] (Figure 4.1)

In this sense the case of György Papp, who was mentioned earlier as the concierge of Szent István park 10, is particularly interesting. The abusive and terroristic language he used with his tenants had been approved by the post-war People's Court. But this was also the building that received

Figure 4.1　A cartoon from summer 1944: the gentleman with a stick is not sure about the time but his friend reminds him: it is enough to look at the gate of a Yellow Star house. The flood of yellow-starred people means it is exactly 11 a.m. (In *Egyedül Vagyunk*, vol. 7, no. 17, 25 August 1944, p. 11)

its Yellow Star designation—partly at least—thanks to the personal famil-iarity of the building manager's wife and the city mayor, who both came from the same town in eastern Hungary.[104] Nevertheless, what makes Mr Papp important here is that besides being the concierge of Szent István park 10, which became a "Swiss house", he held a part-time job at the Budapest Food Inspection Agency. The head of this agency even sent a declaration to the People's Court, which stated that Papp worked there as an aide from October 1935 until May 1945, and he had never observed from him any kind of activity related to the extreme right *Nyilas* move-ment.[105] However, Papp, as the building manager, was accused by the ten-ants of not letting in Christian friends bringing food for those imprisoned to the ghetto house during 1944.[106] At the same time, he was accused of profiting from the starving tenants by selling them food, but the People's Court in its sentence rejected this accusation, stating that Papp sold the food at a standard price even in the days of Budapest's siege.[107] What the sentence does not mention, however, is that the building manager could pick this food up for free at the Food Inspection Agency, therefore he was able to earn a fortune without asking for higher prices, and become even respected by some because of his friendly sales policy.

7   HIERARCHICAL CONTROL STRUCTURE OF THE PROTECTED HOUSE

It seems obvious that in the Budapest apartment houses the October *Nyilas* coup and the setting up of the international ghetto formed and restructured the social space and created new internal power relations. As has been already stated, building managers rose sharply up the social scale, but newcomers also had to find their place. This place was usually below the longer-dwelling tenants, even if they had the necessary papers to reside in the Protected house. In case they did not, or their paper-work was not yet complete, they belonged to a group that Patai called the "*pincések*" [the cellar dwellers], which was seen as the lowest caste in this community. In fact, in the apartment building's hierarchical control struc-ture each group had a different position, rights and obligations connected to its position, which becomes clear from the testimonies. In several build-ings most Jewish Hungarians had to pay taxes to the building manager. As was mentioned before, the concierge of Pannónia utca 24 could receive up to 400 pengő weekly.[108] In Kresz utca 29 the residents democratically accepted the introduction of a monthly payment like this until the end of the war.[109] In the "Swedish house" of Pozsonyi út 33/b the protected individuals, besides paying bribes, were also forced to clean the staircases and do other jobs instead of the *házmester*.[110] The air-raid shelter was a place shared by the building manager and the confined Jewish Hungarians every day, thanks to the frequent bombardment of the city, and this was where the social differences became the most apparent. In Tátra utca 5/c, the tenants remembered the building manager as someone who behaved in this shelter like an empress.[111] Like everybody else, when the Allied bombardments began she also brought down her valuables to the cellar: newly acquired expensive clothes and gadgets caught the tenants' eyes. But a couple of blocks away things developed even further: Tátra utca 24 was under Swiss protection with several hundred inhabitants until 2 December 1944, when the Jewish Hungarians were sent from here to the main ghetto, while some of them were shot into the Danube. Until then, two policemen hired by the concierge maintained inner order, which can be understood as the control of space through a third party. But these policemen also acted as the personal bodyguards of the building manager. Ordinary residents suffered because they were not allowed to directly approach him, while at the same time the presence of these uniformed men also prevented the Arrow Cross fighters' attempted robberies.[112]

When someone wanted to break through this hierarchy, building managers initially threatened the revolting ghetto tenants verbally, and if this was not enough, they were ready to reach out for the help of the new authorities. Nevertheless, as the new power structure had only a vaguely established legal framework, consequently the concierges had only limited formalized procedures for cracking down the rebellion. What they could do was mobilize their social capital, and they also relied on their relatives who had already found positions in the governing *Nyilas* administration. These kinds of cases later provoked post-war criminal investigations, like at Paulay Ede utca 13, where a tenant, Mr Stauber, allegedly called the assistant building manager names in the presence of several other tenants on 16 October 1944. According to the post-war police investigation, there was a connection between this incident and the fact that Mr Stauber was badly beaten on the next day by a *Nyilas* commando, who targeted only him in the entire apartment building.[113] In another case, the People's Court dealt with Vilmos császár út 41, where the Selmecis were the building managers. While they were remembered by the inhabitants as specifically Nazi-oriented Hungarians, in fact only their son joined the *Nyilas* movement officially.[114] When the couple had a conflict with three of the tenants, they turned to their son, who showed up in his *Nyilas* outfit and took the rebelling Jewish Hungarians to the Arrow Cross detention centre on Andrássy út for questioning and subsequent beating.[115]

To sum up, while before setting up the international ghetto the building managers saw themselves as links between the authorities and the residents, following it they found themselves in a much more powerful position and some of them started to act as autonomous agents. Law enforcement agencies were not interested in the inner life of a Protected house, except the Arrow Cross fighters who targeted the capturing of Jewish Hungarian individuals hiding there without the necessary protective papers. As a result, it largely depended on the building managers to set up the rules of living together. There were apartment buildings where the concierge became a law unto themselves and acted as a sovereign ruler, and the nature of the rules introduced by these individual sheds light on the concierges' purposes. One prominent example was the regulations and practice related to access to food, with its double implications: on the one hand, these rules mirrored the intentions of earning large amounts in a short period, on the other hand, they were also the product of considerations for gaining complete authority over the ghettoized people.

NOTES

1. On the *Nyilas* movement, see for example: Éva Teleki, *Nyilasuralom Magyarországon* (Budapest: Kossuth, 1974).
2. At the end, it was only the Vatican, Turkey and Spain whose representatives recognized the Arrow Cross regime as lawful. See this in Karsai, *Vádirat a Nácizmus ellen*, p. 17. See this also in Braham, *The Politics of Genocide Vol. 2*, p. 1237. According to Braham, on 31 October 1944 the *Nyilas* government approved the Swedish protection of 4,500 Jewish Hungarians "in the expectation of diplomatic recognition by Sweden".
3. "Tiz fontos pont" [Ten important points]: in *Magyarországi Zsidók Lapja*, 4 July 1944, p. 3.
4. USHMM Archive, RG-39.016M, Acc. 2008.70, BFL IV.1409/c, box 1867, IX-3203/1944. Note that in this period the Jewish Council was officially already called the Association of Hungarian Jews.
5. Ibid.
6. USHMM Archive, RG-39.016M, Acc. 2008.70, BFL IV.1409/c, box 1868, IX-3350/1944. The buildings referred to in this document are the following: V Szent István körút 4, VI Teréz körút 34, VI Hajós utca 16–18, VII Wesselényi utca 4.

7. Laura Palosuo, *Yellow Stars and Trouser Inspections: Jewish Testimonies from Hungary, 1920–1945* (Uppsala: Uppsala Universitet, 2008), p. 149.
8. Ozsváth, *When the Danube Ran Red*, p. 97.
9. Éva Nádor (ed.), *Csillagos házak: Emberek, házak, sorsok* (Budapest: Nádor, 2015), p. 28.
10. See on these terms and their role in spatial control: David Sibley, *Geographies of Exclusion* (London: Routledge, 1995), pp. 72–136.
11. BFL XXV 1a Files of the Budapest People's Court, case number 86/1945, the case of János Gross, p. 19.
12. BFL XVII/1598, Justificatory Committee Files, box no. 8, the case of Mr Alajos Bankovszky.
13. BFL XVII/1598, Justificatory Committee Files, box no. 8, the case of Mr Alajos Bankovszky, a testimony of Gy. L., on 26 July 1945, p. 111.
14. Ibid.
15. See this in Mr Branstadter's and also in Mrs Bíró's declarations, sent to the Justificatory Committee in July 1945, BFL XVII/1598, Justificatory Committee Files, district VII, the case of János Hofgart.
16. See this is Németh, *A medve utcai polgári*, pp. 22–24.
17. Oral history interview with Nissan Hirschman, conducted by the author on 1 November 2010, in Budapest.
18. Certainly, the majority of the Budapest building managers had only one child, which also becomes clear from the questionnaires filled by them in 1945–46, and held among the files of the Justificatory Committee (BFL XVII/1598, Magyar Házfelügyelők és Segéd-házfelügyelők 291/a. sz. Igazoló Bizottságának iratai). The phenomenon is partly explained by the fact that these people were the first generation who moved to the city: urbanization dragged them out of the network of relatives who could have provided help in sustaining more children. In addition, the usually small size of the concierges' lodges also hindered the bigger family plans.
19. Oral history interview with Nissan Hirschman, conducted by the author on 1 November 2010, in Budapest.
20. BFL XVII/1598, Justificatory Committee Files, district V, the case of József Kakula, Katona József utca 21. See for example this in the minutes of the Justificatory Committee's hearing on 8 June 1945, p. 3.
21. BFL XXV1a Files of the Budapest People's Court, case number 1346/1945, the case of László V., p. 120. In this specific case the family name had to be changed from V. to Turi in the text, in order to protect the identity of the juvenile under criminal investigation.
22. Ibid., p. 95. This document is dated 23 August 1945.
23. Máté Rigó, "Ordinary Women and Men: Superintendents and Jews in the Budapest Yellow-star houses in 1944–45", *Urban History*, 40, no.1, 2013, pp. 71–91.
24. Ibid., pp. 87–88.

25. Oral history interview with Gábor Kálmán, conducted by the author, on 21 December 2012, Washington DC.
26. See this in a letter addressed to the Building Managers' Free Trade Union, dated 15 August 1945. BFL XVII/1598, Justificatory Committee Files, district VII, the case of Mrs Diviki, p. 2.
27. Both testimonies were recorded at the hearing of the Justificatory Committee on 13 July 1945. BFL XVII/1598, Justificatory Committee Files, box no. 8, the case of Mrs Bagarus.
28. BFL XVII/1598, Justificatory Committee Files, district V, the case of Mr Gyula Tóth, the testimony of Dr Aladár F.
29. Braham, *The Politics of Genocide Vol. 2*, pp. 874–876. At the same meeting, the Council of Ministers rejected the offer of the US War Refugee Board, which intended to send food and clothing to the ghetto. See this also in Jenő Lévai, *Fekete könyv a magyar zsidóság szenvedéseiről* [Black book about the Hungarian Jewry's sufferings], (Budapest: Officina, 1946), pp. 192–193.
30. Due to the First and Second Vienna Awards, Hungary regained certain territories which the country had lost after World War I.
31. Some of the protective documents only referred to the holder of the pass as a member of the group whose emigration was approved by both the issuer country and Hungary.
32. This permission was given by the KEOKH, the Hungarian Foreign Police Authority.
33. *Kismama sárga csillaggal* (Budapest: Jaffa, 2015), p. 117.
34. Braham, *The Politics of Genocide Vol. 2*, p. 1238.
35. Cole, *Holocaust City*, pp. 199–201. Cole also lists here other potential reasons for the failure, such as the opposition of "non-protected Jews", and changes in the broader circumstances.
36. Cole, *Holocaust City*, p. 192.
37. Lévai, *Fekete könyv*, p. 189. Lévai explicitly states here that none of the involved parties believed in the reality of a coming emigration.
38. Karsai, *Vádirat a Nácizmus ellen*, p. 32.
39. Referred by Dan Michman in *The Emergence of the Jewish Ghettos during the Holocaust* (Cambridge: Cambridge University Press, 2011), p. 6.
40. Ibid.
41. Bület Diken and Carsten Bagge Laustsen, *The Culture of Exception: Sociology Facing the Camp* (New York: Routledge, 2005), p. 17.
42. W.A. Douglas Jackson, *The Shaping of our World: A Human and Cultural Geography* (New York: John Wiley, 1985), p. 309.
43. Christopher R. Browning, *The Path to Genocide* (Cambridge: Cambridge University Press, 1992), p. 30.
44. USHMM, ACC. 2000.155, box no. 4, the diary of Imre Patai, an entry dated 19 October 1944, p. 2.

45. Ibid., p. 3.
46. Ibid., pp. 3–4. "Exempted" was a reference to the personal intervention of Regent Horthy. He exempted certain Jewish Hungarians—such as heroes of World War I—from the effects of the anti-Jewish regulations.
47. BFL XVII/1598, Justificatory Committee Files, district VIII, the case of Mr Pál Lippárt, a testimony written by Mrs Z. H. on 10 September 1945.
48. BFL XVII/1598, Justificatory Committee Files, district VIII, the case of Mr Pál Lippárt, a letter written by Mrs S.R. without date, confirmed with 11 other individuals' signature at the end of the letter.
49. Ibid.
50. BFL XVII/1598, Justificatory Committee Files, district VIII, the case of Mr Pál Lippárt, a testimony written by Mrs Z.H. on 10 September 1945.
51. Ibid.
52. BFL XVII/1598, Justificatory Committee Files, the case of Antal Herzl, Kiraly utca 67, the letter of six residents, dated 17 July 1945.
53. Ibid., p. 2.
54. Ibid., p. 3.
55. Nádor (ed.), *Csillagos házak*, p. 30.
56. Magda Denes, *Castles Burning: A Child's Life in War* (New York: Touchstone, 1998), pp. 74–75.
57. Karsai, *Vádirat a Nácizmus ellen*, p. 96.
58. BFL XVII/1598, Justificatory Committee Files, box no. 8, district V, the case of Mrs Zsigmond Ványi. See the minutes of the hearing at the Justificatory Committee on 13 June 1945.
59. BFL XVII/1598. Justificatory Committee Files, district VII, the case of Mrs János Hofgart, the letter of Ferenc B., dated 21 July 1945.
60. Ibid. This was confirmed by Mr Jenő B. from apartment III/7 on a hearing that took place on 22 August 1945. Mr B. heard this from his children's nursery governess.
61. Ibid., the hearing of Mr Jenő B. on 22 August 1945. See also, Géza Markó, *"Marok" kereskedők és iparosok szaknévsora*. [MAROK Yellow Pages] (Budapest: Held, 1941).
62. BFL XVII/1598, Justificatory Committee Files, district VII, the case of Mrs János Hofgart, the hearing of Vilmos D. (from Barát utca 11) on 21 September 1945.
63. Ibid., see the letter of Ignác G., dated 10 July 1945.
64. See the questionnaire in Mr Hamar's case, dated 5 July 1945; BFL XVII/1598, Justificatory Committee Files, box no. 9, district VI.
65. Ibid.
66. BFL XVII/1598, Justificatory Committee Files, box no. 9, district VI, the case of Mr József Hamar. See the questionnaire dated 23 June 1945, points 14 and 30. From point 9 we also know that Hamar's wealth grew immensely during the war: he was able to buy a landed property for 7,000 pengő.

67. Ibid, a letter of residents dated 15 February 1945.
68. *Kismama sárga csillaggal*, p. 152.
69. See the original Hungarian version of the police decree in Lévai, *Fekete könyv*, p. 230. See this also in Randolph L. Braham, *A Magyar Holocaust* (Budapest: Gondolat, 1988), p. 215.
70. Cole, *Holocaust City*, p. 199.
71. Braham, *The Politics of Genocide Vol. 2*, p. 1223.
72. Braham, *The Politics of Genocide Vol. 2*, p. 1238.
73. Braham, *The Politics of Genocide Vol. 2*, p. 1237.
74. Braham, *The Politics of Genocide Vol. 2*, p. 1238–1245. The very same numbers are published in Lévai, *Fekete könyv*, p. 189.
75. Lévai, *Fekete könyv*, p. 232.
76. BFL XXV 1a, Criminal cases of the Budapest People's Court, 1945/1500, the case of György Papp, the statement of the defendant, p. 41.
77. Szinnai, *Sötét ablakok*, p. 405
78. Ibid., p 435.
79. *Kismama sárga csillaggal* (Budapest: Jaffa, 2015), p. 158.
80. Karsai, *Vádirat a Nácizmus ellen*, p. 34.
81. Oral history interview with Nissan Hirschman, conducted by the author on 1 November 2010, in Budapest.
82. Cole, *Holocaust City*, p. 199.
83. BFL XVII/1598, Justificatory Committee Files, box no. 5, the case of Mr Antal Szalay, the hearing of the Justificatory Committee on 23 August 1945.
84. See this information in the files of the 1945 census [*népösszeírás*], Pannónia utca 18, registry no. 1.
85. BFL XXV 1a Criminal cases of the Budapest People's Court, 1945/1500, the case of György Papp, the verdict of the People's Court, p. 8.
86. Ibid., see this in Sándor M.'s statement on the trial day on 20 July 1945, p. 45.
87. Phoenix house was registered officially under Pannónia utca 18.
88. BFL XVII/1598, Justificatory Committee Files, box no. 7, the case of Mr Lajos Tőke, a hearing of the Justificatory Committee on 8 June 1945.
89. Ibid. See the mentioning of these regular payments in the letter of Henrik N. and Dr István D. in the same case.
90. BFL XVII/1598, Justificatory Committee Files, box no. 5, the case of Mr Antal Szalay, a letter dated 15 April 1945.
91. Ibid., a letter signed by Árpád F. building warden, without date.
92. See this in Marian Turski, "Bunt skazanych" [Riot of the condemned], *Polityka*, no. 16, 17–23 April 2013, p. 21.
93. Gustavo Corni, *Hitler's Ghettos. Voices from a Beleaguered Society 1939–1944* (London: Bloomsbury, 2003), p. 155.

94. Hanna Krall, *The subtenant, To Outwit God* (Evanston, Ill., Northwestern University Press, 1992), p. 202.
95. See on this for example Palosuo, *Yellow Stars and Trouser Inspections*, p. 109.
96. See on this the 1920/1944.M.E. decree, while on the changes of shopping time, see Szilvia Czingel, *Szakácskönyv a túlélésért* [Cookbook for survival] (Budapest: Corvina, 2013), p. 99.
97. BFL XVII/1598, Justificatory Committee Files, district V, the case of Mrs Kálmán Tóth, the letter of Mrs B., dated 31 May 1945.
98. Ibid., the letter of Mr Murányi, without date, p. 2.
99. Ibid., p. 1.
100. BFL XVII/1598, Justificatory Committee Files, box no. 5, district V, the case of Mr János Kárlecz. A letter signed by Jenő V. and other tenants, dated 31 May 1945, point 4.
101. Ibid, point 6.
102. BFL XVII/1598, Justificatory Committee Files, district VI, the case of Ferenc Auguszt, a letter of the building warden, dated 17 June 1945.
103. Karsai, *Vádirat a Nácizmus ellen*, p. 34.
104. BFL XXV 1a Criminal cases of the Budapest People's Court, 1945/1500, the case of György Papp, pp. 76–77.
105. Ibid., p. 78.
106. See this in the justificatory process: BFL XVII/1598, Justificatory Committee Files, box no. 6, the case of Mrs Papp, a letter by Ármin Rejtő building warden, dated 2 May 1945.
107. BFL XXV 1a Criminal cases of the Budapest People's Court, 1945/1500, the case of György Papp, see the verdict of the People's Court, p. 12.
108. BFL XVII/1598, Justificatory Committee Files, district V, box no. 7, the case of Mr Lajos Tőke, See the mentioning of these regular payments in the letter of Henrik N. and Dr István D. in the same case.
109. BFL XVII/1598, Justificatory Committee Files, district V, box no. 8, the case of Gyula Varga.
110. BFL XVII/1598, Justificatory Committee Files, the case of Mrs K. sH., see the letter of Mr K., dated 3 May 1945.
111. BFL XVII/1598, Justificatory Committee Files, district V, the case of Mrs Kálmán Tóth, the letter of Mr M., without date, pp. 3–4.
112. BFL XVII/1598, Justificatory Committee Files, district V, box no. 6, the case of Mr and Mrs Kaltenecker, the hearing of Mrs K. by the Justificatory Committee on 27 June 1945.
113. BFL XXV 1a Criminal cases of the Budapest People's Court, case number 1945/678, pp. 13–15, p. 26.
114. BFL XXV 1a Criminal cases of the Budapest People's Court, case number 1945/441, p. 4, p. 7.
115. Ibid., p. 4, pp. 6–10.

CHAPTER 5

The Building Managers' Role in Rescue, and Their Ways to Enrichment

Generally bystanders are regarded as passive observers, whose passivity limits their responsibility for the genocide happening next to them. Nevertheless, inaction itself is also a form of action, and Ernesto Verdeja calls those who could intervene to stop the persecution but fail to act "moral bystand-ers".[1] Verdeja rightly points to the "moral bystander" as someone who— being part of the same community—is actually responsible for the actions of their fellow citizens who are becoming perpetrators in their close prox-imity. On the basis of this shared responsibility it is easier to comprehend why some of the ghettoized Jewish Hungarians expected protection from the building managers. However, a building manager could not help all the Jewish Hungarians, thus they had to decide whom to help. In order to be able to understand the choices of the *házmester* in 1944, one has to take into consideration the interwar tradition of tipping. This chapter investigates how this tradition evolved in the critical months of 1944, and it will also describe the ways the building managers managed to provide help for the persecuted residents. While showing the variety of assistance

This chapter was written during a fellowship at the Vienna Wiesenthal Institute, and part of the text was first published as an article in the journal of the Institute: *S:I.M.O.N.—Shoah: Intervention. Methods, Documentation*, vol. 2 (2015) 1, pp. 4–14.

the *házmester* could offer in 1944, this section argues that these concierges were able to bridge the structural holes of wartime society through their extensive social networks.

Of course, this chapter deals not only with those helped, but also with those Jewish Hungarians who were not assisted by the concierge in their struggle for survival. While discussing their stories, one needs to bear in mind that social solidarity towards the so-called Jews was seriously damaged by state-funded propaganda. This misinformation propagated the option of easing Hungary's social problems by using the wealth of the Jewish Hungarians.[2] The *Righteous Among the Nations* award was founded for those who were not misled by any kind of propaganda, and who did not want to remain passive bystanders during World War II, but managed to provide actual help for the endangered people. Like Verdeja's category of the "moral bystanders", the introduction of the Righteous category also divides bystanders into morally accepted and unaccepted groups. The problem with both categorizations, however, is that they are unable to grasp the complexity of the micro-landscapes, where these so-called bystanders acted or failed to act. Therefore, while this chapter explores why the building managers helped certain Jewish Hungarians more than others, it will be also asked what makes an ordinary Hungarian *házmester* become a *Righteous Among the Nations*, and how this categorization can simplify the history of a ghetto building.

1   Righteous Concierges Among the Nations

Since 1962, the Israeli authorities have awarded the title *Righteous Among the Nations* to more than 24,000 people who during World War II helped the persecuted Jews. This number includes 17 Budapest building managers. One prominent example of them is Mrs Rozália Korecz, who, according to *The Encyclopedia of the Righteous Among the Nations*, received recognition in 1998, because 54 years earlier, during the Arrow Cross [*Nyilas*] reign, she bravely hid a doctor called Dr Róna at her place, as well as a certain Mrs Fellner, whom she employed as a maid at home.[3] As the building manager of Kádár utca 5, she also put the four members of the Recht family in an empty flat in the building, from where, according to the same *Encyclopedia*, the inhabitants escaped due to the Russian siege of Budapest. Furthermore, she found shelter in the basement for the Váradi family, and later she admitted to her home the eight-year-old Péter Simon with his mother and grandmother.[4]

The post-war Justificatory Committee file of Mrs Korecz contains much evidence of these good deeds and further elucidates the situation in the apartment building at Kádár utca 5 in 1944. First of all, there is Dr Róna's statement, written on a doctor's prescription form, testifying that Mrs Korecz's helpful acts brought danger to herself and to her own family. The physician was eager to explain that Mrs Korecz not only saved many Jewish Hungarians' lives, but she was so busy dealing with the affairs of those in hiding that her own children often had to wait long hours for food.[5] The head of the Váradi family also wrote to the Committee to give details about how Mrs Korecz allowed him to hide in his apartment, even though the concierge knew that he was an escapee from the labour service. She tolerated his presence and even brought him and his family food. Moreover, she urged him to create a hiding spot behind a large wardrobe.[6] These survivors depict concierge Korecz as a proactive and practical person, who facilitated their hiding. This picture corroborates the *Encyclopedia*'s reference to her opening of an abandoned apartment for the use of the Recht family.[7] From a historical point of view she was not an innocent angel, but a wily and smart woman, and probably exactly these attributes made her successful in helping.

However, not everybody wrote to the Justificatory Committee in favour of concierge Korecz. Imre Fehér, a canned food merchant, for example accused her of arranging immunity for the apartment of a "Jewish lawyer", in return for a radio, carpets and a piano.[8] Accordingly, Mrs Korecz manipulated the apartment's registration: since it became registered as a Christian property, it was exempted from the moving in of the ghettoized Jewish Hungarians. What merits interest here is not so much the allegedly earned asset—although the radio has some significance—but rather how powerful a building manager could grow due to the anti-Jewish legislation.

Imre Fehér, during his hearing at the Justificatory Committee, suggested that concierge Korecz and her husband only helped those inhabitants of the building who could pay for their services. His experience was that the building manager was not in favour of him because he, as a poor man, was unable to pay her considerable tips. Imre Fehér lived in a three-room apartment in Kádár utca 5 until June 1944. Mr Fehér claims that during his absence, due to his resettlement with his wife's relatives, the Korecz couple first simply occupied and then formally requested his apartment from the authorities, thereby maliciously ousting him from it.[9] Mr Fehér also believed that after the war Mrs Korecz tried to make it harder for him to get back his former apartment by forging his pre-1944 registration data. Although the post-war Justificatory Committee, at the end of the day, approved concierge Korecz's wartime acts, it had to formally note that while in the summer of 1944 the Korecz family lived in a studio offered for them as a concierge's lodge, by the time of the post-war justification they already lived in the three-room apartment formerly inhabited by Mr Fehér. Moreover, from the minutes of the Justificatory Committee it is also known that Mrs Korecz sublet one room of the three to subtenants.[10] Therefore, what the justificatory process uncovered here—and what is central to this book—is that after the war the lifesaver Mrs Korecz was in a significantly better financial situation than before helping the Jewish Hungarians. The concierge in many ways acted as a landlord, as an owner, when exercising complete spatial control over the building at Kádár utca 5. She could open empty apartments, force tenants out from the building, and by doing so, she could improve her own living standards significantly. However, perhaps the most interesting aspect of this story is that only the act of occupying Imre Fehér's apartment made it possible for the building manager to accommodate the saved Jewish Hungarians, as it would have been impossible in her small lodge to hide people due to the lack of space. The consequence of this move is actually twofold. Firstly, Mr Fehér's three-room apartment, being substantially bigger than the building manager's one-room lodge, made it possible for concierge Korecz to hide the saved Jewish Hungarians. Secondly, once she moved into the bigger apartment, she could also hide some Jewish Hungarians in the empty lodge. Thus, one may speculate that she could only become a recognized *Righteous Among the Nations* because she was able to usurp the Fehér apartment. But what is not at all speculation is that from the perspective of Imre Fehér this story was much more about losing his home than about saving Jewish Hungarians.

The Budapest building managers worked and lived in intimate microcommunities, where they helped certain members of the community, while they also refused to help other members, or they simply forced the residents to follow the anti-Jewish regulations. The inactivity of the so-called bystanders is often due to their unwillingness to enter the sphere of victims and perpetrators.[11] When concierge Korecz hid the persecuted Jewish Hungarians and brought them food, she stepped out from her so-called bystander role and stepped up against the Nazi perpetrators. However, if she really occupied and requested the apartment of Mr Fehér, she might well be suspected of complicity with the perpetrators. Verdeja is right to describe the existing literature as far too static when it comes to the bystander/victim/perpetrator categorization.[12] He calls for a dynamic approach here, because due to the change of circumstances, over time bystanders could become perpetrators or active helpers.[13] It seems that in the Budapest ghetto houses the building manager often repositioned their role not only over time, but also tenant by tenant. And it also seems that actors like Mr Fehér are missing from the stories of the Yad Vashem's *Righteous Among the Nations.*

2   GREY ZONES

It is disturbing to realize how grey was the zone of rescuers, and it is more than understandable that the Yad Vashem, the official Israeli Authority of Remembrance of the Holocaust, tried to narrow down the group of *Righteous.* However, their choice of criteria, especially the exclusion of those rescuers who intended to profit from helping, goes against the tradition of tipping the Budapest building managers. The next section will show why this categorization does not fit the wartime Hungarian reality, and how Yad Vashem's approach "throws the baby out with the bathwater"—to use a stylistically questionable idiom.

Following the German invasion of Hungary, in a period when the "liberating" Red Army gradually approached Budapest, the ability to hide become crucially important.[14] Immediately after Horthy's naively unprepared attempt to withdraw from the Axis, the German troops handed power to the Arrow Cross leader, Ferenc Szálasi. As it became clear to Jewish Hungarians that they needed to survive only for a couple of months, more and more chose to hide themselves; a strategy in which the building managers played an important part. After some hesitation, in November 1944 Szálasi agreed to loan 25,000 Jewish Hungarian forced labourers to Nazi Germany. These unfortunate people were marched towards Mauthausen for days without food and accommodation. These were the so-called death marches, and the Arrow Cross fighters regularly raided the Budapest ghetto houses to find enough Jewish Hungarians for the deportations. It often depended on the concierge who was taken by the Arrow Cross and who could stay put in the apartment building. A principle aim of this research is to challenge the concept dominant in Hungarian Holocaust literature, which sees rescue efforts performed mostly by foreign diplomats and exceptionally brave members of the Hungarian political and social elite. While recognizing the significance of these actions, this book argues that equally significant assistance was provided by ordinary Hungarians, such as the building managers. Nevertheless, unlike concierge Korecz, in most of the cases these people were never awarded any recognition for their activities, because whilst they helped certain Jewish Hungarians, they often chose not to help or had to report others; and also because they did what they did not so much out of moral consideration as for earning tips. Yet, it does not seem fair to undervalue the courage of the helping building managers when tipping was part of normal life and honouring good service by tipping was the *comme il faut*. It seems that some of the concierges did not unfairly exploit the situation of the persecuted people, but got well-deserved rewards for extraordinary services. The introduction of anti-Jewish laws, and the concierges' suddenly growing authority combined with the longstanding tradition of tipping created a unique setting, where the *házmester* could be rewarded for helping the survival of Jewish Hungarians. Viewing these offerings from the twenty-first century, the tendency to think in black and white terms causes difficulties in making moral judgments over the nature of the saved people's donations. Were these bribes or well-deserved earnings? There are several factors here that have to be considered in order to be able to answer this question.

Yad Vashem lists four criteria for the recognition of a Righteous individual, out of which the third is the most significant from the perspective of the present book. It describes a necessary mental state on the saviour's side, which could not include the expectation of any kind of reward—this is obviously in conflict with an average Budapest building manager's mindset, as they lived largely from tips. Yad Vashem's requirement is:

> The initial motivation being the *intention to help persecuted Jews: i.e. not for payment or any other reward* such as religious conversion of the saved person, adoption of a child, etc.[15]

The other three requirements are:

- Active involvement of the rescuer in saving one or several Jews from the threat of death or deportation to death camps.
- Risk to the rescuer's life, liberty or position.
- The existence of testimony of those who were helped or at least unequivocal documentation establishing the nature of the rescue and its circumstances.[16]

Comparing the data of some 500 recognized Hungarian rescuers who fulfilled these requirements, the historian Sári Reuveni notes that no more than 14 percent of them acted during the spring of 1944, when approximately 432,000 people were deported from the Hungarian provinces, mostly to KZ Auschwitz-Birkenau. This means that the majority of the helping, 86 percent, happened in Budapest in the last phase of World War II.[17] Reuveni also notes differences in the nature of help provided. In the countryside, most assistance involved the temporary sheltering of more or less unknown persons who had escaped from a local ghetto, whereas in Budapest the relationship between helper and helped usually had a longer history.[18]

Reuveni is right to point to the importance of a longer relation between rescuers and rescued in Budapest. Cole and Giordano refer to the same issue, when writing about the higher survival chances of those who, by staying in their apartment buildings, also stayed in a social space where they were known by the non-Jews living in this specific community.[19] In an average apartment building the concierge had very often served for decades those who were hidden by them during the reign of the extreme right Arrow Cross movement. Moreover, even if the concierge was new in the post, their relationship with the tenants was based on an established tradition. And exactly this tradition is what goes against the third criteria set for the *Righteous Among the Nations*, namely that the rescuer could not get any remuneration for helping, and could not act on the basis of the promise of a reward. I believe that the Budapest *házmester* form a special group within the rescuers: in many cases they could legitimately accept money or a present for helping, especially since rewarding their different kinds of services by tipping was a must in Hungary.[20] Tipping them was part of everyday life, which is why one could argue that merely this circumstance should not discredit their importance in rescuing Jewish Hungarians. Moreover, when a building manager helped out a troubled inhabitant, he fulfilled exactly that obligation which Verdeja thinks follows from the helper's social position. Nonetheless, the helped inhabitant also had social obligations, including honouring the services of the building manager with tipping. The custom of tipping made it almost compulsory to reward the services of the building managers, therefore it could have given a negative message if the saviour was not receiving anything from the saved, as the Yad Vashem criteria requires.[21] Nevertheless, as we shall see, this system also resulted in significantly bigger chances of survival on the richer Jewish Hungarians' side.

3   HELPING FOR MONEY

Even though Mr Fehér was deeply disappointed in concierge Korecz, it is easy to argue that her saving of 12 Jewish Hungarians could well earn her *Righteous Among the Nations* recognition. Accepting money for helping, and—from another vantage point—observing the financial progress of Jew-saviours was part of moral normality in Budapest in 1944–45. In a similar case from the Justificatory Committee files, twenty-five residents of Pozsonyi út 16 wrote to the Committee to express their gratitude towards the local building managers, for saving their lives and feeding them during the Arrow Cross reign.[22] Six other Jewish Hungarians, who were only relocated into the building while it served as a ghetto house marked by a yellow star, confirmed that the concierges cooked for the ghettoized people, and when Arrow Cross units raided the building, the concierges hid them in Christian apartments or in the cellar.[23] Mrs S., however, another person who had to move into the building when the ghettoization started, told the Justificatory Committee that the *házmester* indeed served her and all the other residents, but these were paid services.[24] Mrs E. added to this that since she was a widow and could not satisfy the building managers in a financial way, they were quite rude to her, while the same concierges treated her friend who paid them large amounts very well.[25] Therefore in Pozsonyi út 16, similarly to Kádár utca 5, there was a division between the experience of poorer and richer people.

Reading these stories, we are faced with the symbiosis of two seemingly paradoxical practices: the negative discrimination towards the poorer inhabitants was unacceptable (especially in the eyes of the leftists), but paying for the concierges' life-saving services was still widely accepted in Hungarian society in the 1940s. To differentiate between a tip and a bribe is not an easy task. At first glance there seems to be a moral line between the two phenomenon, but what considerations are behind this moral judgment? One factor which is likely to make a difference here is the prospective or retrospective orientation of the person who offers the sum in question. They either want to appreciate the high quality service experienced, or—as Torfason, Flynn and Kupor put it—they want to "encourage good service in the future."[26] After comparing the tipping cultures of various countries, Torfason, Flynn and Kupor maintain that there is a relation between the moral acceptance of bribing and the longer temporal focus of tipping. Their study compares the general attitude towards bribery country by country on the basis of a 2006 Gallup survey.

They found that while for instance Canadians and Indians are similarly willing to tip, Indians are more likely to tip with a prospective orientation, and, at the same time, they find bribing more acceptable than Canadians.[27] Their conclusion is that if someone tips with a prospective focus then this person is likely to show greater tolerance towards bribery. This could be true for the 1940s' Budapest society too. Whereas Jewish Hungarians, who in the interwar period were used to tipping the concierges for their services in the apartment building with a more retrospective focus, in the difficult months of 1944 they started to encourage the same concierges to assist their survival by their supplementary payments and donations. Although this is a bit speculative and the border between bribe and tip stays very blurred, in 1944–45 Hungarian society showed a significant tolerance towards bribing the Budapest building managers.

To assess the difficulty of the contemporary Western comprehension of this moral duality, it is worth quoting an excerpt of a testimony from the Yad Vashem archive. In this interview, Eva Marta Breslauer Schmutz talks about her experiences in a hiding place created under the apartment of a Budapest building manager called Juliska Szvoboda.[28] Mrs Breslauer Schmutz tried to explain to the interviewer that although her relatives paid for the concierge's help, she still merits respect. As she said: "that's true that she got money for helping us. Every time someone arrived at the bunker our grandma gave her either some jewellery or money. But still, she was a very decent person. She helped us."[29] That the interviewer did not seem to accept Mrs Breslauer Schmutz's standpoint becomes obvious from the following excerpt from the same interview:

- And after the war, did you stay in touch with the concierge who hid you during the war?[30]
- [Mrs Breslauer Schmutz:] Yes, after the war she kept living at the same place with her husband, and she did not have any financial problem.
- So [after the war] you kept supporting them financially?[31]
- [Mrs Breslauer Schmutz:] But of course, yes! She saved our lives. For the money or not for the money, she saved our lives.

Obviously, Mrs Breslauer Schmutz saw it as self-evident that they paid the *házmester*, both because honouring the concierge's favour was the custom, and also because the power structure within the apartment building suddenly changed. The building manager, who held one of the lowest positions in the apartment building's pre-war social stratification, suddenly became almost as influential as a building owner. The tenants sensed this power switch, and started to pay them much higher tips for the services provided than they had in peacetime. Those who paid received the necessary assistance from the concierge. Those who were unable to pay were more likely to be drafted to the death marches, or to different kind of work-groups, and were often the subject of the Arrow Cross fighters' brutality. This latter group's experience is what is missing from the stories of the Righteous concierges at Yad Vashem, and for this reason I find these stories incomplete.

4   A Unique Way of Tipping: the Echo of the BBC in the Building Manager's Apartment

Changes in the apartment building's power structure were mirrored in changes in the individuals' wealth. In Kádár utca 5, Mr Fehér accused concierge Korecz of accepting a radio—among other goods—for reregistering someone's apartment in May 1944. A radio was at that time a luxury item, something comparable nowadays to *Apple* computers or expensive plasma televisions. Figure 5.1 is an invoice from 1939, which was issued when a Jewish Hungarian citizen paid 239.94 pengő for a radio produced by the Orion factory. The building manager working at IV, Váczi út 59 earned 180 pengő per month, his colleague at Pozsonyi út 21 got 150 per month, and since no concierge was paid significantly better than them, one can assume that the price of a new radio generally exceeded the budget of an average concierge.[32] This disparity between the radio's high price and the building managers' low income makes the example of the radios suitable for illuminating how the anti-Jewish laws created a new dimension for the tradition of supplementary payments.

My starting point is the translator Tivadar Szinnai's memoir, in which he writes repeatedly about listening to BBC radio with great enthusiasm during 1943–44.[33] Whenever he heard the first sounds of the BBC's Hungarian programme, he felt a shiver down his spine.[34] According to him, the BBC news broadcast gave hope to the Budapest Jews, which is why it was mocked by the rightist Hungarians as "vitamin J".[35] The Jewish Hungarians needed to know where the Allied troops were, how far the Red Army was from the Hungarian capital. Only from this independent news agency could they get this vital information, which

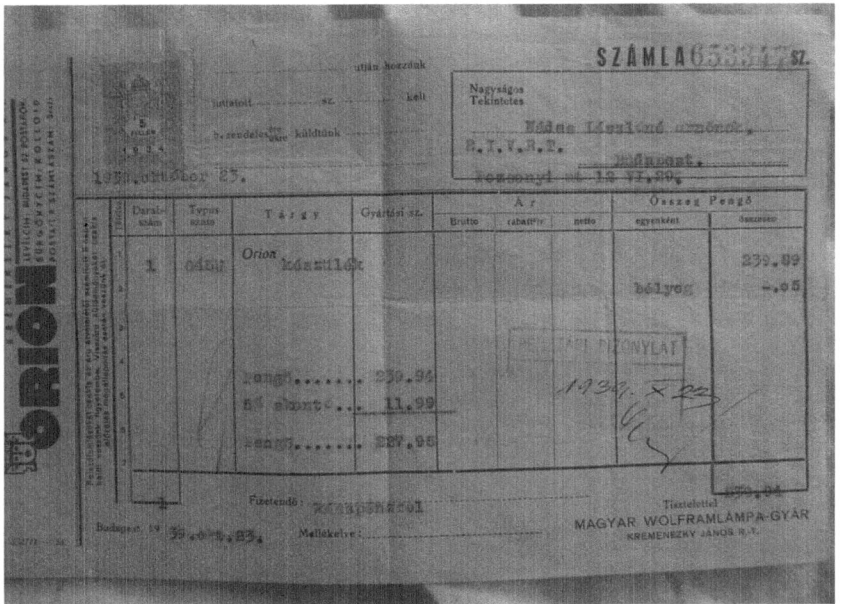

Figure 5.1 An invoice for a radio from 1939 (Private collection of Erzsébet Róna, Budapest, XIII)

told them also how long they had to survive until they could be freed (Figure 5.2).

However, in April 1944, not long after the German occupation of Budapest, Jewish Hungarians were ordered to surrender their radios.[36] On 21 April, the *Magyarország* daily reported that special committees had been formed for this purpose.[37] The members of them first checked whether the radio performed properly, and then gave a receipt to the Jewish owner on which was indicated the estimated value of the machine. Furthermore, even non-Jews had to register each and every radio they got from Jewish Hungarians after 22 March 1944, regardless whether it was a present or whether they had paid for it. Although the decree permitted the non-Jews to keep the radio, nevertheless they were forbidden from selling it under any circumstances.[38]

Figure 5.2 An extreme-right cartoon from 1944 shows those who spread rumours. It is "London" written on the front of the radio, and the listeners' crooked noses meant references to the Jewish origin of the individuals who were interested in the rumours (In *Egyedül Vagyunk*, vol. 7, no. 19, 22 September 1944)

The translator Szinnai, being of Jewish origin, was forced to surrender his radio. As he recalls, he "had a very valuable, modern radio", while the *házmester* of the building where Szinnai lived "had a shabby receiver only good for the local programs".[39] Therefore Szinnai decided to give his radio to the concierge and surrendered instead the building manager's valueless gadget, after which the building manager treated Szinnai and his wife with much greater politeness and attention than before.[40] (Figure 5.3)

Along the same lines, on 22 May 1944, the radical *Magyar Szó* daily condemned the practice of "Jewish manipulation over the radios".[41] As the unknown journalist comments:

if you have a look into the concierges' apartments, almost everywhere you are welcomed by the same picture. [What you can see is] some poor furniture fitting to the concierge, and a luxurious giant radio, which is in sharp contrast to its surroundings, and to the cheap table on which it stands. ... Its Jewish owner evaded the surrender of this radio by giving it to the concierge as a payment in kind. If someone asks this building manager where he got it, he would tell a vague story about the services in return for which the landlord gave it to him a long-long time ago. Let's check these apartments and let's warn these Hungarian concierges that saving and hiding Jewish assets is a form of betrayal and treason. And those who collaborate with them [with the Jews] won't find a place in this cheerful and hard-working new Hungarian homeland.

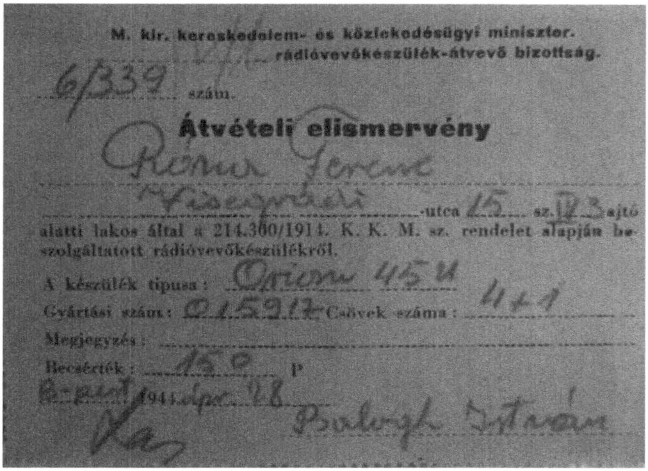
M. kir. kereskedelem- és közlekedésügyi miniszter.
rádióvevőkészülék-átvevő bizottság.

6/339 szám.

Átvételi elismervény

Róna Ferenc

Visegrádi utca 15 sz. I/3 ajtó alatti lakos által a 214.300/1914. K. K. M. sz. rendelet alapján beszolgáltatott rádióvevőkészülékről.

A készülék tipusa: Orion 454

Gyártási szám: 015917 Csövek száma: 4+1

Megjegyzés:

Becsérték: 150 P

B-pest 1944. ápr. 28

Balogh István

Figure 5.3 Proof of receipt after a surrendered radio from 28 April 1944 (Private collection of Erzsébet Róna, Budapest, XIII)

Several building managers took this risk, nevertheless, as is frequently recalled in the survivors' testimonies. One of them, Karolin Schwartz testified in favour of building manager Pál Benedek, stating that "the residents always listened to the English radio with him" in Csáky utca.[42]

Listening to BBC radio broadcasts put Jews and non-Jews equally under threat. Less than two weeks after the German occupation, the Hungarian government forbade listening to radio programs aired by the Allies. Anybody who breached this decree could be sentenced to up to six months imprisonment and faced the confiscation of the radio.[43] For example, Imre Béri, building manager at Mártírok útja 34, was denounced and taken by the Arrow Cross just "because of listening to the English radio".[44] His denunciation gives us an idea why secret meetings for radio listeners were organized in the dark in the building managers' apartments. József Hegedűs, a concierge from Nagykörút, when sharing the identity of his secret guests with the post-war Justificatory Committee, recalled a regular get-together like this in the ghetto house: "the English radio broadcast news at half past 11, the Russians at midnight. The other tenants knew nothing about who was at our place [in the building manager's lodge], because when the listed tenants entered our apartment, neither did we switch on the light in the apartment nor outside in the corridor."[45]

The post-war Justificatory Committee formally inquired about the wartime financial gains of the concierges. Between 1945 and 1947, representatives of the Justificatory Committee used three types of questionnaires to investigate the activity of the building managers. There were quite a few questions which appeared on all three. No doubt, at first sight, the odd ones out among them were questions like "Did you acquire any radio from Jews? If yes, when and for what reason?" However, the answers given reveal how valid these questions were. Mrs Német was a concierge in the residential area called Zugló. She used the questionnaire to complain to the Justificatory Committee when she wrote: "I got one [radio] from the landlord, but when he got home from the deportation, he asked for it back and now I don't have any."[46] Mr Csányi, who worked as the building manager of Aradi utca 61, answered that he received a radio from the *Jews* "as a present".[47] The very same answer was given by Mrs Henk from Abonyi utca 10—the building where Zsuzsanna Ozsváth's memoir takes place.[48] Another *házmester*, Mrs Csoknyai, "swapped" her radio with a Jewish tenant, potentially in a similar way to the above-mentioned translator, Tivadar Szinnai.[49] The most fascinating is, however, is the case of István Kaufmann, who retells Szinnai's story but from the perspective of the building manager. As he explains, he exchanged his radio with a Jewish tenant: "I gave a smaller one for a bigger [radio] receiver, when the Jews had to surrender theirs."[50] In my view, this short sentence explains how an agency was formed between Jewish Hungarians and non-Jews against the effect of an anti-Jewish order.

Writing about the radios, one has to keep in mind that it was not only a valuable item, a symbol of modernity and wealth, but it was also the single source of reliable information for those who were locked up in a ghetto house. In 1944, the question for Jewish Hungarians was no longer who was going to win the war, but when the Allies' victory—which promised the end of persecution—was going to reach them. This is why the radio became a means of survival in Budapest, and this is how dozens of radios formerly owned by Jewish Hungarians were gifted to the building managers, avoiding the compulsory surrender of them. In return the building managers not only allowed the Jewish Hungarian tenants to illegally listen to it from time to time, getting first-hand information about the progress of the Allies, but they also provided preferential treatment to the radio donors. Although the radio is only one example, nevertheless it represents a broader phenomenon of 1944 Budapest, where the peacetime tradition of supplementary payments could turn into the wartime bribing of the building managers, a process which pointed towards the levelling of the financial differences between concierges and their tenants.

5 HELPED AND HURT BY THE SAME BUILDING MANAGER

The average Budapest building managers undoubtedly helped certain Jewish Hungarians, but at the same time—provided that they fulfilled all their duties—they could not avoid making life harder for some of the others. Therefore, encountering a concierge during World War II meant two different experiences: a positive one for those whom they helped, and a negative one for those on whom the *házmester* enforced the Nazi rule of law. Consequently, the reconstruction of the history of an apartment building depended largely on the decisions of the post-war authorities, on whose voice to hear and whose experience to leave out. Here I want to turn again to the case of Szent István park 10, where Mr and Mrs Papp took over the concierge post from the previous building manager in the middle of 1942. Regarding the actions of concierge Papp, two official post-war processes—a police inquiry and a trial at the People's Court—tell two completely different stories. A third one, the Justificatory Committee's long-lasting investigation, sheds light on an ongoing battle between the tenants behind the scenes. In Szent István park 10, as was mentioned before, Mrs Papp, through her pre-war connections to the city mayor, Doroghi Farkas, actively contributed to the designation of the building as a Yellow Star house. Her husband, György Papp, however, stood trial after the war, because he had allegedly used anti-Jewish language during the autumn and winter of 1944, when Szent István park 10 was a Swiss Protected house. According to the accusers, Papp refused to let into the building those who sought immediate shelter, he robbed food from the inhabitants and repeatedly accepted bribes from them.

Thanks to the court procedure, we know far more about György Papp than the average concierge. He was 40 years old in 1945, the father of two, and, like his wife, was born in Hajdúdorog, a small town close to Hungary's eastern borders. He and his wife became the building managers of Szent István park 10 when their predecessor, Jenő Rózsa, had to leave this post because of his Jewish origin.[51] To give the reader a full picture, György Papp kept his other job during the examined period: he was working as an aide at the Budapest Food Inspection Agency, where he had access to foodstuff. It was perhaps related to Papp's engagement elsewhere that he, in spite of the anti-Jewish regulations, secretly reemployed Mr Rózsa, the previous building manager as his assistant in the winter of 1944, providing him a place to stay and also some crucial income.[52] Because of this employment the Jewish Hungarian Jenő Rózsa became a lifetime ally of Papp. On 22 November 1945 he was interviewed by the 291/a Justificatory Committee, where he explained that he got to know György Papp when he needed to pass on to him the building manager post in 1942. The second time the two met was when Mr Rózsa returned to Szent István park 10 as a holder of a Swiss *schutzpass*. Later, however, his Swiss protection was revoked for an unknown reason, and the former concierge was relocated to the main ghetto. He escaped from the ghetto and yet again he returned to Szent István park 10, where György Papp registered him as an assistant concierge and stoker, while his wife was also registered as an assistant concierge. In this narrative, Rózsa underlines the fact that Papp took a considerable risk when he registered him and his wife as *őskeresztény* [a prime Christian].

The post-war police investigated the Papp case in a short, four-day-long period at the end of May 1945. The inspectors had in their hand a denunciation written by Mrs Jenei from the fifth floor of the building, blaming Papp for not admitting a Jewish family seeking shelter in early December 1944.[53] By that time the Yellow Star house was transformed into a building under special Swiss protection, where only the holders of a Swiss protective paper [*schutzpass*] were allowed to stay. As was discussed in the previous chapter, these documents certified that the holder of this pass was eligible for the issuer country's citizenship, or had at least an immigrant visa there, and therefore they were under the protection of this particular state. As a result, the protected [*védett*] individual could live in an apartment building supervised by the state's embassy. The foreign diplomats had agreed a quota with the Hungarian officials for this kind of document; nevertheless, due to the over-issuing of the protective papers, buildings like Szent István park 10 became unimaginably overcrowded. From Papp's statement at the court room it is known that 540 people lived here, which compared to the pre-1944 number of inhabitants (60) explains why people were forced to sleep even on the staircase, and why new arrivals mentioned in the denunciation could have only worsened the situation.[54] The denouncer Mrs Jenei claimed that in this situation the placing of protected Jewish Hungarian individuals was a well-paying business for concierge Papp. Allegedly, for those who had paid for this, the building manager was able to find a place even in the most congested apartments of the Protected house, if necessary by using violence. However, as her acquaintances did not pay Papp, they were not allowed to stay in Szent István park 10.[55]

The police officer who led the investigation against Papp referred to the events of December 1944 in his report, stating that the building manager violently kicked out the refuge-seekers from the building, which indirectly led to their imminent death. Nevertheless, this police report does not take into account the crowded nature of the apartment building.[56] Discussing the same incident, the verdict of the People's Court emphasizes that, first, those wanting to enter during this incident had had no valid Swiss papers, and second, that the Arrow Cross raids regularly checked that only those stayed in the apartment building who actually possessed the Swiss protective documents. Furthermore, the verdict points to the Swiss embassy, which specifically forbade building manager Papp to let in anyone not holding a *schutzpass* issued by the embassy's employees. The embassy workers thought that the presence of a person like this could cause the deportation or the death of all Jewish Hungarians who lived in Szent István park 10.[57] This was a wholly new circumstance, which did not show up in the police documents at all, and on the basis of this it is not surprising that the People's Court had a different judgement of the same incident than the police.

There is much more behind the striking dissonance between the police report and the court verdict, which represents well the difficulties of interpreting the recent past in 1945. According to the police files, several inhabitants of the Protected house complained about their bad treatment by Papp. Someone remembered the building manager shouting, "I won't tolerate stinky Jews avoiding compulsory work."[58] Another woman recalled that Papp had given her a slap when she was unable to go for the daily work. She said that it was the *házmester* who picked the members of this work-group, but those who had given him regular tips were never chosen for the duty.[59] Both of these witnesses described scenes when uniformed *Nyilas* men had had drinks with the concierges, and had fun during events organized in the building manager's ground floor apartment. These were the people Papp kept company with. The police report describes Papp's behaviour towards the inhabitants of the Swiss house as violent and brutal. It was alleged that Papp not only intimidated a group of the unfortunate residents, but also assaulted them.[60] The minutes of Ármin R.'s hearing by the police, dated 28 May 1945, confirms that Papp regularly threatened to hand over the Jewish Hungarians to the Arrow Cross. Moreover, Papp physically attacked this older man, Mr R.[61] Countering the dark picture drawn up by the police, the members of the People's Court were of the opinion that the building manager's anti-Jewish speeches and threats "served exclusively the saving of the Jewish residents".[62] One may read their interpretation as something more comparable to a cost analysis than to a legal decision, where they simply labelled all the suffering of Papp's accusers as an unavoidable necessity. The judges hurried to add that the neighbouring building's concierge was famous for his Arrow Cross sympathy, which is why all the Jewish Hungarians were deported from there. Their conclusion is that Papp did very well when he acted unfriendly towards the Jewish Hungarians, by this hiding his true "Jew-friendly attitude". The People's Court maintained that the majority of the residents were certain that Papp was in fact not at all dangerous to them, but just disguised his helping attitude, which was perfectly justified in a malignant situation.[63]

From a longer historical perspective it seems certain that building managers like György Papp treated different groups of tenants completely differently, while the immediate post-war police officials and judges were looking for an unambiguous picture. As the investigation proceeded, more and more details appeared that shed new light onto the previous testimonies. Mrs Jenei, for example, accused *házmester* Papp of leading an Arrow Cross fighter into her apartment, where they called her to give them her last piece of bacon, which the Arrow Cross man seized from her. Mrs Jenei simply could not comprehend why the building manager had not given his own food to the *Nyilas* man, since he had much more to give. As she added, he had to be aware that Mrs Jenei had not been able to leave the building for several days to do any kind of shopping.[64] However, in the courtroom Papp presented a longer version of this visit to Mrs Jenei, explaining that one day four Arrow Cross militia members had entered his lodge, and one of them declared himself to be hungry. His wife, Mrs Papp, had straightway wanted to feed this person, who refused the offer and insisted to "fetch food from the Jews instead".[65] As Papp explained, he had only accompanied the Arrow Cross man in the apartment building to prevent any kind of violence. In order to limit the possible damage, Papp himself entered Mrs Jenei's larder and took 200 grams of bacon from there. He added that the Arrow Cross man received other goods from other apartments too.[66]

The People's Court in its verdict accepted the building manager's arguments that by his acts he simply wanted to save the tenants and protect them from violence and persecution. The decision to tacitly pardon the building manager was based on the pragmatic thought that the end justifies the means, and such small sacrifices as 200 grams of bacon are not taken into account at the end of the day. On another note, several residents remembered that Papp brought food for them to the ghetto house.[67] It was also Papp who through his personal connections organized the escape of nine residents from the main ghetto in December 1944.[68] Perhaps the best overview of the situation was given by Mrs Szobovits, who had spent the period in question outside of Szent István park 10, but returned there immediately after the war. As she told the court, "the end of last year I haven't spent at home, I don't know how the defendant treated the persecuted inhabitants ... but by the time I have arrived back, most of the residents were praising him, while a minority was angry at him."[69]

Comparing the files of the police and the court inquiries, one could conclude that the police investigation presents the exclusive voices of the victims. Its focus is solely on the inhumanity of the building manager, so much so that it gives the impression the police officers left out all other information from the testimonies. Consequently, this narrative seems more intense than the other, especially because the Jewish Hungarians were encouraged in it to talk about their traumatic experiences. On the contrary, what the People's Court does in its verdict is to sweep aside the victims' complaints, on the assumption that the building manager just wanted to save as many Jewish Hungarians as possible, and keep the "cost" of the Arrow Cross' reign and visits in Szent István park 10 low. It does not deny that the incidents happened, rather it understands them as acceptable behaviour in a difficult situation.

It is difficult to integrate cases like that of concierge Papp into the existing Holocaust literature because of the ambiguous behaviour pattern observed in them. It seems that the building manager was much more than a passive "bystander": the holder of this post was an active agent, who could intervene either to decrease or to increase the suffering of the Jewish Hungarians living in Budapest in 1944. As many building managers did both, it is extremely problematic to adjudicate on their wartime behaviour. It might seem slightly exaggerated to draw a comparison between their role and Regent Miklós Horthy's, but the governor too was responsible for legitimizing the German invasion in March 1944, and not stepping up against the deportation of more than 400,000 people from the Hungarian provinces. However, he was the one who stopped the deportations in early July 1944, by this saving—at least temporarily—the Jewish Hungarians living in Budapest.[70] Not by accident did the post-war Hungarian government instruct the judges of the People's Court to take into account that the accused workers (including by this also the building managers) were bewildered by the Horthy regime's elite.[71]

6   WHOM DID THEY HELP?: THE CASE OF ISTVÁN BARKO[72]

Radio and different kinds of donations, emotional closeness—among other things—could make concierges help. In this longer section, in addition to the query "why help?", the question of "whom to help?" is also raised. Building managers obviously had some sort of a preference list while assisting the Jewish Hungarians' survival during World War II. Besides analysing the data of subsequent censuses in Budapest from 1941 and 1945 to map the Jewish Hungarians within the ghetto houses who were helped, this part aims to reconstruct the history of a particular apartment building with the help of immediate post-war testimonies. In Visegrádi utca 60, as early as on 27 April 1945, 12 residents, as well as the assistant concierge, signed a denunciation of the building manager István Barko. They reported him to the police because he was not willing to give back the belongings of the Jewish Hungarian tenants, although ten weeks had already passed since their return to the building from forced relocation or from labour service.[73] When the police searched the *házmester*'s apartment, they found several pieces of cloth with the initials of the tenants on them and further personal belongings, which made the building manager's wrongdoing unquestionable.

The initial accusation sent to the police was followed by another report, this time addressed to the Building Managers' Free Trade Union, in which approximately the same group of tenants listed their detailed objections. The police search provided enough proof for them to state that the building manager entered their apartments during their captivity, and took their goods from there. They went on to claim that "although immediately after the freeing of Budapest the building warden had called the concierge to return all stolen goods [promising him amnesty], he failed to react to this call."[74] They recalled also how "a denunciation followed by a search of the premises resulted in the finding of many of our valuable belongings in the Barko family's apartment by the police." Finally, they made it clear that the concierge did not seem to be ready to adjust to the new *democratic* values: "[t]here are serious concerns as well over their [the concierge's and his family members'] political behaviour..."[75]

To defend himself, and to balance somewhat the negative comments, the building manager collected supportive reference letters from other former and current tenants, who described the noble deeds of Barko in their declarations. Strikingly, most of these were written by the members of the upper middle classes, and some even were submitted on company letterhead. This could indicate two things: either the building manager helped rich people more, or he thought the richer and the better connected his supporter was, the better it looked to the Justificatory Committee. For example, the director of the Dreher brewery and chocolate factory, moved to Visegrádi utca 60 on 3 July 1944, and stayed there only until the middle of November. In the summer of 1945, he addressed his words to Barko, who had obviously turned to him for a recommendation for the justificatory process. As he wrote about his days in the ghetto building, "[d]uring this period I got to know you through our conversations, and by these chats it became clear to me your counter-Faschist[sic!] and counter-German attitude, and your democratic and socially sensitive worldview. During the time I spent there, you have done invaluable services for us, Jewish residents of the house."[76]

These letters suggest a variety of help provided by Barko during 1944: an elderly lady got Christian food ration cards from him instead of the less valuable "Jewish" ones.[77] Another tenant, György G. was taken to Komárom, a town north-west of Budapest, for forced labour service, while his wife, trapped in Visegrádi utca 60, sent letters and a parcel to her husband through Barko. In addition, when in November 1944 the Arrow Cross movement collected Jewish women from the area—theoretically for forced labour, in practice for the so-called death marches—Barko managed to save György's wife from being drafted.[78] Approximately a month later, in December 1944, both György and his spouse were hiding in the building with the *házmester*'s approval, and as György recalled, "when the Arrow Cross fighters entered the building, he [meaning the concierge] warned us and assisted us in finding an escape route. By this, he really saved me and my wife from being dragged away and from death."[79]

Behind this second raid of the Arrow Cross fighters in Visegrádi utca 60 laid the intention of the Szálasi government to relocate all remaining Jewish Hungarians—or at least those who did not possess any protective papers from neutral countries—to the newly established main ghetto in the VII district.[80] Barko, thanks to his connections, knew in advance about this second raid in early December and informed one of the richest tenants in the building, Róbert Stern, a wealthy paint merchant. Providing information as a means of help sheds light on the building manager's social capital.[81] He had useful contacts at the police, links to influential persons elsewhere, and by helping well-to-do Jewish Hungarians he built important new relationships. This continuous networking was then of help to him again when the post-war investigators analysed his case. Only in this context can one explain why both Róbert Stern and his mother, Mrs Weiss, recognized Barko' wartime services by writing supporting letters in the early post-war period on the letterhead of the Ármin Stern Paint, Oil and Industrial Stock. The mother, Mrs Sándor Weiss, gave a deeper insight when stating that Barko, "during the German occupation and the Arrow Cross era, as the building manager of Visegrádi utca 60, fully understood the problem of the Jewry, and if it was possible, he always offered a helping hand. ... My son, Róbert Stern spent most of the *Nyilas* period hiding in our apartment. Barko knew about it, he agreed to it, moreover, when the *Nyilas* fighters asked explicitly whether any Jew was staying in this apartment, Barko declared that no Jew was left there."[82] Above all, when a *Nyilas* army unit arrested the Jewish residents, Barko guaranteed that Mrs Weiss was not Jewish, therefore she was left in the building.[83]

What is worth noticing here is that the building manager was clearly in the position of influencing who was taken and who was not by the Arrow Cross, although obviously he could not rescue everyone. Nevertheless, he chose to help some people more than others, and these people appeared to be richer than those who later complained over Barko's and his family members' ill-treatment. Róbert Stern's account adds to this the following: "...with some breaks I [illegally] spent November and December 1944 in the building and you were aware of this. Before the tenants were taken to the ghetto from the building, you warned me that an order for emptying the Yellow Star houses had just been issued. Despite the fact that at this times it was forbidden to let out Jews from the building, with your help we managed to leave it. With this act you greatly contributed to my survival..."[84] The Stern family, just like György G. and his wife, successfully fled from Visegrádi utca 60, thanks to the well-informed building manager, by contrast with the others who were taken from there by the Arrow Cross forces. These other residents were much less satisfied with Barko's wartime actions and intended to cause the building manager and his family serious trouble during the justificatory process.

7   AT THE HEARING OF THE JUSTIFICATORY COMMITTEE

Following the non-helped residents' denunciation, and the opposing documents submitted by the building manager, the Justificatory Committee had to hold hearings before deciding about concierge Barko's fate. The minutes of these hearings give a comprehensive picture of the activities of the building manager and his family. This was also the forum which provided the most personal insights into the life of the tenants. While Róbert Stern, in late July 1945, gladly wrote about István Barko as his saviour, some two weeks later, in front of the Justificatory Committee, he added less positive memories about the building manager and his family. He made the following statement about the police search in the concierge's lodge: "during the aforementioned police action I also recognized my books and neckties among the things they found at the Barkos'. Barko himself told me that he was going to check and if there was anything else that belonged to me, he would return it. I did not hurry him and to this day I have not got anything back. Last November, when the Jews' movement was very much limited, I, as a forced labourer, often tried to come home, and in most of the cases Mrs Barko tried to block me in this. However, I have nothing against István Barko, he was always at my disposal. On the basis of this, I even wrote him a statement of support."[85] Although Róbert Stern's words certainly could be understood in different ways, it is worth picking up here on his post-police action inactivity. I argue that this inactivity was just another way of tipping, another expression of deep gratitude: Mr Stern knew very well that Barko unjustly held his belongings, however, he did not urge him to give these goods back because he and his family were thankful to Barko for warning them before the Nazi raid the previous December. His gratitude simply stopped him from causing further trouble for the Barko family.

And, in what seems to be a general pattern, there were other witnesses as well who testified against the wife of the building manager, at the same time emphasizing that they had no complaints against Barko himself. For instance, Mrs Roth declared at the Justificatory Committee that "my daughter worked for the Swedish legation, hence both she and I were exempted from the obligatory wearing of the yellow star badge, and we were not bound by the movement restrictions. I have no problem with the building manager István Barko, much more I have something against his wife. She despite our exemptions did not let in my daughter who visited me, preventing her from bringing me bread and other kinds of food. When we witnessed the search of premises in the concierge's apartment with the building warden, we found there numerous assets of ours, including even furniture. After all of this, as several of my belongings are still missing, I can well suspect that my loss is related to the family of the building manager."[86] When stating this, Mrs Roth probably had in mind the 29 November 1944 ghettoization decree, which explicitly made the building managers and the building wardens responsible for the safekeeping of all valuables left behind in the former Yellow Star houses by the inhabitants who were moved to the so-called main ghetto.[87]

The building warden, Sándor Gonda was also questioned by the Justificatory Committee members, whose interest concerned the particular moment when the policemen had searched through the concierge's lodge in April 1945. As the building warden replied to them, "soon after the police arrived, they found in the lodge's larder [tenant] Lajos Erdei's preserved fruit and canned vegetables. Although at the liberation [mid-January 1945], when Lajos Erdei was starving, he asked for food from the Barko family, they refused him saying they did not have it either."[88] The building warden Gonda also recalled that he tried to convince Barko in February 1945 to voluntarily return all stolen goods, in vain. Seemingly the building manager repeatedly avoided admitting any stealing committed either by him or his loved ones. If he covered up for his wife and children this would be understandable; however, explaining and excusing are two different issues. Nevertheless, if one thing seems sure it is that István Barko was in a difficult situation, partly (if not completely) because of his family's behaviour in 1944. His troubles grew further when the Justificatory Committee heard Ms Piroska Kern's testimony on 13 August 1945. This tenant explained that she had "no political objections against István Barko, contrary to his wife and his son, who both publicly used several times anti-Jewish expressions, which might refer to their Arrow Cross affiliation."[89] The witness was present, for example, when Mrs Barko refused to talk to one of the female tenants, saying "I am not willing to converse with any kind of Jewess." Similarly, Mrs Füle testified that "I cannot judge the political behaviour of István Barko, however, there were many complaints against his wife and his son."[90]

Perhaps the most serious accusation against the Barko family came from Zsuzsanna Ökrös, who—due to the general mobilization—was ordered to leave Visegrádi utca 60 and perform forced labour work in Isaszeg. From there she escaped in mid-November 1944, and after hiding in various places she returned to the building. On 4 December an Arrow Cross militia collected young Jewish Hungarians from Visegrádi utca, and to avoid the round-up, the seventeen-year-old Zsuzsanna hid in the elevator's tube.

As she explains, "I stayed in there the whole night, and at the first light I ran up to Mrs Lajos Varga, living on the fifth floor, and begged her to accompany me to a safe place. Of course, the main entrance of the building was closed at that time, so we rang for the building manager. Mrs Barko came out and seeing me she was very upset and rejected my request to leave the building, so I had to stay there. I asked the assistant concierge to hide me, who indeed helped. But at the same time, the Barko family alerted the *Nyilas* militias, who came for me and found me. They beat me up and took me to their headquarters in Vadász utca."[91] (Figure 5.4)

Figure 5.4 The entrance of Visegrádi utca 60, which remained closed for Zsuzsanna Ökrös in the early hours of 5 December 1944 (A photo by the author, taken in 2011)

Although the above quoted testimonies reveal the intricacy of the situation in the wartime apartment building, they say little about why *házmester* Barko and his wife had completely different approaches towards Jewish Hungarians. Behind this difference could lie an incident which endangered the everyday life of the Barko family. In late October 1944, concierge Barko was arrested and transferred to the Gestapo's local detention centre for lending his revolver to one of the Jewish Hungarian residents.[92] The arrest of the concierge put an end to the good relations between the Barko family and a significant part of the inhabitants. As one of them, Mr Pál Felkai remembered, "...until the building manager was taken away and beaten by the *Nyilas* commando, even his wife was providing preferential treatment to us tenants. Only after this incident did she start to change..."[93] Since the complaints over the building manager's family started from this late October and early November period, it could be argued that Barko's arrest evoked a pro-Nazi attitude from his wife and children. However, this attitude could be also viewed as more self-protective than a real expression of pro-Nazi and anti-Jewish sentiment.

8   Mapping the Survivors Within the Building

Analysing the data of the 1941 and 1945 censuses can help to understand more about the complex setting between the supporters of the concierge and the group which targeted his dismissal from his job. In 1941 the owner of the apartment block, Mrs Grün, lived on the first floor of the building.[94] Her religion was "Israelite", which corresponds to the later designation of Visegrádi utca 60 as a Yellow Star house. She survived the war, and four years later she was still registered in the same flat. Imre Kiss—to whom Barko lent the firearm in October 1944—lived on the ground floor, in apartment 2/a.[95] Barko himself was registered on the 6th flat-sheet, and lived on the ground floor of the building with a direct view both of the main entrance and the courtyard, as had almost all the Budapest concierge lodges. Mrs Barko's maiden name remains unknown, but it is revealed that she was born in 1903, and she abandoned her studies after four years of public schooling. Barko was a locksmith; he was born in 1902, the father of two. The flat-sheet lists the premises that belonged to the concierge's lodge as two rooms, a kitchen, a hallway, a bathroom and a larder. This is the larder where in April 1945 the police found Lajos Erdei's canned food.

There were significant differences between the rental fees paid by the denouncers and those who stood behind the building manager. The Erdei family had lived in apartment number 9 on the second floor since 1939, and for their four-room unit they paid 1,700 pengő rental fees per annum.[96] Mr Erdei was a technician and he was born in 1888, which is interesting as his wife was eight years older than him. On the same floor lived the Stern family, the paint merchants who after the war supported Barko during the justificatory process.[97] Mrs Füle, who signed the denunciation against Barko moved to Visegrádi utca 60 in May 1938, and lived in a three-room apartment on the third floor.[98] Piroska Kern, the widow of a physician, who recalled at the Justificatory Committee hearing Mrs Barko using anti-Jewish expressions, lived with her daughter and the daughter's husband in the three rooms of apartment no. 16.[99] Both she and her son-in-law signed the denunciation. Sándor Gonda, the building warden—who distributed all the goods found at the Barko residence during the post-war police search—lived in a relatively small, two-room apartment on the fourth floor.[100] In accordance with the size of the unit, the rental fees were also low, 900 pengő per annum, whilst Mr Stern, who was saved by the concierge, paid almost double for his apartment. Nevertheless, even 900 pengő was too high for this insurance agent's financial situation, which is why he rented a bed to a young lady, Mrs Monoki, who made a living from cleaning offices. Both Mr Gonda and his subtenant signed the denunciation, which was most probably initiated by the former.

In post-war apartment buildings there was frequent antagonism between the building manager and the building warden. The latter was democratically elected by the tenants right after Budapest's liberation, as an achievement of the new "democratic" system, while the building manager was regarded as a representative of the owner, and many times as the representative of the already invalid morals of the previous political regime.[101] It seems true for Visegrádi utca 60 too that the building warden orchestrated the attacks against the *házmester*, Barko. Not only was his signature centrally placed on both reports on the concierge's alleged crimes, but he also made the second document signed by his subtenant, Mrs Monoki. Furthermore, the building warden indicated that she lived on the first floor, although in reality Mrs Monoki lived with him on the fourth.[102] Why might someone in his position do this? Two considerations seem to be possible here: he either wanted to hide the connection between him and Mrs Monoki, or rather he wanted to give the impression that the whole building—all the floors—were behind the denunciation.

But this was not at all the case, as everybody who was hesitant to join the second initiative against the building manager was from the first floor or from the ground floor. In Visegrádi utca 60, it was the richer families who backed Barko the building manager, those who lived closer to the ground floor and who probably paid for the concierge's extra services during the Holocaust. The *házmester* provided help for them in various ways: he was a courier, he let people out when they were supposed to stay in the ghetto building, and he let them hide and stay inside when they were supposed to leave the building. He could provide food ration cards with better value than the "Jewish" ones, and when it was needed, he even could lend a gun to one of the neighbouring residents. Just as payment for services was a regular method in peacetime conditions as well, it seems possible that during 1944 it was the wealthy Jewish Hungarians' reflex to tip the building manager for his special services. These payments increased significantly this group's survival chances, even if there could have been also non-financial elements here which played a part, such as friendship, or respect for certain tenants.

There were four apartments situated on the fifth or top floor. In the smallest lived the assistant concierge, who cleaned the staircases and put out the rubbish for collection. [103] Next to her lived the Varga family, in apartment 29. They moved here as late as 25 November 1942.[104] The husband, Lajos Varga was a musician and his wife—who also signed the denunciation—was the one who accompanied Zsuzsanna Ökrös on 5 December 1944, when Mrs Barko refused to let them out of the building. In apartment 26 lived the Binder family and their two subtenants.[105] Their neighbours were the Szegi family, four people living in a two-room apartment.[106] As both of these families, as well as the assistant concierge, signed the denunciation against the Barko family, one can assume that the denouncers resided on the upper floors, in the cheaper units, while the concierge's supporters lived closer to the ground floor, in the more expensive apartments.

Well-documented cases in other apartment buildings across the Hungarian capital show that the concierges hurried to save among the first ones the owners and supervisors of their buildings. Even if these people's survival was the building managers' direct professional interest, nevertheless, this tendency underpins my argument that the *házmester* contributed more to the survival of the rich Jewish Hungarians than to the poorer ones. This is what happened, for instance, in Lázár utca 11, an apartment building close to the famous Budapest opera house. This building was designated exclusively for non-Jews, but with the help of concierge István Allmann, the Jewish Hungarian owner could hide here and survive. For the justificatory process, the owner described how the concierge brought them food and firewood, and provided a hiding place for them.[107] Only a couple of blocks from here, in Nagymező utca 36, *házmester* Udvardy kept the building owner's money and assets safe.[108] In early December 1944, from Szondi utca 42c the concierge Dávid Sipos showed great courage by entering the already sealed ghetto of Budapest. There he passed his own identity documents to his boss, the building supervisor Béla Czigler, and by this he effectively saved Mr Czigler's life.[109] There is no reason to think that these building managers only helped the building owners. In fact, Allmann, Sipos and Udvardy actively backed the hiding of others as well. One counter-example is the survival of Ágota Sebő, whose mother became friends with the assistant building manager, a poor lady who lived close to them. The latter's son, Jancsi Fischer did shopping for Ágota Sebő and her mother when they had to move into a ghetto house.[110] Moreover, following the Arrow Cross takeover the Fischers even provided a hiding spot for Ágota and her mother. In this case, clearly the emotional connection was the driving force behind helping, even though Ágota remembers that after the war her mother gave money to Mrs Fischer, and they kept bringing them oranges and other gifts for Christmas. In spite of these evident counter-examples, it seems that the building owners, supervisors and the other richer or influential tenants were more likely to be among the ones saved by the concierges than the poorer inhabitants. In addition, a further difference is that the assistance provided for the richer residents by the concierge was likely to be offered for a longer period than the occasional help offered to the poorer ones.

Surely, building manager Barko facilitated the survival of the richer and more influential tenants of Visegrádi utca 60, where the post-war actions of the Justificatory Committee divided the residents into two groups. The supporters and the denouncers seemed to represent approximately equal parts of the inhabitants, which not only made the building deeply divided but also undermined Barko's post as a building manager. These groups differed from each other both in their financial situation and in their location within the building. The denouncers occupied mostly the upper floors and were led by the newly elected building warden, while the wealthier supporters of the building manager lived in the more spacious and more expensive lower apartments of the building. These groups remembered the past differently, especially in terms of the *házmester*'s role in it, and they also had completely different scenarios for the future. When they wrote in the second denunciation's last sentence that the Barko family's "political behaviour" was problematic, they suggested no less than that the building manager embodied the old, reactionary regime of Regent Horthy.[111] Contrary to this pre-war world controlled by the representatives of the haute-bourgeoisie, in 1945 they could imagine building a new democratic Hungary, where the working class would play a leading role.

In the autumn of 1945, concierge Barko began to understand the nature of the new age, and started to strengthen his position with leftist political declarations: a practice which became widespread only when the communist dictatorship consolidated. On 11 September 1945, the Social Democratic party unit of Csillaghegy declared that Barko had been a member of their party.[112] On 4 October, department IX of the Budapest Mayor's office issued the following certificate: "We certify that István Barko … as a skilled worker working under Gábor Waltz locksmith, is continuously performing locksmith jobs at the kitchen of department IX of the Mayor's office, therefore his work is indispensable."[113] To be fair, it is worth noting that Mr Waltz also lived on the ground floor of Visegrádi utca 60, right next to *házmester* Barko. But this fact has not came into the Justificatory Committee's attention, and less than two weeks later, on 16 October 1945, István Barko received the resolution justifying his wartime acts.

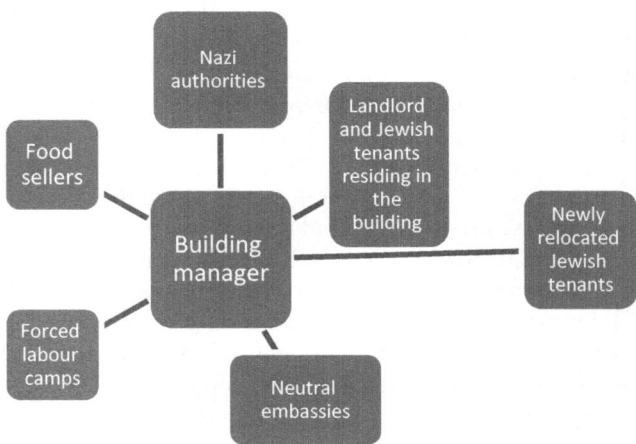

Diagram 5.1 Budapest building managers were at the centre of social networks and functioned as focal points

This basic diagram shows how a Budapest building manager could bridge the structural holes between the ghettoized tenants and other elements of 1944 Hungarian society, thanks to their social position. According to Ronald S. Burt, "structural holes are an opportunity to broker the flow of information between people, and control the projects that bring together people from opposite sides of the hole."[114] Budapest building managers bridged structural holes when they, for instance, bought food for the ghettoized people. Concierge Barko delivered a package to György G., in a labour service camp, sent by his wife living in the ghetto house at Visegrádi utca 60.[115] When the ghetto building was due to be emptied, it was the building manager, who—thanks to his network connections—knew in advance about the coming Nazi raid in early December. He quickly informed Róbert Stern, a wealthy paint merchant residing in the building, who then escaped, thereby avoiding this round-up.[116] By spanning the structural holes these individuals gained competitive advantage, which is the metaphor of social capital.[117] The diagram also shows that the landlords and certain other Jewish tenants—residing already for years in a building that later was turned into a ghetto house—had closer ties with the building manager than those individuals who were forced to move here only because of the ghetto regulations. Their prior contacts often resulted in a higher level of trust. In addition to this, the building managers knew the background of the older residing tenants much better. Consequently, they could easily pick a richer one from whom a higher remuneration could be expected. This cherry-picking could be based also on earlier larger tips received by the concierges. It obviously made sense to save those tenants first who were willing to—and able to—better tip the concierges.

Building managers also provided a link between the authorities and the tenants. This function, however, characterised them already in earlier years of the war too, and to a lesser extent in the interwar years. It is enough to think about their role in the compulsory address registration, or their distributing assignments with the food rations cards. Nevertheless, while prior to ghettoization the Jewish tenants could also contact directly the authorities, this became extremely difficult once they were confined to a closed ghetto building. The *házmester*'s role as the focal point between the authorities and the tenants already in the interwar era gave concierges extensive experience with policemen, postmen, municipality officers and so on. This is why they knew how to approach them, and they were very often entrusted with otherwise classified information during World War

II. This factor can also partly explain the building managers' high success in helping the survival of those Jewish Hungarians who were in hiding.

Concierge Barko' acting like a postman with a package sent to a forced labourer was not a unique case. There were other building managers as well, who remained focal points between the forced labour servicemen and their wives even after the women had to move forward. This is exactly what happened with the Szinnai couple. In the middle of November 1944, Tivadar Szinnai's wife, Vera, moved from a Yellow Star house to a Swiss protected building. Before leaving, she left a letter with the concierge, Mrs Balla, in which she explained her next location to Szinnai.[118] What is even more interesting is that the building manager from their original home (Pekarek) appeared in these days at their Yellow Star house, asking in what ways he could help his former tenants. Szinnai's wife gave this *házmester* a package with Szinnai's clean clothes, some money and cigarettes, so that if he went to this building first, he would find everything he needed there.[119] Thus this building manager took note of the address where his former tenants moved (perhaps he had written it into the registry book of residents), and he also was aware of the deadline when protected Jewish Hungarians had to move out from the Yellow Star houses. This example shows how the Budapest concierges intended to keep tabs on their tenants, which is best understood if we regard the *házmester* as an entrepreneur. They were interested especially in maintaining their social networks, as this provided them with financial income.

The last chapter of this book will look at the actions of the Justificatory Committee in more detail, to be able to assess what made this organization condemn or pardon certain building managers. It will also investigate some of the People's Court cases concerning the concierges, because this was where the most serious war criminals landed, among them several Budapest *házmester*. What is more, forums like the Justificatory Committee played an important role in the post-war reconciliation process, which is why it is important to look at the Jewish Hungarian tenants' participation in these procedures.

NOTES

1. Verdeja, "Moral Bystanders and Mass Violence", p. 154.
2. Kádár and Vági, *Self-financing Genocide*, pp. 91–92, and p. 90.
3. Sara Bender and Pearl Weiss (eds.), *The Encyclopedia of the Righteous Among the Nations: Rescuers of Jews during the Holocaust, Europe (Part I) and other countries* (Jerusalem: Yad Vashem, 2007), p. 261.

4. See on this: Frojimovics Kinga and Molnár Judit, *A Világ Igazai Magyarországon a második világháború alatt* (Budapest: Balassa, 2009), p. 226.
5. BFL XVII/1598, Justificatory Committee Files, box no. 5, the case of Mrs Korecz, a statement submitted by Dr Róna, dated 9 June 1945.
6. Ibid, Mr Váradi's letter, dated also 9 June 1945.
7. Bender and Weiss, *The Encyclopedia of the Righteous Among the Nations*, p. 261.
8. BFL XVII/1598, Justificatory Committee Files, the case of Mrs Korecz, a letter of Mr Imre W., dated 2 June 1945. In this section, the original name of the denouncer of the concierge, Imre W. was changed to Imre Fehér to protect this person's privacy.
9. Ibid, see Mr W.'s testimony at a hearing of the Justificatory Committee, on 20 June 1945.
10. Ibid, see Lóránt V.'s testimony at a hearing of the Justificatory Committee, on 20 June 1945.
11. Verdeja, "Moral Bystanders and Mass Violence", p. 157.
12. Verdeja, "Moral Bystanders and Mass Violence", p. 157. Here Verdeja actually talks about the philosophical works, not about the historical ones.
13. Verdeja, "Moral Bystanders and Mass Violence", p. 157.
14. Krisztián Ungváry, *Budapest ostroma* [The Siege of Budapest] (Budapest: Corvina, 2001), pp. 223–224.
15. See this on the website of Yad Vashem: http://www.yadvashem.org/yv/en/righteous/faq.asp#1, last accessed on 23 September 2014
16. Ibid.
17. Sári Reuveni, "Magyar fák az Igaz Emberek erdejében" [Hungarians trees in the forest of the Righteous Among the Nations] in László Karsai (ed), *Küzdelem az igazságért: Tanulmányok Randolph Braham 80. Születésnapjára* [Fight for Justice: studies for the 80th birthday of Randolph Braham], (Budapest: Mazsihisz, 2002), p. 568.
18. Ibid.
19. Tim Cole and Alberto Giordano, "On Place and Space: Calculating Social and Spatial Networks in the Budapest Ghetto", *Transactions in GIS*, vol. 15, no. 1, July 2011, pp. 148–149.
20. For decades concierges were rewarded for opening the gate of an apartment building between 10 p.m. and 6 a.m. by at least a set sum per occasion, and by law they had to be paid for providing the elevator on demand, therefore it is natural that they were paid for their rescue activity too. See more on the tradition of tipping in Chapter 1.
21. As a Holocaust survivor notes in her recollections, even rejecting a tip was an insult in interwar Budapest. See this in Szilvia Czingel, *Szakácskönyv a túlélésért*, p. 31.

22. BFL XVII/1598, Justificatory Committee Files, district V, the case of Mrs Pozsár, see a letter dated 17 June 1945.
23. Ibid.
24. Ibid, see the testimony of Mrs S., given at the meeting of the Justificatory Committee, on 9 July 1945.
25. Ibid., see Mrs E.'s testimony at a hearing of the Justificatory Committee, on 16 July 1945.
26. Magnus Thor Torfason, Francis J. Flynn and Daniella Kupor, "Here's a Tip: Prosocial Gratuities are Linked to Corruption", *Social Psychological & Personality Science*, vol. 4, no. 3, 2013, pp. 348–354.
27. Ibid., pp. 350–353.
28. Yad Vashem Archive, Collection O.3, File number 12504.
29. Ibid., p. 9.
30. Ibid., a question on page 13, on the 12th line from the bottom.
31. Ibid., a question on the 9th line from the bottom.
32. See the questionnaire in the case of Gyula Babsch, dated 27 June 1945, BFL XVII/1598, Justificatory Committee Files, box no. 1. Also see the case of L. Koltay, BFL XVII/1598, box no. 5, the letter of Mr B. N., dated 23 May 1945.
33. Szinnai, *Sötét ablakok*, pp. 61–62.
34. Ibid., p. 61.
35. Ibid.
36. It was the 1600/1944 decree of the Hungarian government that ordered the surrender of the radios owned by Jews on 16 April 1944. However, interestingly, László Endre, as a subprefect of Pest county already ordered the confiscation of radios from the local Jewish Hungarians in March 1944, which shows the volume of institutional rivalry within the Hungarian administration for seizing the Jewish assets. See this in Kádár and Vági, *Self-financing Genocide*, p. 75. Moreover, the Ministry of Defence also issued a decree about the surrender of radios under 33.000/1944 number.
37. "Be kell szolgáltatni a zsidók rádiókészülékeit" [The radios of the Jews have to be surrendered], *Magyarország*, vol. 51, no. 89, 21 April 1944, p. 5.
38. See this in 1.490/1944 M.E. decree
39. Szinnai, *Sötét ablakok*, p. 132.
40. Ibid.
41. *Magyar Szó*, vol. 3, no. 114, 22 May 1944, p. 5: "Sárga csillag–Rádió" [Yellow Star–Radio].
42. BFL XVII/1598, Justificatory Committee Files, district V, the case of Mr Pál Benedek.
43. *Virradat*, vol. 9, no. 14, 3 April, p. 4: "Hat hónapig terjedő elzárás és internálás az ellenséges rádiók hallgatásáért" [Six months internment for listening to the enemies' radio].

44. BFL XVII/1512. Budapesti Kerületi Elöljárósági Igazolóbizottságok Iratainak Levéltári Gyűjteménye. Házfelügyelők és Segéd-házfelügyelők 271/a. sz. Igazoló Bizottságának iratai, [Municipal Justificatory Files, the files of Justificatory Committee no. 271/a, building managers and assistant building managers]; the case of Mr Imre Béri.
45. BFL XVII/1598, Justificatory Committee Files, district V, the case of József Hegedűs.
46. BFL XVII/1598, Justificatory Committee Files, district XIV. See the questionnaire in the case of Német Jánosné, Zászlós utca 6.
47. BFL XVII/1598, Justificatory Committee Files, district VI. See the questionnaire in the case of István Csányi, Aradi utca 61.
48. BFL XVII/1598, Justificatory Committee Files, district XIV. See the questionnaire in the case of Mrs Zs. Henk, Abonyi utca 10.
49. BFL XVII/1598, Justificatory Committee Files, district VI. See the questionnaire in the case of Mrs P. Csoknyai, Izabella u. 62–64.
50. BFL XVII/1598, Justificatory Committee Files, district VI. See the questionnaire in the case of István Kaufmann, Bulcs u. 25/a.
51. BFL XVII/1598, Justificatory Committee Files, box no. 6, the case of Mrs Papp, the minutes of a hearing at the Justificatory Committee on 22 November 1945.
52. Ibid: the case of Mrs Papp. See the testimony of Jenő Rózsa in the minutes of the Justificatory Committee, dated 22 November 1945.
53. In this section, the original name of the denouncer, Mrs. J., was changed to Mrs Jenei to protect her privacy.
54. BFL XXV 1a Criminal cases of the Budapest People's Court: 1945/1500, the case of György Papp, the statement of the defendant, p. 41.
55. Ibid: the case of Mrs Papp. See the testimony of Mrs László J. in the minutes of the Justificatory Committee, dated 20 October 1945.
56. Ibid., p. 34. See the police report, dated 30 May 1945.
57. Ibid., the verdict of the People's Court, p. 10.
58. Ibid., see on this the testimony of Zsuzsanna S., pp. 28–30.
59. Ibid., the testimony of Mrs Be., p. 33.
60. BFL XXV 1a Criminal cases of the Budapest People's Court, 1945/1500, the case of György Papp, a police report dated 30 May 1945, p. 34.
61. Ibid., the testimony of Mr R., p. 38.
62. Ibid., the verdict of the People's Court, p. 8.
63. Ibid., p. 8.
64. Ibid., p. 19, a denunciation submitted by Mrs J., dated 12 May 1945.
65. BFL XXV 1a Criminal cases of the Budapest People's Court, 1945/1500, the case of György Papp, see the statement of the defendant, p. 41.
66. Ibid.
67. Ibid., p. 48, p. 61, and p. 64.

68. Ibid., p. 61, and see also the letter of support written and signed by numerous inhabitants of the Protected house, pp. 76–77.
69. Ibid., the testimony of Mrs Szobovits, p. 63.
70. On Horthy's role see Krisztián Ungváry, *A Horthy rendszer mérlege* [The balance of the Horthy era] (Budapest: Jelenkor, 2012).
71. Tibor Zinner, "Háborús bűnösök perei. Internálások, kitelepítések és igazoló eljárások 1945–1949."
    [Trials of war criminals: internments, resettlements and justificatory processes, 1945–1949] *Történelmi Szemle*, no. 1, 1985, p. 121.
72. In this section, the original names of the concierge and the inhabitants living in Visegrádi utca 60 were changed or modified to protect their privacy.
73. BFL XVII/1598, Justificatory Committee Files, district V, box no. 3, the case of Mr István Barko, a denunciation signed by 13 residents, dated 27 April 1945.
74. Ibid., a letter of the residents addressed to the Building Managers' Free Trade Union.
75. Ibid.
76. Ibid., Elemér G.'s letter, written on 3 July 1945.
77. Ibid., Mrs. Ke.'s letter, written on 18 June 1945.
78. Ibid., György G.'s letter, written on 23 June 1945.
79. Ibid., György G.'s letter, written on 23 June 1945.
80. See on this Cole, *Holocaust City*, p. 218, J. Lévai, *A Pesti gettó története* (Budapest: Officina, 1946), p. 66.
81. On the nature of social capital, see Pierre Bourdieu, "The Forms of Capital" in J. Richardson (ed.) *Handbook of Theory and Research for the Sociology of Education* (New York: Greenwood, 1986), pp. 241–258.
82. BFL XVII/1598, Justificatory Committee Files, district V, box no. 3, the case of Mr István Barko, see a letter written by Mrs W., dated 24 July 1945.
83. Ibid.
84. Ibid., Róbert Stern's letter, written on 24 July 1945.
85. Ibid., see Róbert Stern's testimony on 2 August 1945.
86. Ibid., see G. Roth's testimony on 10 October 1945.
87. Lévai, *A Pesti gettó története*, p. 55.
88. BFL XVII/1598, Justificatory Committee Files, district V, box no. 3, the case of Mr István Barko, see Sándor Gonda's testimony on 2 August 1945.
89. Ibid, see Piroska K.'s testimony on 13 August 1945.
90. Ibid, see Klára F.'s testimony on 13 August 1945.
91. Ibid, see Miss Zsuzsanna Ö.'s testimony on 13 August 1945.
92. Ibid., see this in detail in Mrs D.'s testimony on 10 October 1945.
93. Ibid., Mr. Pál F.'s testimony on 10 October 1945.
94. BFL IV/1419/J Az 1941-es Népszámlálás lakásívei, 359/b II. számlálójárás, [Flat-sheets of the 1941 Census, 359/b II. counting unit] Flat-sheet no. 12, Visegrádi utca 60, apartment I/3.

95. Ibid., Flat-sheet no. 4, Visegrádi utca 60, apartment 2/a.
96. Ibid., Flat-sheet no. 18, Visegrádi utca 60, apartment II/9.
97. Ibid., Flat-sheet no. 20, Visegrádi utca 60, apartment II/11.
98. Ibid., Flat-sheet no. 23, Visegrádi utca 60, apartment III/14.
99. Ibid., Flat-sheet no. 25, Visegrádi utca 60, apartment III/16.
100. Ibid., Flat-sheet no. 33, Visegrádi utca 60, apartment IV/24.
101. Ágnes Nagy, "Lakóközösség kontra háztulajdonos...", pp. 167–169.
102. BFL XVII/1598, Justificatory Committee Files, district V, box no. 3, the case of Mr István Barko, see the second denunciation signed by 12 residents, dated 19 June 1945. See the second line in the list of the tenants at Mrs János M: I/6.
103. Ibid., Flat-sheet no. 32, Visegrádi utca 60, apartment V/28.
104. Ibid., Flat-sheet no. 33, Visegrádi utca 60, apartment V/29.
105. Ibid., Flat-sheet no. 35, Visegrádi utca 60, apartment V/26.
106. Ibid., Flat-sheet no. 36, Visegrádi utca 60, apartment V/27.
107. BFL XVII/1598, Justificatory Committee Files, box no. 8, district VI, the case of István Allmann the letter of Dr György S., dated 13 August 1945.
108. BFL XVII/1598, Justificatory Committee Files, box no. 7, see the questionnaire in the case of István Udvardy.
109. BFL XXV 1a Files of the Budapest People's Court, case number 1945/200, the case of Dávid Sipos, the statement of Béla Czigler, p. 33.
110. Oral history interview with Ágota Sebő, conducted by the author on 4 February 2014, in Budapest.
111. BFL XVII/1598, Justificatory Committee Files, district V, box no. 3, the case of Mr István Barko, a letter of residents addressed to the Building Managers' Free Trade Union.
112. BFL XVII/1598, Justificatory Committee Files, box no. 3, the case of István Barko: see the declaration of the Social Democratic Party's Csillaghegy unit on 11 September 1945.
113. Ibid., the declaration of department IX of the Budapest Mayor's office on 4 October 1945.
114. Ronald S. Burt, "The Social Capital of Structural Holes" in Mauro F. Guillén, Randall Collins, Paula England and Marshall Meyer (eds), *The New Economic Sociology* (New York: Russell Sage Foundation, 2005), p. 155.
115. BFL XVII/1598, Justificatory Committee Files, box no. 3, the case of István Barko. See Mr. György G.'s letter, written on 23 June 1945.
116. Ibid., see Mr. Róbert S.'s letter, written on 24 July 1945.
117. Burt, "The Social Capital of Structural Holes", p. 149, p. 155. See on this also: Ronald S. Burt, *Brokerage and Closure: An Introduction to Social Capital* (Oxford: Oxford University Press, 2013), pp. 4–5, and pp. 10–24.
118. Szinnai, *Sötét ablakok*, p. 403.
119. Ibid.

CHAPTER 6

Calling the Building Manager to Account: The Colourful Palette of Retribution in Early Post-War Budapest from People's Court to Justificatory Committee

This chapter is about a power struggle between various groups: tenants, concierges and others, who all had to find ways of living together in the new setting brought about by the Red Army in early 1945. In the beginning, it seemed like the Jewish Hungarian tenants were successful in reclaiming the upper hand in the Budapest apartment houses. However, through their connections and ability to adapt, the building managers found ways to whitewash their past, and to connect to the political left, which gradually took over government. The sources reflect how quickly the concierges built good relationships with the occupying Russian forces, strengthening by this their positions both inside the apartment building and outside of it. The chapter also maps the contemporary judgement over the problem of the "non-interfering" attitude, by which could be described thousands of ordinary Hungarians in 1944, and whether trying to stay out of the anti-Jewish atrocities as a bystander was legally punishable in 1945–46. Finally, from the decisions made by the retribution authorities we can discern an immediate post-war position on what should have been done in 1944. Concerning the building managers' wartime activity, this was a highly complicated question, as for instance, one of them was reprimanded for not warning a tenant that the Gestapo had been looking for him, with the result that this person was arrested the next day.[1] To judge an action—or more precisely inaction—like this correctly took a lot of consideration, and the different institutions, like the People's Court and the Justificatory

© The Author(s) 2016   147
I.P. Adam, *Budapest Building Managers and the Holocaust in Hungary,*
The Holocaust and its Contexts, DOI 10.1007/978-3-319-33831-6_6

Committee, differently evaluated the building managers' behaviour in this setting. Before analysing their decisions, it is worth having a closer look at why these institutions had so much information on the building managers' wartime acts, or in other words, why the tenants collected memories on the concierges at all.

1   MUTUAL PREPARATION FOR A POWER CLASH

That the Jewish Hungarian tenants of the Budapest apartment buildings during World War II developed a strong and long-lasting appetite for justice is well shown by the fact that they purposefully collected implicating memories about the building managers. They came out with these reminiscences in the immediate aftermath of the war when they thought the time was ripe for a calling to account. Although in the ghetto period the tenants seemingly lived in an inactive captivity, in reality they were active in preparing for a post-war charging of the incriminated concierges. In this agency they may have seen a chance of gaining something back from their lost social respect and self-esteem. Hence, the shared intimacy of the inner life of an apartment building, the chance to closely observe the lives of the concierges, empowered the Jewish Hungarian residents for the post-war retribution process. Besides their self-esteem, these people also wanted to get back their apartments, their assets, and the former Jewish Hungarian building managers additionally wanted their jobs back too. Well-documented cases show how they made steps to force the return of their goods and posts, and the first step in this long process was usually to recall what the building managers did to them. For some reason, a striking number of the negative memories recalled after the war relate to the concierges' behaviour at the moment when the Arrow Cross came into power. Thus, it seems that the tenants experienced this day (15 October 1944) as a kind of "moment of truth".

Thinking about why the Jewish tenants remember so often this moment, or the beginning of the Nazi German occupation (19 March 1944), one has to realize that these were the instances when everyday Hungarians not only could express freely their willingness to directly profit from the anti-Jewish regulations, but could even be proud of an anti-semitic arrogance. The expression of this readiness by their fellow-citizens, like neighbours, building managers and others, shocked Jewish Hungarians, and not only them. Similarly to them, Sándor Márai, one of the most popular Hungarian authors of all time, in his book entitled *Memoir of*

Hungary mentions his shock at his own friends. Márai held a dinner party to celebrate his name day on 18 March 1944, where he reports the following comment from one of his guests in the course of a heated debate over the political developments: "'I am a National Socialist,' he shouted. 'You'—he pointed at me—'can't understand this, because you are talented. But I'm not, and that is why I need National Socialism.'"[2] This quote resonates with an earlier entry in Imre Patai's wartime diary, where he describes the younger Hungarian workers at his company. According to him, "there is not a lot of appetite for work in these youngsters. This generation envies the living standard of the *Jewish directors*. Even though they are lacking any talent, they want to live to the same standard [as the *Jewish directors*]."[3] These kinds of general statements suggest that the contemporaries saw how and why many Hungarians joined the anti-Jewish movements to find a shortcut towards the upper social classes. These general statements were later put into context by István Bibó, the only immediate post-World War II thinker who gave serious thought to why and how the Hungarian Holocaust could happen. He was concerned with the entire Hungarian population's attitude, because, as he sadly acknowledged, during the war "actions targeting the effacing of the Jews from their economic positions enjoyed strong support all over the country."[4] Since Hungarian society was stuck in a hierarchically feudal stage, it was extremely difficult to move upwards on the social scale, which is why—argues Bibó—slogans like "the Jewish question has to be solved", for the majority of the population meant a progressive step towards social equality.[5] Bibó obviously was not familiar with Wolfgang Benz's theory about the nature of anti-Jewish sentiment in Eastern Europe, which explains that in times of crises anti-semitism could symbolize much more than simply an animosity towards Jews.[6] In these historical moments anti-semitism serves as a complete set of solutions that suggests reorganizing the world in an allegedly more logical system. Furthermore, it also provides an "instrument of communication" that allows the masses to better understand each other and to find a common denominator.[7] Talking about Hungary in particular, Benz underlines that anti-semitism is and was an integral part of national identity. He refers to the alleged Jewish–Communist alliance, a myth that was successfully propagated in the interwar era, and that anti-semitism's excluding effect created a stronger feeling of community among many Christian Hungarians.[8] Although Bibó could not be familiar with this concept, it fits perfectly his description of wartime Hungary, where millions demanded the "solving of the Jewish question", effectively the redistribution of the Jewish-Hungarians' wealth and positions. As Bibó observed, with the introduction of the widely supported anti-Jewish regulations, large groups of ordinary Hungarians realized that this was the moment when they could get a better position for themselves without working hard for it. Bibó maintains that "from this moment broad groups of Hungarian society got used to the fact that positions were not only achievable by hard work and entrepreneurship, but also by choosing someone else's already existing position and by denouncing this person."[9] But the circle of people who benefitted from these anti-semitic regulations was even wider than those intentional applicants. Opportunities opened up for everyday non-Jews just because Jewish Hungarians were dismissed from their jobs, or because they were not allowed to continue their businesses any longer. One of them, Mrs Kardos, the former concierge of Katona József utca 26, complained to the post-war authorities with these words: "because of the anti-Jewish laws I was dismissed from my position. Now here I am standing with my little daughter: we have no home, and I cannot make ends meet, which is why I request my job back."[10] Similarly, Márton Icskovics recalled in 1945 that "thanks to the order issued on 15 June 1942, which forbade Jews from remaining as building managers, my employment was cancelled."[11]

Many people regarded as Jews, like Mrs Kardos or Mr Icskovics, lost their jobs and homes in the early 1940s. In this process, the so-called Second Jewish law, Act IV of 1939 was the key—says Bibó—which the political elite regarded as a necessary sacrifice.[12] The conservative governing forces thought that by offering this act to the extreme right, they could put off for a long time the popularity of the Arrow Cross and the Imrédy parties. But they badly miscalculated the situation, and the extreme right became much more powerful, successfully advocating for the acceptance of more and more anti-Jewish regulations.[13] The anti-Jewish resentment further deepened as these regulations mostly left untouched the biggest Jewish Hungarian investors, because the big entrepreneurs were closely tied in economic terms to the governing non-Jewish conservative political elite.[14] This process went on for several years and resulted in a complete socio-economic transformation on the level of the middle and lower-middle classes. These changes had strong effects on the Budapest apartment buildings as well, where in the middle of 1942 Jewish Hungarian building managers lost their jobs, while Jewish Hungarian tenants experienced hardship, especially after the Nazi German forces arrived in Budapest in March 1944. In this respect, the days of the Nazi German invasion (19 March 1944) and the Arrow Cross takeover (15 October 1944) were crucial, as these were the times when the already suffering Jewish Hungarians' defencelessness culminated. When on these very days, previously lowly ranked individuals like the building managers expressed their political affiliation towards National Socialism, then the differently value-oriented Jewish Hungarians naturally took these expressions badly, and recalled them during the post-war evaluation of the concierges' wartime behaviour. From these moments onwards, they were not regarded anymore as potentially helpful building managers, but as political enemies of the Jewish Hungarians, and accomplices in an institutionalized plunder. Pro-Nazi sympathy expressed in these moments was understood symbolically by the Jewish Hungarians as blatant betrayal. From their perspective, the concierges—who previously lived for years on the tenants' tips—unscrupulously joined their enemies, the Nazis, in order to profit from the situation. These people wanted to break out so vehemently from their lower social positions that it did not matter for them much that the Nazi-led socio-economic rearrangement also meant unfair and inhuman treatment for the Jewish Hungarians.

To what extent these socio-economic changes could shake the community of a Budapest apartment building is shown in the case of József Kása, a concierge from VIII district, Lujza utca 22. This building manager admitted a significant growth in wealth on the Justificatory Committee's questionnaire. Accordingly, during the war his assets doubled from 5,800 pengő (1 January 1937) to 11,600 pengő (1 January 1945), which is remarkable given it was a relatively small building in a not especially rich area of Budapest, and perhaps his income grew even more than he was willing to confess.[15] In this case, a tenant called Jenő Katz wrote to the Justificatory Committee and argued against the concierge's approval, raising two scandalous issues related to his wartime activity. In his letter Mr Katz states, first, that both the building manager and his wife "expressed joy and used anti-Jewish words on the occasion of the German occupation".[16] Second, they used the tenant's belongings, which he gave them for safekeeping, "for their own purposes".[17] I find it remarkable that Mr Katz writes first about the pro-Nazi attitude of the concierge and only after this about his own losses. As for the losses of Jewish residents in the building, another tenant, Henrik Schmergel criticized the building manager in relation to a box full of clothes he posted to a forced labourer relative of his in June 1944, just before moving out from his apartment to a ghetto building.[18] In a way, he tried to get around the June ghetto order and escape with some of his clothes. This gesture could give a lot to the relative in need, but the only problem was that the army unit where this person was serving refused the delivery. Hence the package was sent back to the original address, to Lujza utca 22, but by this time the sender Mr Schmergel had been moved from here to the designated ghetto building. Later Mr Schmergel managed to get the delivery record from the 72nd post office of Budapest, which says that the building manager took the returned box from the postman. However, József Kása, the concierge, denied that he took the package. This account appeared to be especially dubious after the war, when the letter writer Mr Schmergel had seen the son of the building manager dressed in one of the shirts he originally had sent in the package to his relative in June 1944.[19] After this unexpected incident, the building manager reluctantly agreed to return some of Mr Schmergel's belongings, and indeed had given the tenant several items of clothing. In a further twist, it later emerged that most of the clothes given to Mr Schmergel originally belonged to another tenant of Lujza utca 22, named Pölcz, who had been told by the concierge that her family's clothes had been stolen by the incoming Russian troops.[20] So, the building manager's misappropriations mingled and created unsolvable situations in the immediate aftermath of the war, when basic means of life were missing for the returning Jewish Hungarians. But Mr Schmergel lost much more than part of his wardrobe. According to his letter, by the time he returned from the ghetto, his entire apartment was already inhabited by the building manager's godfather.[21] This was only possible because, in June 1944, the concierge forced out Mr Schmergel's non-Jewish subtenant, who after the war even gave a testimony about this to Mr Schmergel, stating, "due to the [anti-]Jewish laws, my main tenant had to move to the ghetto. I, as a Christian wanted to stay in the apartment, but because Kása *házmester* continuously was bothering me, I had to give up and move out from it."[22]

Besides noting how the concierge turned everything upside-down in the building and made selfish use of the anti-Jewish regulations, it is also worth noticing what an enormous effort it took to turn these happenings into documents. Mr Schmergel—now forced to flat-share with the hated concierge's godfather—had to quickly find out where his former subtenant's post-war location was, and ask her to write a declaration about her 1944 experiences. The case of József Kása demonstrates this challenge of creating paperwork from alleged criminal behaviour versus wartime support performed by the building manager. In Lujza utca 22, when the Justificatory Committee's denazification process reached the building, tenants broke into two groups: the supporters and the enemies of the concierge. Kása's file even contains a form, where tenants who wanted to keep the concierge in his post were listed on the left side (25 persons), while those who requested his dismissal were listed on the right side (three persons).[23] The building manager also attached an official criminal record form issued by the VIII district police headquarters, certifying that he was not convicted of any kind of crime in the recent past.[24] The concierge also added to this a supportive declaration signed by a tenant, Mrs Chaim Luszthaus, who lived in an apartment situated on the ground floor of Lujza utca 22, which means she was a direct neighbour of the building manager.[25] Both the Jewish Hungarian tenants and the concierge prepared documents for a post-war power clash, which in this building was won by the returning Jewish Hungarians. On 27 August 1945, the Justificatory Committee decided against approving Kása's wartime activity, firstly because it found that the building manager was pro-Nazi Germans, and only secondly because of his cruelly acquisitive behaviour.[26] This practice of listing arguments against a corrupted concierge indicates that the authorities were keener on listening to the tenants' complaints if they gave accounts about the building manager's pro-Nazi or pro-Arrow Cross sentiment. They were, perhaps, much less interested in assisting the Jewish Hungarians in gaining back their losses, and this preference made many aspects of the socio-economic changes irreversible.

Therefore, both the shock of the Jewish tenants over the unreliability of the concierges, and the retribution authorities' interests, facilitated the emergence of accounts about the openly expressed anti-semitic attitude of the building managers. For instance, in the middle of October 1944, one of the first decrees of the Arrow Cross leader Szálasi was to seal all the ghetto buildings. This was carried out, for example, in Podmaniczky utca 29, where the Jewish Hungarian residents were closed in the cellar. Here, on 16 October building manager Alajos Bankovszky went down to the captured people and gave them a speech, declaring that he belonged to the *Hungarista* Nazi movement, and to the Arrow Cross.[27] He was also often seen drinking wine and eating together with the Arrow Cross men during these days.[28] The first report about this building manager confirms the theories of Benz and Bibó. Nevertheless, the details in the second report rather reveal how much the inner yard of a Budapest apartment building as an intimate space worked two ways: on the one hand the concierges kept an eye on the Jewish Hungarians, but on the other hand, the Jewish Hungarians also continuously observed the concierges.

One Jewish Hungarian tenant recalled that in downtown Budapest, in Alkotmány utca 29, a party started spontaneously in the building manager's apartment immediately after the radio announced that Horthy was arrested and the Arrow Cross had taken over the governing power.[29] Mrs Ferenc Auguszt, concierge of VI, Horn Ede utca 6 celebrated in a publicly right-wing non-Jewish tenant's apartment on 15 October, 1944, which account tells us that the inhabitants of the ghetto building also observed the non-Jews who stayed in these buildings despite their Jewish designation.[30] In VI Laudon utca 5, András Váradi assisted her mother, Mrs Váradi in fulfilling the tasks of a building manager. Although both of them strictly implemented the anti-Jewish regulations, they did good things as well. They kept the valuables of various Jewish tenants safe, and helped the building supervisor's sister to survive when she was locked up starving in the main ghetto of Budapest.[31] However, their reputation was seriously damaged by their 1944 pro-Nazi attitude, which is why they later lost their positions too. It is known from the testimony of a resident that "on 15 October, when Szálasi came into power, there was loud partying in the apartment of the Váradis until late at night".[32] Tenant Mr Kőszegi heard clear applause and celebration from the lodge that night, and as he added, the younger Váradi believed wholeheartedly in the Nazi-German triumph, and spread news about the magical weapon they had developed in Csepel Sziget, an industrial area of southern Budapest.[33] Another resident, József Árvai confirmed the building managers' friendly attitude towards the German soldiers. The army men often dined at a canteen set up in the house, and Mr Árvai even saw the older concierge, Mrs Váradi, kissing these soldiers, which shows how intimate these accounts could be.[34]

2   PREPARATIONS ON THE CONCIERGES' SIDE LEAD TO THE EMERGENCE OF THE JUSTIFICATORY COMMITTEE

Just like the tenants, building managers were also preparing for a postwar calling to account, first individually and later collectively, in organized forms. Even their individual help offered to certain Jewish tenants has been interpreted by historian László Karsai as conscious efforts to counter their previous vicious acts. Karsai argues that saving Jewish Hungarians became a habit of the concierges only after the Arrow Cross coup, demonstrating their selfish intentions.[35] As Karsai rightly points out, unlike in wartime Poland, in Budapest bystanders who assisted the fleeing Jewish Hungarians did not risk capital punishment, but the possibility of internment and heavy fines.[36] While in Warsaw, the Nazi Germans' decrees threatened with death the rescuers of the persecuted people as early as in 1941, in Budapest only after the middle of October 1944 was the same penalty in use by the ruling Arrow Cross movement. In the fact that in Budapest, exactly after this point, an increasing number of ordinary Hungarians engaged in "Jew-saving", Karsai sees an escape route, namely that they "may have thought that by saving Jews they might save themselves as well in the new regime."[37] Perhaps the exact reasons behind helping someone were more complex, but surely there was an intention among the concierges, an agency that countered the Jewish Hungarian tenants' intention to punish all the wrongdoers. These acts, however, had limited effects and needed documentation, which generally got the form of a supporting declaration signed by those saved, as we have seen in the case of Kása, or in the Barko case in Chapter 5.

The organized preparations of the building managers had much more influence on the entire process of post-war retribution. As was mentioned in Chapter 1, building managers always had associations, from which, as early as on 7 February 1945, a trade union was formed along a Soviet pattern.[38] Although, the name of this organization was new, it was registered to the same address as the Building Managers' National Alliance during and before the war (Semmelweis utca 4). Moreover, some of the new functionaries had even held leading positions during the Horthy era. The head of the new Building Managers' Free Trade Union was János Boldis, who, for instance, between 1941 and 1944 took part in the concierges' most prestigious events as the conductor of their choir. The wake-up call for the new leadership was the public concern over the entire building manager craft: it seemed that these people shared a collectively negative image at the end of World War II, and the public demanded vengeance against them. To respond somewhat to this popular demand to punish the petty war criminal *házmester*, or rather to alter and minimize it, in early 1945 the new communist mayor of Budapest announced the forming of a Justificatory Committee of the Building Managers under the control of the Building Managers' Free Trade Union.[39] The Committee's members were delegated by the Building Managers' Free Trade Union, and the five political parties, which made up the *Magyar Nemzeti Függetlenségi Front* (MNFF), a Soviet-backed umbrella organization of the anti-Fascist political powers.[40] They were led by the skilful guidance of a professional lawyer. Another driving force behind the setting up of the justificatory committees was the occupying Allied forces' request for the denazification of the Hungarian bureaucracy and public life.[41] This request was expressed both in the truce agreement and in the Hungarian interim government's programme as a need to cleanse the civil services of members of the Arrow Cross movement and "other betrayers of the national good".[42] In accordance with this, the Justificatory Committee was primarily searching for those building managers who were members of the Arrow Cross or any other extreme-right party, or those who aimed to achieve the goals of a party like this. It wanted to also identify those concierges who by their wartime actions "hurt the interest of the Hungarian people".[43] Lastly, the Justificatory Committee had to hunt down those *házmester* who "instigated hatred against a certain part of the society", which meant obviously the Jewish Hungarians.[44] This list and its emphasis explain why so many Jewish Hungarians reported primarily the pro-Nazi sentiment of the Budapest building managers.

No doubt, the preference of the leaders of the trade union was to find as few corrupted concierges as possible. This desire was expressed in the official journal of the trade union entitled *Házfelügyelő*, where president Boldis predicted that the denazification process was going to prove the building managers were not in any way more immoral than the representatives of any other professions.[45] According to him the negative connotation the people felt towards the concierges was due to the fact the *házmester's* activity during the war was much more public than anyone else's. As he added, per se pardoning them, the building managers had to execute the Nazi orders, and they had no opportunity to sabotage them.[46] It says a lot about how this investigation was conceived that the building managers were not expected to need a lawyer in this process, except if a convicted concierge intended to challenge the Justificatory Committee's decision.[47] The only group that took this investigation really seriously was the former tenants of the apartment buildings, especially the Jewish Hungarians, who wrote hundreds of letters to the Justificatory Committee.

Consequently, the forming of the Justificatory Committee of the Building Managers in early spring 1945 was partly down to the agency of the concierges, who wanted to survive in their posts. In effect, the concierges achieved that they were regulated by an internal investigation. Even though outsiders had to be involved with this check, it was a much better deal than a thorough screening organized by an independent organization. This was, one might argue, an obvious result of the concierges' effective relationship-building with the post-war authorities.[48] It is worth noting that the Building Managers' Free Trade Union held its first general meeting at the headquarters of the local Communist Party unit on 7 July 1945. The statement of their director, a certain Mr Juhász, is even more telling. "In a democratic country"—he said—"there is a need for democratic building managers, who can adjust to the current situation of the country."[49] The concierges' journal which published this quote also had some more direct suggestions for the building managers. In an article entitled "Things worth learning", it explains the meaning of words like democratic, reactionary, socialism and communism.[50] The same journal published the following call under the headline, *The days of the parties:* "we call all our colleagues' attention that every Tuesday is a party day in the Communist and Social Democratic Party units. These events include public lectures, and it is greatly advised to attend these days in as high numbers as possible. More information can be found in *Népszava* and *Szabad Nép* [dailies] every Tuesday." These lines and also the speeches were channelling a message, and this message was clearly to encourage building managers to orient themselves to the political left. The new leaders of the building managers wanted to limit the space for the rightist and conservative elements among them, because they had realized that these people could discredit the whole concierge profession. Therefore— and here lies the second part of the leaders' agency—they wanted to use denazification to eliminate those colleagues who were not willing to give up their right-wing or conservative affiliations.

By the summer of 1945, most of the building managers understood that they had to adjust to the political developments. For instance, the residents of Dobozi utca 17 remembered their concierge, K. Felföldi, as someone who in 1944 openly favoured the Nazi Germans over the Russians, living in symbiosis with his father-in-law, who worked for the local Gestapo.[51] In a dramatic change, however, a resident noted on 12 August 1945, that the same building manager had just become a member of the Social Democratic Party a couple of weeks before.[52] In May to July 1945, when the building managers were obliged to fill out the Justificatory Committee's questionnaire as the initial phase of the denazifying process, most of them already could make a good guess at the expected answers. It is enough to think about those questions, which inquired about their reading habits, asking what kind of dailies they had been reading during the war, and what they were reading at the time of the justification [*Milyen napilapokat olvasott és olvas*]. The vast majority responded with *Szabad Nép*, the newspaper of the Communist Party, and *Népszava*, a daily closely connected to the Hungarian Social Democratic Party. The survey also inquired about the concierges' membership of parties, trade unions and other organizations during the Horthy era. The most common answer here was membership of the building managers' association [*Házfelügyelők Szövetsége*], but hardly anyone confessed Arrow Cross Party membership. Instead, for instance, István Bándy depicted himself in the interwar years as a member of the Social Democratic Party, who spread leftist propaganda among his fellows [*a szocializmus érdekében fejtettem ki agitációt*].[53] After the war Ferenc Ackermann from district IV became a Communist party member, who even wore a party badge on his clothes every day.[54] The very last section of the survey provided space for additional remarks.[55] This is where János Kondorosi from VI, Bajcsy Zsilinszky út 27 wished to prove his long-lasting faith in the communist movement. As he wrote, "following the repression of our freedom fight in 1919, I was taken to an internment camp at Pardubice."[56] By this the concierge refers to his connections to the first Hungarian Soviet Republic, which came into being at the end of World War I. Concierge Kondorosi was a member of Béla Kun's army, which was finally defeated by the Entente powers in summer 1919. He thought his captivity under the occupying Czechoslovakian forces, and his suffering for the leftist political cause in 1919, could earn him some good points in the eyes of the 1945 rulers. Along the same lines, Ferencz Markovits from Teréz körút 27 went back even further in time, when he stated on the questionnaire that in 1897, for the occasion of the twenty-fifth anniversary of the Paris Commune, he wrote a commemorating article about Leo Frankel, who was of Hungarian origin and had held a leading position in the Commune.[57]

Reading these statements in the twenty-first century, they all seem to be attempts to adapt to the new social and political conditions, while the tenants' conflicting accounts about the building managers' pro-Nazi sentiments often show that many of the same building managers adapted well to the previous political background too. In VI, Lehel utca 19, the *házmester* cooperated in 1944 with the Arrow Cross army men and allegedly handed the Jewish tenants over to them without hesitation.[58] But despite all this, in January and February 1945 the same building manager billeted Russian soldiers in the apartments of the former Jewish tenants, and he also provided place for a newly-met couple, a Red Army soldier and his girlfriend, the daughter of another building manager.[59] Elsewhere, a post-war police investigation against Mrs Róth, the building manager of XIV Benkő utca 7, uncovered that she burnt her Arrow Cross membership card in the air-raid shelter at the end of the war.[60] Mrs Mohácsi, a tenant who witnessed this burning remembered that the concierge commented: "this doesn't suit the time anymore, soon we are going to get Communist membership cards". Indeed, soon after this, the witness, who had seen the Arrow Cross badge on the concierge during the war, realized that both Mrs Róth and her husband had started to wear red armbands. To conclude, in the first post-war months the building managers performed a spectacular turn-around in their political preferences. This process had a top-down incentive, but it showed a bottom-up direction too. Jewish Hungarian tenants understood that this was about the building managers' intention to keep their positions, and wrote their own accounts in response.

3   THE PEOPLE'S COURT AND ITS DISTINGUISHABLY DIFFERENT PRIORITIES

Another retribution forum the Jewish Hungarian tenants could and did turn to in order to bring justice through official channels was the People's Court. However, its sentences suggest that guilt meant something else for the judges working here than for the Justificatory Committee's jury. Deliberate and active contribution by the building managers to the deportation, death, torture or detention of the victims was the only type of action for which the People's Court charged the *házmester*, while the survivors in Budapest wanted justice in much more delicate situations. They wanted the concierges to be condemned for using publicly anti-semitic expressions, for situations where they did not show the usual respect towards the tenants, or where they stole everyday goods from the tenants' vacated apartments. In this respect, there were two entirely different conceptions of the denazification of the *házmester* profession in the minds of Jewish Hungarian tenants and in the actions of the People's Court. It is little surprise that the tenants far too often left the court rooms disappointed.[61] The Justificatory Committee set its stance somewhere between these two fundamentally conflicting positions. This is why, instead of the People's Court, it was the Justificatory Committee of the Building Managers that offered an opportunity for Jewish Hungarian tenants to speak about their embarrassing experiences with the concierges. Sometimes this Committee worked like a transitional justice reconciliation forum within the microspace of the apartment building, sometimes more like a buffer zone, where even pre-war conflicts of a tenement house could get new meaning due to the new political developments.[62] In these days a certain journalist called Fedor visited the Building Managers' Free Trade Union's building, where the Justificatory Committee's hearings were taking place. He called the building simply the "house of hatred", from where he reported the following:

> Since the Justificatory Committee invites the concierges at the same time with the pro- and counter witnesses, on the corridors there are groups formed of 8–10 individuals from every building. From their clothes and style an experienced Pest citizen can figure out the exact street where the specific building stands from where these people arrived here today. You can guess whether for example they are from the jam-packed Peterdy utca or from the elegant Molnár utca. These people two years ago barely knew each other, now they stand here either angrily looking or swearing at one another. Two years ago they were only saying hello politely each other, giving small tips to the *házmester* ... The empowerment of these concierges started in the air raid shelters, and this was also where the inhabitants started to better get to know each other. And now here stand the building managers, once making life-and-death decisions, now they are surrounded by their tenants like the main actors of a Greek drama are surrounded by the choir. [63]

This descriptive account of a journalist suggests that the hearings of the Justificatory Committee provided space for more emotionally heated debates over the concierges' activity than the trial days of the much more legalistic People's Court.

To illustrate the differences between the People's Court's and the Justificatory Committee's actions, I turn to Pannónia utca 22, where tenants saw the Arrow Cross badge on the concierge's son, and remembered his wife as someone who openly favoured the Nazi German invasion in 1944.[64] But the tenants had much more to report about concierge István Zseni himself. This *házmester* disgraced himself when, although he had known that the Gestapo was searching for a resident of the building, Mr Gáspár, he did not warn him about this life-threatening danger. Moreover, on the day before this tenant was arrested, in the late evening the concierge went up to his apartment to make sure that Mr Gáspár was in fact at home.[65] Situations like this had to be very delicately assessed after the war. The building manager presumably did not do much more than his job required when he checked the homecoming of the tenant, and therefore the People's Court could not prosecute him. Nevertheless, the resolution of the Justificatory Committee argues that by not warning tenant Gáspár that Gestapo officers were inquiring about him, the concierge crossed the line of immoral behaviour. By stating that Zseni "did not give Mr Gáspár a chance to escape the deportation", the Justificatory Committee reasoned that the concierge should have been aware of the consequences a Gestapo arrest could bring.[66] It made things even worse that although Mrs Gáspár begged the concierge to say why exactly he came up to their apartment on that night, his answer was just a flippant remark: "you are going to find out it in the morning".[67] What is remarkable here is that the act the Committee members decided to penalize in Zseni's behaviour was only a little bit more than mere bystanding. The concierge in these circumstances was reluctant to warn a potential victim of potential danger, and surprisingly in this case—partially because of the tragic outcome of the incident—the bystanding led to the post-war dismissal of concierge István Zseni. What Zseni did was not a crime, therefore his case was not transferable to the People's Court, but it was enough for the Justificatory Committee to deprive the building manager of his job and as a consequence, from his home as well. The Justificatory Committee had the authority to dismiss the building managers, or to suspend them from their job temporarily (up to five years). If they found a war criminal, they had to notify the public prosecutor office and were obliged to send the file to the People's Court.[68] But what is more, the Justificatory Committee also had the right to propose the internment of those who did not commit actual crimes during the war, but because of other, non-specified reasons were "a danger to the rebuilding of the country in democratic terms".[69] Thanks to the vague definitions the Committee worked with, various political and social connections could appear to be decisive at this level, unlike the People's Court, which worked on a much more accountable base.

In contrast to the Justificatory Committee's more general focus, the People's Court was exclusively prosecuting the war criminals of Hungary. The connection between the two forums was that the rulings of the Justificatory Committee could be appealed against, and the appeal court was the National Council of the People's Court (*Népbíróságok Országos Tanácsa*), the top of the denazification system's hierarchy. Compared to the Justificatory Committee, the People's Court was more bound by legal procedures in evaluating the evidence. This explains why inconsistency characterizes the Justificatory Committee much more than the People's Court, which was able to convict only those building managers whose professional complicity resulted in the arrest, deportation or physical abuse of the victims. Almost all the convicted building managers were found guilty of one of two similarly built criminal law constructions. One was the 81/1945 M.E. decree of the prime minister on the jurisdiction of the People's Court [*Népbíráskodásról szóló rendelet*], section 13, part 2, which ordered the punishment of those who "provided help for an army-like organization in committing violent crimes against individuals and assets".[70] The other legal reference was section 10 of 1440/1945 M.E. decree of the prime minister, which ordered to punish everyone who provided data for an organization that persecuted certain parts of society.[71] In fact, the latter law is an early modification of the former, and it says that "a person who acted as an informer of such fascist and counter-democratic organizations, which targeted the persecution of a certain part of society is guilty of war crimes."[72] This fairly impersonal legal parlance fitted perfectly the wartime actions of almost all the Budapest building managers. Those working in buildings designated for non-Jews by law had to report on Jewish Hungarians hiding in their buildings. While those concierges serving in the ghetto houses by law had to keep a list of the Jewish Hungarians, and were forced by a resolution of the Szálasi government to give this data to the Arrow Cross once it came into power in 1944. However, in practice, for the People's Court a building manager's complicity only meant the act of deliberately calling the attention of the Nazis to hidden Jewish Hungarians. For example, Dávid Sipos was sentenced to six months in prison and lost his post as the building manager of Szondi utca 42c.[73] Mr Sipos was charged under section 10 of the 1440/1945 M.E. decree, because on 26 December 1944, he went to Andrássy út 60 to say that there was a Jewish woman hiding in apartment 7 on the second floor of his apartment building, and by this act he caused the otherwise avoidable detention and sufferings of tenant Mrs Fülöp.[74] Andrássy út 60 was the most infamous centre of the Arrow Cross movement.[75] Mrs Fülöp was taken here by two Arrow Cross fighters, who were accompanied to her hiding spot by the concierge.[76] During the arrest, these two men beat her badly and forced her to give them her valuables.[77]

4   FURTHER DIFFERENCES BETWEEN THE ACTIVITY OF THE PEOPLE'S COURT AND THE JUSTIFICATORY COMMITTEE

Other kinds of crimes were only exceptionally discussed by the People's Court if they occurred on the side of the war criminal. This was the case in a trial against Mr and Mrs Koppány.[78] Here the denunciation was filed against both the husband and the wife, hence the investigation initially started against both *házmester*. The inspectors found incriminating data against both of them, but while Mr Koppány—as a war criminal—got five years in jail for assisting purposefully in the deportation of a Jewish tenant, his wife got a shorter jail term for misappropriation and stealing.[79] Mr Koppány's crime was that he realized that when the Arrow Cross men took the Jewish Hungarians from the ghetto house where he served, they "mistakenly" left one person called Mr Glaser, and to correct this error, he himself walked this individual to the assembly point.[80] The sentence underlined that the building manager was not obliged to hand the tenant over to the Arrow Cross, nobody forced him to do this, and also that tenant Glaser disappeared during the deportation.[81] The latter circumstance was decisive in terms of the length of the time in prison. Although the building managers had little influence on what happened with the Jewish Hungarians they handed over to the Arrow Cross, if the person died this triggered severe penalties. This rule was laid down in the 81/1945 M.E. decree of the prime minister on the jurisdiction of the People's Court, which in section 13 says that if a victim suffered injuries that took more than 20 days to heal, then the maximum punishment was three years, while if the victim had died, then the person who reported him or otherwise handed him over to the paramilitary unit [this meant the Arrow Cross] was punishable by up to ten years in prison.[82]

The Koppány case represented a unique exception in another sense too, because in this trial the People's Court proceeded against both the building manager and his wife, while in general it preferred to take legal action against only one individual. This was a notable difference compared to the Justificatory Committee's practice, which tended not to look into the guilt of the male *házmester* and his wife separately [in Hungarian *házmesterné*], which is understandable, as this job required more than one person. The reasons behind this dissimilarity could be that it was much easier to prove one person's indisputable guilt in war crimes than two, as for instance even Mrs Koppány was cleared of this accusation, and was only convicted of ordinary crimes.[83] On the contrary, the legalistically less precise Justificatory Committee of the Building Managers was more concerned with creating liveable situations in the apartment buildings. For example, a non-vacated lodge could have been blocking the employment of a new concierge. Furthermore, it is also easy to imagine that if a convicted concierge's spouse managed to hold on her job, she would have needed to work under fire of the denouncers of the already dismissed husband. In order to provide a clean sheet for the *democratic future* of the apartment buildings, the Committee tried to kick out the entire family of the corrupted building managers, which happened, for instance, at Csáky utca 21. Here, a tenant called Klára B. wanted to return to her home at the end of the war, but was stopped at the main gate by the building manager's wife, János Dolmányos.[84] Investigating the building manager's behaviour, the hearing of the Justificatory Committee unveiled that by the end of the war Mrs B.'s apartment was already inhabited by the younger brother of the concierge's wife, which perhaps explains why she did not let the tenant into the building when she had just returned from the ghetto.[85] Another tenant, József J. told the Committee's jury that in the Yellow Star house period, Mrs Dolmányos only let out the Jewish tenants from the building for a substantial payment.[86] She was also accused of stealing several of the tenants' assets in 1944.[87] Strangely enough, when the Committee members asked the witnesses about the building manager, János Dolmányos' actions, it appeared that he was in the army during the entire period.[88] In the light of this, it is especially interesting that the Justificatory Committee suspended János Dolmányos from his post as a concierge for five years, which also meant that he and his family had to move out from the concierge's apartment. The reasoning of the resolution says that the Committee ascertained Mrs Dolmányos' guilt, which—from a legal point of view—was inseparable from Mr Dolmányos' position.[89] This is how János Dolmányos, the man who was not even present, became guilty of crimes committed against the Jewish Hungarian tenants during the Arrow Cross era at Csáky utca 21.

The Justificatory Committee understood the concept of guilt extensively on a regular basis, claiming that crimes committed by husbands or wives triggered the firing of their spouses. Sometimes when doing this it even referred to the decree of the Budapest mayor on housing matters, and its 62nd section, which says that the crimes committed by a concierge affect his or her spouse as well.[90] This is how it found concierge Dezső Tordai responsible for the actions of his family members. The resolution sanctioning his dismissal hints that in 1944 Tordai's daughter worked for the SS, and left Hungary with the retreating Nazi German army. The conclusion of the jury was that "although no incriminating evidence occurred against Dezső Tordai, yet he has to bear the consequences of his family members' crimes and pro-German acts. It is because as a head of the family he should have used his disciplinary rights and blocked his family members' actions."[91] This argument underlines the special responsibility a husband and a father had, giving an idea of how patriarchal Hungarian society was at this time. Similarly, István Halay was condemned because, according to the Justificatory Committee, "as the head of the family he could have used some disciplinary action to stop his wife, who caused unnecessary suffering for the persecuted people."[92] In my understanding, this reasoning is the first step the retribution authorities took on the path leading to recognizing a morally reprehensible bystander behaviour. The problem is that although they were willing to recognize this within a family unit, there were only one or two cases where the authorities addressed the question of guilty inaction in larger communities, or in the society as a whole.

5   INACTION AND BYSTANDING IN THE RULINGS OF THE PEOPLE'S COURT AND THE JUSTIFICATORY COMMITTEE

Inaction is perhaps the most problematic moral behaviour to judge around the World War II period. This statement is especially true for Budapest, where after the Arrow Cross coup the Holocaust meant an ongoing plunder and mass killing in the heart of the city. A large-scale murder happening day by day had to meet the eyes of the locals, while far too many people failed to offer help to the victims. This is perhaps why the post-war authorities preferred to depict the ordinary Hungarians as innocent bystanders. It was just not possible to make criminals from so many people, therefore in most of the post-war investigations the question of fatal inaction did not appear at all. Consequently, neither the Justificatory Committee, nor the People's Court discussed this question in detail, but both touched on it in some of their resolutions. One illustration here is a caution, with which the Justificatory Committee of the Building Managers decided to close László Kovács' case. A caution was a rare exception among resolutions. The Committee only issued this sanction in situations where there was something disturbing that had to be noted, but there was not enough negative data to deprive a building manager of his position. László Kovács was the concierge of Szent István körút 18, a building not far from such landmarks as the Margaret Bridge and the Danube promenade. Surprisingly, the reasoning of the resolution suggests no less than that the building manager missed the chance to help the persecuted. Literally, he was condemned because of bystanding, which is so unusual that it is worth quoting here the original words. Accordingly, "László Kovács did not show the slightest willingness to help, which could be expected from everyone in these kinds of times. But this [helpful attitude] could especially be expected from someone who was a building manager, and who therefore had such rights which were close to the rights of the authorities. Nevertheless, the Committee did not find on László Kovács' side any consciously malicious will in the discussed instances, which is why it decided to issue the slightest possible sanction."[93] Reading this text, one starts wondering what makes the difference here. If when talking about bystanders it was so clear to the investigators that they dealt with a moral nonfeasance, why did they not consider this in other instances? The resolution was signed as in most cases by Oszkár Büchler, the head of the Justificatory Committee, and there is no reason to think that it was the product of a unique mixture in the members of the Committee. It is also clear that the majority of the residents stood behind the building manager; at least an attached declaration signed by 46 tenants can be read that way. They testified that the concierge helped everyone suffering during the war, and he was recognizably against the Nazi Germans and the Arrow Cross.[94] In the archival file of Kovács there is also a testimony that describes the everyday harmony lived through in the war years with the building manager. It mentions that "once the Jewish radios had been already surrendered, we listened to the evening news from Moscow and from London together in the concierge's apartment", a widespread phenomenon discussed earlier in Chapter 5.[95]

On the darker side, the Committee members were faced with a complaint from tenant Mrs Freyer, who indirectly blamed the building manager for the loss of her brother. Mrs Freyer's younger brother received a call to join the juvenile army unit, the so-called Leventes.[96] Mrs Freyer's brother did not want to report to the army; however—as was confirmed by another tenant, Mrs Bányai—it was the threatening concierge who convinced the young man to follow the conscription order.[97] Mrs Freyer adds to this that her brother escaped from his battalion, and wanted to hide in Szent István körút 18, but because of the building manager's warnings this was not feasible.[98] Thereby, Mrs Freyer's younger brother went missing in action.[99] So what has happened here is that the building manager did his job when trying to limit the possibility of anyone staying illegally in the building supervised by him. Contrary to this, the Justificatory Committee made the point that he should have turned a blind eye, and let the young man hide.[100]

Another resident, Mr Balázs J. specifically complained about the concierge's inaction: Balázs, arriving back from forced labour service, realized that his subtenant had left with the majority of his furniture.[101] As Balázs pointed out, the building manager had to be aware that the furniture belonged to him, yet he did nothing to stop the subtenant robbing the apartment. To his biggest surprise, when after the war Balázs went to have a word with the concierge, he saw in Kovács's lodge two silver candle-holders belonging to him, which he then managed to reclaim from the concierge.[102] To conclude, the concierge was not willing to assist an escapee from the army, and did not interfere when a Jewish Hungarian tenant's apartment was looted. This means two instances of not wanting to leave the role of a bystander, which were rightly condemned by the Justificatory Committee. Nevertheless, to find someone guilty for overseeing and not acting was absolutely exceptional. This explains why the concierge got so upset when he received his caution—even though it did not have any further consequences—and decided to appeal against the decision.[103] The People's Court rejected the appeal, because it was only possible to overturn a resolution if it dismissed an individual.[104] Two questions arise here: first, why the Justificatory Committee found it necessary to issue a caution; and secondly, and this is the larger point, if they were conscious of how many malicious things the building managers had overseen, and in how many situations they failed to help, why did they not address the problem of bystanding in other cases? Seemingly, the answer to the latter question is that in general they did not intend to go that far in denazification. Yet, and this answers the first question, in this specific situation they felt an urge to act, because Mr Freyer was the building warden, therefore the young man who had disappeared in the war was the building warden's brother-in-law.[105] The flipside of the coin is, though, that if there was no one impor-tant involved in a case like this where inaction caused a major loss, there was very little chance of calling a building manager to account for accusations of failing to help.

The People's Court by default dealt only with active complicity when investigating war crimes, which obviously excluded from its focus pas-sive bystanding, even if the inaction caused tragedies. Nevertheless, when the tribunal discussed the gravest offences, interestingly this was when it encapsulated in its verdict the question of fatal inaction as well. Such was the case of Mrs Reményi, where the People's Court took it as an aggra-vating circumstance that the defendant, precisely because of her job as a building manager was in the position to provide help for the persecuted Jewish Hungarians.[106] Instead of helping, she caused otherwise avoid-able losses. Mrs Gyula Reményi, as the building manager of VII, Dohány utca 16–18, was present on 13 November 1944, when the Arrow Cross fighters assembled the Jewish Hungarian inhabitants of this ghetto building.[107] Among the people forming lines in the courtyard, before starting a long march towards the German concentration camps, were Mr and Mrs Lunczer. They were so sick that the Arrow Cross men allowed them to go back to their apartments. However, hearing this, the concierge went after them and sent them back to the gathered Jewish Hungarians, shouting, "you are not going to stay here as my responsibility."[108] The couple left with the group and Mr Lunczer vanished.[109] On the same occasion, the building manager forced two ladies around the age of 54 to report downstairs as well, even though they protested because the Arrow Cross came only for Jewish Hungarians between the age of 16 and 50. As the People's Court verdict states, "to this day they have not returned and there is no any available data concerning their fate".[110] It was also the concierge who went up to Oszkár Gergely's apartment to bring him down to the assembly point. This time she had to fend off the objection of the building warden, who cried out, "let him stay, he is over 60 years old", but all dispute was in vain. Oszkár Gergely was taken by the Arrow Cross and, as a result, he went missing.[111] Obviously, many more people died from the group of tenants taken this day from VII, Dohány utca 16–18, but the People's Court only listed those four individuals, for whose death it found the building manager accountable. Additionally, the People's Court heard how the concierge led the Arrow Cross fighters to the hidden valuables of the Jewish Hungarian residents in the cellar of the building, out of which several pieces were found in her lodge after the liberation of Budapest.[112] At the same lodge were hidden those objects that the building manager took from the Lunczers' apartment following their departure in November 1944.[113]

The 42-year-old Mrs Reményi was arrested on 14 June 1945, and exactly two months later the People's Court sentenced her to death by hanging.[114] She was found guilty of war crimes (81/1945 M.E. decree of the prime minister, 13§, point 2) and of stealing (criminal code 333§ and 336§, point 3). The defendant denied all accusations, saying that she only followed the Arrow Cross militiamen's orders.[115] Disagreeing with this, the People's Court was of the opinion that Mrs Reményi from her own will, without any kind of coercion, caused the death of Mr Lunczer (58), Ms Goldman (54), Ms Gluck (54), and Mr Gergely (60).[116] They all went down to the courtyard because of Mrs Reményi's threats, even though the Arrow Cross was not keen on taking them.[117] The Court added to this that, in the autumn of 1944, Mrs Reményi refused to distribute the Swedish protective papers that were sent to the building, and tore these documents apart.[118] Her motivation for enrichment was seen as an aggravation, just as was her position.[119] The verdict underpins that Mrs Reményi assisted the Arrow Cross even more than was required, "although exactly because of her position as a building manager—if she had acted in good faith— she could have helped the persecuted inhabitants of the building in their trapped situation."[120] It is important to dwell a little longer on this reasoning. The significance of this last sentence is that it rues the missed chance for helping, but at the same time it also presents a behaviour pattern that could have been expected from everyone employed as a building manager in 1944 Budapest. Thousands of concierges missed the chance of providing essential help, still, they did not let the opportunity of gaining assets go so easily. Thousands of them worked in these years in the Hungarian capital, but only a handful of them appeared at the People's Court, even though, as this verdict suggests, the judges recognized the extent of guilt behind bystanding. Mrs Reményi got the harshest possible punishment, although the appeal court, the National Council of the People's Court (*Népbíróságok Országos Tanácsa*), turned her sentence into life imprisonment.[121] Even though she took an active role in the persecution of some of the tenants, at the same time she was judged as a morally responsible bystander because of her inaction in the ill fate of others.

6   Ordinary People

The reason why Mrs Reményi was not executed is that the judges found her very low level of education to be an extenuating circumstance. They felt that this could be the reason why she was unable to resist the pressure of the Arrow Cross system.[122] During the trial it appeared that the defendant had finished only the first four classes of elementary school.[123] But since the position of *házmester* was not exactly a job for intellectuals, the researcher starts wondering how much this was an excuse instead of a real problem. Out of 27 trials of Budapest building managers at the People's Court, there was only one defendant who had entered a grammar school, which was the first step towards the acculturation to the petty bourgeoisie.[124] Although no legislator ever tried to assess how many years of schooling, if any, were needed to be able to recognize the destructive and immoral nature of Nazism, this dubious concept of some kind of reduced responsibility was widely applied. The People's Court argued with it when it reduced to six months the jail term of Mrs Csibor, the building manager of XIV Nürnberg utca 43, who disclosed the Jewish origin of a tenant to an Arrow Cross functionary living in the same apartment building.[125] This concierge dropped out of school after only three years.[126] On the same basis Mrs Fejes' sentence was shortened to one-and-a-half years, even though she had under her belt the basic six years of schooling.[127] Mrs Fejes found a three-membered Jewish Hungarian family hiding in her building, revealed their hiding spot, and while publicly naming them Jews, handed the three individuals over to a policeman.[128] In another case the National Council of the People's Court in its verdict established that the accused Mrs Kerekes, who did not attend any schooling, had a "primitive soul".[129]

The capacity of thinking independently was an issue addressed also by post-war political leaders, usually if they wanted to pardon ordinary Hungarians. On 18 July 1945, *Szabad Szó*, the daily of the National Peasants Party reports that a thousand so-called *kis-nyilas* or petty members of the Arrow Cross Party were released from internment camps.[130] The journalist noted that interior minister Ferenc Erdei, and his communist state secretary, Mihály Farkas, had decided to pardon these people, because they recognized how these unfortunate members of the workers' class and peasantry were just misled by the Arrow Cross propaganda.[131] The reporter also mentions those masses who the Red Army took with it to work in Siberia and other distant parts of the Soviet Union, claiming that they were taken there in order to learn the lesson that fighting against the Soviets was a mistake.[132] Shortly after the Nazi Germans left Budapest, thousands of civilians fell victim to Russian army men hunting for forced labourers, among others ethnic Germans, but also those believed to be the supporters of the Nazi regime.[133] This was a third pillar of retribution, the least legitimate and, at the same time, the most brutal. The author Sándor Márai knew an ordinary Hungarian in Buda, who was carried by this wave to the distant city of Yekaterinburg. He writes:

> For example, there was a baker in our neighbourhood, at Zerge Stairs and the corner of Attila Street. True to his trade, he baked bread for the military in his ground-floor flat. He wasn't a Nazi, but he feared the Communists, and so when he had to declare his position, he joined some "wondrous stag" group. He knew doing so would subject him to surveillance and get him into trouble when the time of the identity check arrived. Yet, when many left Budapest because the bridges over the Danube were blown up and artillery rumbled in Újpest, this baker did not go anywhere; he stayed in his shop in

Buda. Apprentice bakers had been conscripted, or they had fled. What will a baker do at the end of the Second World War when he realizes that for him the war was lost? He pondered the matter and, like Montaigne, made his decision: he stayed in his shop and continued to ply his trade.

... On the last morning, when the Germans and Hungarians had moved on and given Buda up, the baker took off his white work apron, extinguished the fire in the oven, sat down beside the kneading trough, leaned the long-handled paddle with which he pushed the loaves into the oven against the wall, rolled a cigarette and lighted up. He waited for the Russians thus. They arrived at noon and promptly hailed him away, because a zealot living in the neighbourhood denounced him as a war criminal. This notion was easily extended, and in the early days after the war's end, large numbers of people who survived were called war criminals. The finger-pointing lasted for years; the baker had time in Yekaterinburg, where he was taken from his shop, to reflect on whether he was really guilty or not. It is not easy to determine the truth in the baker's case. Nor in the cases of the writers, kidney surgeons and shoe-top stitchers who survived a lost war. Possibly everyone is guilty, the entire human race. For this reason, it is best to win, because the victor gains a statue. The one who loses is hanged or hauled off to Yekaterinburg.[134]

Just like this baker, thousands of other so-called bystanders were collected by the Red Army and deported to Siberia, including a few Budapest building managers. Stories like the one Márai outlined here pop up in the files of the Justificatory Committee. The female concierge of VI Aradi utca 31, a former Yellow Star house, notes on the last point of the trade union's questionnaire that "my husband is in Russian custody since 25 January, when he was arrested on the street. In spite of the fact that I am not aware of his current location, I demand his justification too."[135] Elsewhere it was only a piece of paper fixed neatly on a file which informs that a *házmester* couple from Návay utca 5 did not show up at the hearing of the Justificatory Committee as "they were taken by the Russians, and replaced by a certain Mr Csernyi."[136] These people faced an undefined term deprived of their freedom, and unlike those whose cases were discussed by the Justificatory Committee and the People's Court, they did not have any chance to turn to an appeal court.

In the outcome of 27 cases where building managers appeared as accused at the People's Court, one can find a significant difference between the verdicts on first and second instances in terms of leniency. In eight out of

27 the first sentences were already acquittals. Add to this those nine trials where neither the concierge nor the public prosecutor challenges the decision of the People's Court. However, out of the remaining ten files we can find only one where the National Council of the People's Court did not change the first verdict in favour of the defendant.[137] Therefore it seems that the further in time from the end of World War II the decision was made, the less harsh are the punishments given to the accused building managers. In addition, in 1946–47 the People's Court also turned around many resolutions of the Justificatory Committee that ordered the dismissal of the building managers. One reason behind this tendency could be Péter György's theory, which is that as the Communist Party gradually took over governing, there was less and less will to call everyday people to account. György comes to the conclusion that the communists decided to play on the despair of the Hungarian middle and lower classes over the crimes committed against the Jewish Hungarians during World War II. The communist leaders did not intend to criminalize the acts of myriads of Hungarians, because they knew that leaving the masses in shame made them accomplices in the sense that they had no moral grounds to demonstrate against the unlawful brutality of the coming left-wing dictatorship.[138] Reading the trial materials, one can add to this that the Jewish Hungarian accusers also had begun to stay away from the People's Court trials, as if they had had enough of these long drawn-out procedures. Some of the acquittals were actually due to the fact that the key witnesses did not show up on the trial day.[139] Seemingly, the whole calling into account became less and less important. As one of the Jewish Hungarian tenants— who suffered deportation because of the concierges informing the Arrow Cross in December 1944—phrased it on 23 October 1946 at the People's Court: "[w]hen the accused caused my detention, I got very angry at her. Even when I was in Germany, I have just been praying all the time to be able to come home and call her to account. When I arrived home, I could not find her in her lodge and this was her luck, because if I had found her, she would not be here today. But in the meantime my anger faded away. I don't want to hurt the accused anymore."[140]

7   AN EPILOGUE OR THE LIMITS OF THE JUSTIFICATORY PROCEDURE

In the thousands of files left behind by the post-war Justificatory Committee, there is only one case in which a tenant appealed against the resolution. Although this is far from being the richest case in terms of research material, I still perceive it as important as it shows the limits of the retribution process. It also clarifies that this was not a forum where Jewish Hungarians could seek rehabilitation and justice for minor atrocities suffered during the Holocaust. Mihály Szita and his wife were the building managers of Zoltán utca 10, a building some two blocks away from the Hungarian Parliament. The accusers of the concierge, a 76-year-old art historian professor called Dr Béla Lázár and his wife, heard the news about the forming of the Justificatory Committee of the Building Managers. They most probably read one of the adverts the Building Managers' Free Trade Union posted in dailies, like the one which was published on 13 April 1945, less than three months after Budapest's liberation in *Népszava*. It says only: "we call all the V district inhabitants to report about the building managers' and assistant building managers' behaviour in the past."[141] This advertisement is vague enough to create the false impression that the officials were interested in all kinds of "past behaviour", potentially from any time in the past. All in all, after going through thousands of retribution files, I can well guess that the trade union leaders expected to hear different complaints than the one filed by Dr Lázár.

My interest in this case was partly due to the inadequate complaints, but also due to Dr Lázár's career. The Hungarian Jewish Lexicon notes that he was born in 1869 in Nagyvárad, today Oradea in Romania. While becoming a fairly famous art historian, he studied at various universities in Pest, Munich, Paris, Berlin and Jena. In the interwar era he was for a decade the director of the Ernst museum in Budapest, a collection specializing in modern art.[142] He published more than 15 books. I have found a couple of them in a second-hand bookshop next to my Budapest home. In one of them he explains how he became a friend of Henrik Ibsen, whose dramas he translated into Hungarian, or how he drank absinthe with Oscar Wilde in Paris in 1900.[143] I know from the file of the Justificatory Committee that Dr Lázár moved to Zoltán utca 10 in August 1942, to the first floor of the building. The placement of his apartment indicates that despite the anti-Jewish regulations, he still had enough money to afford the more expensive rentals. Both on the basis of this, but also on the basis of his social position, he could expect some kind of respect from a lowly ranked building manager. He was particularly annoyed when he did not get anything from this, which becomes clear when one reads the letter that Dr Lázár decided to write to the Justificatory Committee on 22 May 1945. What is stunning is that he did not formulate life-threatening accusations against the concierge. This case is not about participation in murder or even in plunder, much more about class dimension. It was Dr Lázár's human dignity at stake here, and the visions of what a new democratic Hungary should look like, and who deserved the chance to take part in the building of this new state.

Dr Lázár recalled that during the war he wanted to employ a maid, but the concierge always made sure that the candidates were informed about the Lázárs' Jewish origin, and this piece of information resulted in potential employees declining all kinds of job offers.[144] Once, in 1944, for four consecutive days the building manager did not collect their rubbish. Moreover, when finally Dr Lázár called him for his duties Mr Szita replied angrily: "if only Dr Lázár were not an old man he would knock him on the head."[145] Dr Lázár simply could not understand how was it possible that he, who worked for 50 years for Hungarian culture, was the subject of such assaults by a *házmester*. This remark indicates that Dr Lázár suffered the insult as a Hungarian intellectual, even though it might target his imagined Jewish self. As he disappointedly added, the Szitas never said hello to him, only now they did so when their justification was due, and even then did not do it with the proper respect.[146]

In the autumn of 1944, Dr Lázár and his wife left their home at Zoltán utca 10 for a Spanish Protected house. He returned from there in the second half of January 1945, when the Russians had taken control of Pest and fighting was restricted more and more to Buda, on the other side of the Danube. From time to time, the Pest side still received some shrapnel, and when the air-raid alarms started to ring, building manager Szita did not let Dr Lázár and his wife enter the air-raid shelter in Zoltán utca 10, claiming that "there was no place for Jews."[147] While the Lázárs were relocated from their home due to the ghetto order, a non-Jewish Hungarian family requested to be allowed to settle in their apartment. Szita helped the new tenants to move all the belongings of Dr and Mrs Lázár—including a complete library, furniture and paintings—to the tiniest room normally kept for the maid.[148] Dr Lázár and his wife moved into this single dark room in January 1945, as all the other parts of their apartment were taken by the new tenants, with whom they now had to share their bathroom and toilet. And even in this situation, the former museum director turned to the concierge for help in rearranging and cleaning this room to make it liveable, but the building manager refused to help. He even rejected Dr Lázár when he asked permission to use the concierge's kitchen to make tea.[149]

Dr Lázár finished his letter with the conclusion that this sort of fascist, pro-German anti-semite was not fit for the building manager post, especially not in a house "where Jews or people of Jewish origin live, because with them life could turn into hell".[150] Reading Dr Lázár's words it becomes clear that his experience of the Holocaust was completely different than those recollections generally used to describe the Nazi Germans' or Nazi Hungarians' brutality. Nevertheless, this sort of tragedy, a sudden degradation on the social scale, was also part of the events dubbed the Hungarian Holocaust. But there are two more issues in Dr Lázár's letter besides the loss of popular respect. First, the letter reports Mr Szita as someone who simply does not understand the winds of change. In fact, building managers could be confused in the first hours of the post-World War II period. This is why Mr Szita seems stubborn and hard-line in this story, when it came to the question of whether to let Jewish Hungarians into the air-raid shelter just days before the Nazi troops surrendered Budapest. To understand what the new set-up meant regarding the so-called Jews was less obvious then we would think in the twenty-first century. On 18 January 1945, on the day of Pest's liberation, Mrs Kerekes from Dob utca 108, for instance, told the former tenants returning from the main ghetto that she was not letting them in until an official decree ordered her to do this.[151]

Second, there are two expressions used in the last part of Dr Lázár's letter—"I served Hungarian culture for fifty years" and "where Jews or people of Jewish origin live"—which could be understood as hints of Dr Lázár's assimilated status. Most probably this highly cultured man, whose books were frequently published in the interwar era both within and outside the country, was shocked that someone as low ranked as a *házmester*, an ordinary man, could question the success of his integration into the Hungarian people. This shock played a part when Dr Lázár reported the Szitas to the Justificatory Committee, which set a date for the hearing of the art historian.

The minutes of this hearing survived in detailed form, perhaps because the acting president of the no. VI committee was not Oszkár Büchler who regularly led the Justificatory Committee's activities, but a judge, Dr Zoltán Szilágyi. It was on 20 June 1945, in Szent István körút 27, where the committee questioned the professor and his wife as the key witnesses of the case. Here, the Lázárs recalled again the alleged offences. The only case of interest to the Committee was the instance when the building manager denied Dr Lázár use of the air-raid shelter. During the same hearing, Szita explained that he did not reject Dr Lázár because of his Jewish origin, but "because the shelter was full and the professor, being a sick man, wanted to use the sofa."[152] Shortly after this, the president of the Justificatory Committee called Mrs Lázár to leave the room as "the witness was disturbing the hearing."[153] This act of the head of the Justificatory Committee is symbolic: it is a clear message from the representative of the new society about what is interesting and what is not. Although Dr Lázár's letter mentions a series of humiliations, the Justificatory Committee was used to hearing much more severe crimes. When close to 600,000 Jewish Hungarians lost their lives, nobody cared about the hurt feelings of an old man. For the same reason the Committee rejected Dr Lázár's request to hear other witnesses, who lived in front of their home, in Zoltán utca 11. Instead they listened to the testimony of someone brought by the building manager, who declared that in the second half of October 1944, Szita saved her life by registering her under a false name in the registry book of Zoltán utca 10.[154] This statement was more than enough for the Justificatory Committee, which immediately cleared Szita from all charges, and with this he successfully passed the justification.

Surprisingly, Dr Lázár did not give up and appealed against the resolution, which created a unique situation. The Justificatory Committee screened thousands of the Budapest building managers, but never again did it happen that a tenant appealed against its decision. Finally the People's Court had to reject Dr Lázár's appeal, referring to paragraph 9 of the 4080/1945 M.E. decree, according to which only the subject of the justificatory process and the members of the Justificatory Committee had the right to appeal against the Committee's resolution.[155] This legal construction and the rigidly legalistic practice of the People's Court took the necessary tools from Holocaust survivors to effectively fight for their rights, and placed them into a subordinate status within the retribution procedures concerning the Budapest building managers. As a result, most building managers, like Mihály Szita, were cleared of a string of charges, and stayed on in their posts. Nevertheless, the way Dr Lázár fought to reclaim something of his lost social respect reveals how hard it was sometimes for the Jewish Hungarian tenants to move on.

The justification of the Budapest building managers in particular, but broadly speaking the whole denazification of the Hungarian public life in general, is judged as far too lenient. Historian Tibor Zinner concludes that in Budapest, between March and October 1945, justificatory committees working in various professions investigated 41,602 cases, all of which ended with approval except 7,583, a percentage well above 80 percent.[156] As the contemporary journalist István Kemény notes it, "the clean out is a total failure. Almost everybody is here with us about whom we thought they were going to disappear through the trapdoor. The cleaning has failed, as did the entire justificatory procedure."[157] Sixty years later, Éva Standeisky adds to this that a general rejuvenation was not possible because the new rulers could not afford to alienate the masses. The post-war political parties did not even consider campaigning to call each and every beneficiary of the anti-Jewish policies into account, as they would have risked losing numerous potential supporters. Standeisky thinks that almost exclusively the top of the former political elite was severely punished as war criminals in show trials, whereas most everyday Hungarians were regarded as misled by these wartime leaders.[158] Finally, as the influential historian István Deák assesses, the punishment of wrongdoers "gradually lost political and moral significance".[159]

NOTES

1. BFL XVII/1598, Justificatory Committee Files, box no. 8, district V, the case of István Zseni, a resolution dated 21 July 1945.
2. Sándor Márai, *Memoir of Hungary, 1944–1948*, (Budapest: Corvina, 1996), p. 6.
3. The diary of Imre Patai, an entry dated 28 June1942, p. 2, United Sates Holocaust Memorial Museum (USHMM) Archive, ACC. 2000.155, box no. 4.
4. Bibó, *Válogatott tanulmányok*, p. 630.
5. Ibid., p. 631–632.
6. Wolfgang Benz, "Anti-Semitism in Europe. Traditions, Structures, Manifestations." (Uppsala: Uppsala University Press, The Hugo Valentin Lectures III, 2004), pp. 13–36.
7. Ibid., p. 29.
8. Ibid., pp. 24–25.
9. Bibó, *Válogatott tanulmányok*, pp. 632–633.
10. BFL XVII/1598, Justificatory Committee Files, district V, the case of Mrs Sándor Kardos, see a questionnaire dated 16 July 1945.
11. The referred order was the 1942/3530 B.M. decree. BFL XVII/1598, Justificatory Committee Files, district VI, the case of Márton Icskovics.
12. Bibó, *Válogatott tanulmányok*, pp. 626–627.
13. Ibid.
14. Ibid., p. 627.
15. BFL XVII/1598, Justificatory Committee Files, box no. 22, the case of József Kása, VIII Lujza utca 22, see the questionnaire dated 9 July.
16. Ibid., a testimony of Jenő Katz, dated 28 August 1945.

17. Ibid.
18. Ibid., a letter from Henrik Schmergel, dated 8 August 1945.
19. Ibid., Mr Schmergel's letter, p. 1.
20. Ibid.
21. Ibid., Mr Schmergel's letter, p. 2.
22. Ibid., see the declaration of Ms Anna Simon, dated 7 August 1945.
23. BFL XVII/1598, Justificatory Committee Files, box no. 22, district VIII, the case of József Kása, VIII Lujza utca 22, see a document titled *Nyilatkozat* [Declaration] and divided vertically into two equal parts, dated 9 August 1945.
24. Ibid., *Erkölcsi bizonyítvány* [Criminal Record Form], dated 21 August 1945.
25. Ibid., see the letter of Mrs Luszthaus dated 23 August 1945.
26. Ibid., the resolution of the Justificatory Committee dated 27 August 1945.
27. Ibid, the case of Alajos Bankovszky, the letter of Mrs Árpád M., dated 21 June 1945.
28. Ibid, the testimony of György L. at the Justificatory Committee on 26 July 1945.
29. BFL XVII/1598, Justificatory Committee Files, box no. 4, district V, the case of Ferenc Hegedűs, V Alkotmány utca 29, see the hearing of the Justificatory Committee, dated 10 July 1945. Another witness, József K., confirmed this on 14 September.
30. BFL XVII/1598, Justificatory Committee Files, box no. 8, district VI, the case of Ferenc Auguszt, the testimonies of Mihály Sz. and Antal B. on 6 July 1945.
31. BFL XVII/1598, Justificatory Committee Files, box no. 8, district VI, the case of András Váradi, see the letter of six tenants, dated 8 July 1945.
32. Ibid., Mihály Kőszegi's testimony on 20 July 1945.
33. Ibid.
34. Ibid., the testimony of József Árvai at the Justificatory Committee on 30 July 1945.
35. László Karsai "The Hungarian Holocaust as Reflected in the People's Court Trials in Budapest" in *Yad Vashem Studies*, vol. 32, 2004, pp. 59–96.
36. Ibid., p. 79. See on this also Attila Lajos, *Raoul Wallenberg: mítosz és valóság* (Budapest: Minerva, 2007), p. 67.
37. Karsai, "Hungarian Holocaust as Reflected in the People's Court Trials", pp. 79–80.
38. *Házfelügyelő*, vol.1, no. 1, August 1945, p. 1.
39. Nagy, "Lakóközösség kontra háztulajdonos...", p. 164.
40. The *Magyar Nemzeti Függetlenségi Front* [Hungarian National Independence Front] was formed on 2 December 1945 in Szeged, south-

east Hungary. It was founded by the following parties: Független Kisgazdapárt, Magyar Kommunista Párt, Szociáldemokrata Párt, Nemzeti Parasztpárt and Polgári Demokrata Párt.

41. A truce agreement signed in Moscow on 20 January 1945 explicitly ordered the new Hungarian authorities to arrest the war criminals and either imprison them or hand them over to the victorious Allies. See on this Ildikó Barna and Andrea Pető, *Political Justice in Budapest after World War II* (Budapest: Central European University, 2015) p. 14.

42. See this in detail: Zinner, "Háborús bűnösök perei", pp. 118–140.

43. The denazification law was quoted in BFL XVII/1598, Justificatory Committee Files, box no. 8, district VI, the case of István Allmann. See also the decree of the Mayor of Budapest, numbered 143.451/1945-IX, in *Fővárosi Közlöny*, vol. 56, no. 18, 26 May 1945.

44. Ibid.

45. *Házfelügyelő*, vol. 1, no. 2, September 1945, p. 3.

46. Ibid.

47. Nagy, "Lakóközösség kontra háztulajdonos....", p. 164.

48. President Boldis uses the phrase in his article: "our request was heard by Mayor Zoltán Vas, who on 28 April regulated the relations of the building managers in a decree". See this in *Házfelügyelő*, vol. 1, no. 1, August 1945, p. 1.

49. *Házfelügyelő*, vol. 1, no. 1, August 1945, p. 1.

50. *Házfelügyelő*, vol. 1, no. 1, August 1945, p. 2. "Amit jó tudni".

51. BFL XVII/1598, Justificatory Committee Files, box no. 21, district VIII, the case of K. Felföldi, the letter of Edit Z., dated 12 August 1945.

52. Ibid.

53. See the questionnaire in the case of István Bándy, dated 6 August 1945, BFL XVII/1598, box no. 1.

54. See the questionnaire in the case of Ferenc Ackermann, dated 9 August 1945, BFL XVII/1598, box no. 1.

55. The question of this section was simply put: "What else would you like to add?"[Mit kíván még előadni?].

56. See the questionnaire in the case of János Kondorosi, dated 15 July 1945, BFL XVII/1598, box no. 11.

57. See the questionnaire in the case of Ferencz Markovits dated 16 June 1945, BFL XVII/1598, box no. 11. Note that the short-lived Commune existed only in 1871, therefore 1897 could not be the twenty-fifth anniversary.

58. BFL XVII/1598, Justificatory Committee Files, the case of Mr Bicsédy, a letter written by Árpád Benedikt, pp. 2–6.

59. Ibid., pp. 9–11.

60. BFL XXV.1.a - 952/1945. A Budapesti Népbíróság büntetőügyei [Criminal cases of the Budapest People's Court] The case of Mrs Ferenc Róth. See the hearing of Mrs Mohácsi, p. 9.

61. Barna and Pető also are of the opinion that the Jewish Hungarians were disappointed in what the People's Court could offer them. They note that since very high number of cases ended in acquittal (43 percent), these court procedures could not serve as a tool in processing the trauma of Holocaust. However, they see general causes behind this disappointment, such as the anomalies and paradoxes of the political justice system, while I rather argue that the limits of wartime criminal activity introduced by the post-war People's Court did not meet the expectations of the Holocaust survivors. See this: Barna and Pető, *Political Justice in Budapest after World War II*, pp. 104–109.

62. See on this Nagy, "Lakóközösség kontra háztulajdonos...". Nagy in this article explains the post-war conflicts of people living in the apartment buildings. However, she does not address issues related to the Holocaust, but post-war roles of building wardens, landlords, concierges and tenants.

63. See this in an article entitled "Házmesternék civilben" in *Haladás*, vol. 1, no. 1, p. 6.

64. BFL XVII/1598, Justificatory Committee Files, box no. 8, district V, the case of István Zseni, the letter of Mrs Mangold, dated 21 June 1945.

65. BFL XVII/1598, Justificatory Committee Files, district V, the case of István Zseni, a resolution dated 21 July 1945.

66. Ibid. Here the original Hungarian text of the resolution is: "*nem adott módot arra, hogy Gáspár megmeneküljön a deportálás szörnyű szenvedéseitől*".

67. BFL XVII/1598, Justificatory Committee Files, district V, the case of István Zseni, the hearing of the Justificatory Committee on 9 July 1945.

68. See for example: BFL XVII/1598, Justificatory Committee Files, box no. 22, district VIII, the case of Mrs Lackó, the resolution of the Justificatory Committee dated 26 September 1945.

69. Zinner, "Háborús bűnösök perei", pp. 119–120. It was the political police who decided about the proposed internment on the basis of the 138.000/1945 B.M. decree.

70. See this for instance in BFL XXV 1a Budapesti Népbíróság bünetőperes iratok [Files of the Budapest People's Court] the case of Katalin Farkas, case number 678/1945, p. 39 and also on p. 43. [The text in the original Hungarian form is the following: "katonai jellegű alakulat részére személy és egyben vagyontárgy ellen elkövetett erőszakos cselekményben segítséget nyújtott."]

71. 1440/1945 M.E. § 10, point no. 5.

72. See on this decree 1440/1945 M.E. § 10, point no. 5. [The precise Hungarian text of the modification is the following: "népellenes

bűntettben bűnös az is, aki a fasiszta és a demokráciaellenes törekvéseknek vagy a társadalom egyes rétegei üldözésének célját szolgáló hivatalos szerv, párt vagy társadalmi szervezet besúgójaként működött vagy annak számára adatokat szolgáltatott."]

73. BFL XXV.1.a, case number 202/1945. A Budapesti Népbíróság büntetőügyei [Criminal cases of the Budapest People's Court], the case of Dávid Sipos. See the verdict on p. 46. The length of the punishment was relatively short, partly because it appeared that the assistant concierge put Sipos under pressure in order to force him to contact the Arrow Cross.

74. BFL XXV.1.a—case number 202/1945. See the verdict on p. 47.

75. On the historical role of the building under Andrássy út 60, see Krisztián Ungváry and Gábor Tabajdi, *Budapest a diktatúrák árnyékában* [Budapest in the shadow of dictatorships] (Budapest: Jaffa, 2012), pp. 44–45 and 59–61.

76. BFL XXV.1.a, case number 202/1945, p. 5, p. 15, p. 47.

77. Ibid., p. 3.

78. Another case like this was the investigation against Mr and Mrs Grosz (BFL XXV.1.a 86/1945), although here only the female concierge was convicted in the end, while her husband was acquitted of all charges. See the first verdict dated 13 April 1945 (pp. 85–87) and the second one from 23 May 1945 (pp. 88–89).

79. BFL XXV.1.a, case number 234/1945. A Budapesti Népbíróság büntetőügyei [Criminal cases of the Budapest People's Court], the case of Mrs György Koppány, the verdict of the court of first instance, dated 19 June 1945, p. 11.

80. This assembly point in late October 1944 was a sports field in XIV district, the so-called KISOK pitch, with legendarily horrendous sanitary conditions.

81. BFL XXV.1.a, case number 234/1945. A Budapesti Népbíróság büntetőügyei [Criminal cases of the Budapest People's Court], the case of Mrs György Koppány, the verdict of the court of first instance, dated 19 June 1945, pp. 11–14.

82. 81/1945. ME decree, section 13.

83. BFL XXV.1.a - 234/1945. A Budapesti Népbíróság büntetőügyei [Criminal cases of the Budapest People's Court], the case of Mrs György Koppány, the verdict of the court of first instance, dated 19 June 1945, see the acquittal on p. 12.

84. BFL XVII/1598, Justificatory Committee Files, box no. 4, district V, the case of János Dolmányos, the letter of Ms Klára B., dated 19 June 1945.

85. Ibid., the minutes of the Justificatory Committee, dated 24 June 1945, pp. 1–2, see the testimony of Ms Klára B. and Mrs Antal F.
86. Ibid., pp. 2–3, the testimony of József J.
87. Ibid.
88. Ibid., p. 3.
89. Ibid., the resolution of the Justificatory Committee, numbered 375/a.I.B.I.945.
90. See this decree quoted for instance in the case of József Fersli, resolution dated 10 July 1945. BFL XVII/1598, Justificatory Committee Files, VI district, box no. 9.
91. BFL XVII/1598, Justificatory Committee Files, box no. 7, district V, the case of Dezső Tordai, resolution dated 17 June 1945.
92. BFL XVII/1598, Justificatory Committee Files, box no. 9, district VI, the case of István Halay, resolution dated 1 October 1945.
93. BFL XVII/1598, Justificatory Committee Files, box no. 5, district V, the case of László Kovács, Szent István körút 18, see the resolution dated 27 July 1945.
94. Ibid., see the document entitled "Declaration", and dated 12 July 1945.
95. See this in the letter of Mrs Bányai, dated 10 May 1945.
96. Ibid., the hearing of Mrs Freyer at the Justificatory Committee on 20 July 1945.
97. Ibid., the letter of Mrs Bányai, dated 10 May 1945.
98. Ibid., the hearing of Mrs Freyer at the Justificatory Committee on 20 July 1945.
99. Ibid.
100. BFL XVII/1598, Justificatory Committee Files, box no. 5, district V, the case of László Kovács, see the resolution dated 27 July 1945.
101. See the statement of Balázs J., dated 16 June 1945, and his hearing at the Justificatory Committee on 12 July 1945.
102. Ibid.
103. The president of the Justificatory Committee, Oszkár Büchler sent all the documents to the People's Court on 17 August 1945, because the concierge had announced that he intended to appeal.
104. The number of the People's Court document is Nb.Ig. XIV. 260571945-2, and it is dated 9 September 1945.
105. Mr Gy. Freyer's position as a building warden is mentioned during his hearing at the Justificatory Committee on 12 July 1945.
106. BFL XXV.1.a - 1481/1945. A Budapesti Népbíróság büntetőügyei [Criminal cases of the Budapest People's Court], the case of Mrs Gyula Reményi, the verdict of the court of first instance, dated 14 August 1945, p. 1.
107. Ibid., p. 2.
108. Ibid., p. 2.

109. Ibid., p. 1 and p. 5.
110. Ibid. p. 2.
111. Ibid., p. 2–3.
112. Ibid., pp. 3–4.
113. Ibid., p. 4.
114. Ibid., p. 1.
115. Ibid., p. 5.
116. Ibid., p. 5.
117. Ibid., p. 6.
118. Ibid., p. 8.
119. Ibid.
120. Ibid.
121. Ibid., p. 11, the date of this second instance verdict is 15 April 1946.
122. The case of Mrs Gyula Reményi, the minutes of the People's Court's closed meeting on the request for mercy, p. 46.
123. The case of Mrs Gyula Reményi, p. 46.
124. BFL XXV.1.a, case number 2779/1945. A Budapesti Népbíróság büntetőügyei [Criminal cases of the Budapest People's Court], the case of Mr Sándor Erdélyi, VIII, Rákóczi út 51.
125. BFL XXV.1.a, case number 947/1945. A Budapesti Népbíróság büntetőügyei [Criminal cases of the Budapest People's Court], the case of Mrs János Csibor, the verdict of the court of first instance, dated 20 July 1945, p. 7.
126. Ibid., p. 7.
127. BFL XXV.1.a, case number 1285/1945. A Budapesti Népbíróság büntetőügyei [Criminal cases of the Budapest People's Court], the case of Mrs Imre Fejes, the verdict of the court of first instance, dated 20 July 1945, p. 3.
128. Ibid., p. 1.
129. BFL XXV.1.a, case number 2724/1945. A Budapesti Népbíróság büntetőügyei [Criminal cases of the Budapest People's Court], the case of Mrs János Kerekes, p. 114.
130. József Horváth, "Ezer kis-nyilas", *Szabad Szó*, 18 July 1945.
131. Ibid.
132. Ibid.
133. Tamás Stark, "Málenkij Robot: Hungarian Forced Labourers in the Soviet Union (1944–1955)", in Győző Cholnoky (ed.), *Minorities Research: a collection of studies by Hungarian authors* (Budapest: Lucidus, 1999), pp. 155–167.
134. Márai, *Memoir of Hungary*, pp. 156–158.
135. BFL XVII/1598, Justificatory Committee Files, district VI, the case of Mrs Károly Rippner (Aradi utca 31), a questionnaire dated 16 June 1945.

136. BFL XVII/1598, Justificatory Committee Files, district V, the case of Mr Péter Bagi and Mrs Mária Bagi.

137. BFL XXV.1.a - 86/1945. A Budapesti Népbíróság büntetőügyei [Criminal cases of the Budapest People`s Court], the case of Mrs János Grosz. Strangely enough, here the verdict of the court of first instance was acquittal, but the appeal court sentenced the defendant to six months in jail. Contrary to this, Katalin Farkas first got six years, whereas the appeal court acquitted her (BFL XXV.1.a - 678/1945); Dávid Marosi's 12-year penalty was reduced to six years after his appeal (BFL XXV.1.a - 550/1945); Sándor Erdélyi got only a year in prison instead of the original ten-year punishment (BFL XXV.1.a - 2779/1945); the same happened in the case of Mrs János Kerekes, the first verdict ordered ten years in prison, while the second instance reduced this to a single year (BFL XXV.1.a - 2724/1945), and so on.

138. Péter György, Apám helyett [Instead of my Father] (Budapest: Magvető, 2011), pp 30–31, pp. 23–24.

139. See this for example in the case of Péter Deli (BFL XXV.1.a - 748/1945), p. 37, or in the case of Mrs Ferenc Róth (BFL XXV.1.a - 952/1945), p. 26, see the verdict on pp. 136–138.

140. BFL XXV.1.a - 2724/1945. A Budapesti Népbíróság büntetőügyei [Criminal cases of the Budapest People's Court], the case of Mrs János Kerekes, the hearing of Ms Aranka K., p. 75.

141. Népszava, 13 April 1945, vol. 73, no. 46, p. 6. The original Hungarian text included also the address, where the written reports were expected: "Felhívjuk az V. kerületi lakosokat, hogy a házfelügyelők és segédházfelügyelők múltban tanúsított magatartásáról írásbeli jelentést tegyenek, V. Szent István körút 27. I. 2. szám alatt a Házfelügyelők Orsz. Szabad Szakszervezetének V. kerületi helyi csoportjánál."

142. Péter Újvári (ed.), Magyar Zsidó Lexikon (Budapest, 1929), p. 524.

143. Béla Lázár, Írók és művészek között [Among writers and artists] (Budapest: Pallas, 1918).

144. BFL XVII/1598, Justificatory Committee Files, box no. 7, district V, the case of Mihály Szita: a letter to the Justificatory Committee from Dr Béla Lázár, written on 22 May 1945, p. 4.

145. Ibid., p. 4.

146. Ibid., p. 5.

147. Ibid., p. 2.

148. Ibid., p. 3.

149. Ibid., p. 3.

150. Ibid., p. 5.

151. BFL XXV.1.a, case number 2724/1945. A Budapesti Népbíróság büntetőügyei [Criminal cases of the Budapest People's Court], the case

of Mrs János Kerekes, police hearing of Mrs Mária K., dated 12 July 1945, p. 42.

152. Ibid, the case of Mr Mihály Szita: the minutes of the Justificatory Committee's hearing on 20 June 1945.

153. Ibid.

154. Ibid.

155. BFL XVII/1598, Justificatory Committee Files, box no. 7, district V, the case of Mihály Szita, a resolution numbered Nb. Ig. XIV. 3511/1945-5.

156. Zinner, `Háborús bűnösök perei`, pp. 118–140.

157. István Kemény, *Világ*, 8 June 1945, pp. 1–2.

158. See more on this: Éva Standeisky, "Erkölcsök 1945-ben" [Morals in 1945] *Mozgó Világ*, vol. 31, no. 2, 2006.

159. István Deák, "Political Justice in Austria and Hungary after World War II" in Jon Elster (ed.) *Retribution and Reparation in the Transition to Democracy* (Cambridge: Cambridge University Press, 2006), p. 125.

Conclusion

To sum up, being a building manager in Budapest was a minor role until the early interwar years, when the social and technical developments accumulated more and more tasks for a concierge. These assignments required the constant presence of a full-time employed *házmester*. Moreover, in bigger apartment buildings the well-coordinated work plan of an entire family was needed to fulfil all the jobs required. It seems that the vast majority of the Budapest building managers were not born in Budapest, rather they picked this position as a beginning of their urban city life, taking advantage of the free lodging which by law had to be provided by the landlord. This was more than crucial in a newly built metropolis like Budapest, where rental prices were rising sharply. This gives the concierge's position a transitional character. Nevertheless, the free accommodation was compensated by a lower-than-average basic salary. The low fixed income was a prevailing problem for the building managers throughout the entire first half of the twentieth century. This problem was all the more frustrating as the concierges' importance grew sharply, thanks to the technical and urban developments, but also because of the special circumstances of the war. In addition, they were not given the necessary authority by which they could have done a good job. It was precisely these tensions that made the building managers aspire to authority, but also because of this many concierges started to support such radical movements that targeted the redistribution of "Jewish wealth", above all the Arrow Cross movement.

© The Author(s) 2016   187
I.P. Adam, *Budapest Building Managers and the Holocaust in Hungary*,
The Holocaust and its Contexts, DOI 10.1007/978-3-319-33831-6

During World War II, building managers took part in the intensified surveillance. Furthermore, the Ministry of Defence assigned both the maintenance of the air-raid shelters and the check of the lights-out regulations to the Budapest concierges. They were picked for these roles only because of their social position—the same way as they were later named as the guards of the ghetto houses—and it is surprising to see how unconditionally the state officials trusted them, without checking their ability and reliability in-depth. The only condition the Hungarian government made was laid down in the 3.530/1942 B.M. decree, which from the middle of 1942 declared illegal the employment of Jewish Hungarians as a *házmester*. Two years later, the Budapest building managers played a prominent part in setting up individual ghetto buildings, the so-called Yellow Star houses. From this moment they could directly influence the survival chances of the Jewish Hungarians. At the same time, they could financially benefit from the precarious situation, where, although they did not officially belong to any authority, nevertheless, on a daily basis they were responsible for enforcing discriminative regulations. They acted as intermediaries between the authorities and the Jewish Hungarian residents, which gave them much wider latitude than other bystanders.

In my book I argue that the empowerment of the building managers happened as a side-effect of the anti-Jewish legislation. They had held a rather lower rank in the apartment buildings' pre-war social stratification, but due to the wartime issues and especially because of the choice of a dispersed ghetto setting—where the basic ghetto unit became the apartment building—they were handed an unprecedented power. The Nazi authorities could make good use of these people because they were a perfect fit for a watchdog in a ghetto building: they had extensive practice in territorial control and they knew everything about both the building itself and its inhabitants. Nevertheless, their already existing social network combined with their new social position made them critically important also in the Jewish Hungarian tenants' fight for survival. Here it is necessary to point to the interwar tradition of tipping the building managers. In the 1920s and 1930s this was essential, because the basic salary of the concierges was set very low, and only a complicated system of supplementary payments made it possible for them to make ends meet at all. For instance, for decades they were rewarded for opening the gate of an apartment building between 10 p.m. and 6 a.m. by at least a set minimum per occasion, and by law they had to be paid for providing the elevator on demand. But the tradition was to pay a better tip for the polite and well-serving concierge. It was natural, therefore, that they were paid for their rescue and other helping activities too during 1944. This seems logical, as the sources make it clear that paying for saving lives was morally acceptable in wartime Hungary, and in general, there was a high level of tolerance towards bribery around this time in society. When asking questions about responsibility for the improper behaviour of everyday Hungarians such as the concierges during the Holocaust, one has to point also to the upper classes, who for decades did not pay a proper salary to the building managers, and who also blocked most channels of individual advancement in the hierarchical structure of society. Therefore, turning to the final chapter of World War II, the Budapest concierges lacked money; however, they were rich in social connections, and they were experienced in dealing with all kinds of authorities. By using their connections and experiences they were now able to help the survival of thousands of Jewish Hungarians, who honoured their services with tips and bribes. Thus, by helping the upper-class Jewish Hungarians, the building managers also improved their own financial situations, which perhaps should have been improved much earlier with fairer salaries and employment rules.

I had difficulties in deciding whether in 1944 these supplementary payments worked in fact as tips or as bribes; however, the temporal focus could be decisive in these cases. It is likely that one can talk about tips where there was a clear sign that the donor wanted to appreciate a service retrospectively, while giving supplementary payment with a prospective orientation could hint the intention of buying assistance in the fight for survival. In any case, the anti-Jewish regulations paved the way for the enrichment of the building managers, which I explained through the case of the radios: once the surrender of the Jewish-owned radios was ordered, dozens of these machines were donated to the Budapest building managers. It happened simply because it made much more sense to give the radio to the *házmester* than to hand it in to the authorities. In return the building managers not only allowed the Jewish Hungarian tenants to illegally listen to the radio from time to time, getting first-hand information about the progress of the Allies, but they also provided preferential treatment to the radio donors. Although the radio is only one example, nevertheless it represents a broader phenomenon of 1944 Budapest, where the combination of the anti-Jewish regulations and the tradition of peacetime tipping could turn into the wartime bribing of the building managers. Tips, radios, valuable jewellery and other makeweights were given to the Budapest building managers by the Jewish Hungarian tenants for various types of services, and the nature of most of this assistance was that by acting the building managers bridged a structural hole in a social network. This was a common feature that occurred in almost all Budapest apartment buildings, but the most plausible examples we saw from Barko building manager in Chapter 5 at Visegrádi utca 60.[1] In general, concierges preferred to save longer residing tenants and not the newly relocated ones, because the pre-1944 contacts often resulted in a higher level of trust. In addition to this, the building managers knew the background of the older residing tenants much better, and consequently they could easily pick a richer one from whom a higher gratuity could be expected. These people proved to be valuable in the social networks too, so the building managers were more interested in their survival. As a result, class status mattered and the richer Jewish Hungarians had better survival chances in most Budapest apartment buildings.

The sources prove that most *házmester* took part actively in enforcing the anti-Jewish regulations, and often tried to benefit from these rules. This was the case even with those concierges who otherwise saved Jewish Hungarians' lives, as was shown in the case of Mrs Rozália Korecz. In her apartment building in Kádár utca we were faced with two conflicting stories: one which was told to the Justificatory Committee by a former tenant, and another one published in *The Encyclopedia of the Righteous Among the Nations*.[2] The latter version does not tell of those not assisted by the concierge, which is why I dubbed the stories of Yad Vashem incomplete. In ghetto buildings turned into "Protected houses" of neutral embassies there is a sign of even greater activity of concierges. Here, in the late autumn of 1944, some of them autonomously set new rules for the micro-community, including exploiting the Jewish Hungarians' pitiful situation through an internal tax. A great number of building managers developed a strict control system over the access to food, because having the monopoly to provide food not only meant extraordinary income, but it gave also more power over the ghettoized people.

Finally the Red Army brought liberation for the Jewish Hungarians, and in the early post-war months the former ghetto buildings' inhabitants stepped up to call the building managers to account. Nevertheless, there was a competing agency of the concierges, which tried to downplay the accusations, whilst at the same time building close ties with the now-governing political left. Their collective efforts were particularly successful in this matter, and they only needed to sacrifice those colleagues who were not willing to change their right-wing, anti-communist or antisemite mindset. Their official denazifying organ, the Justificatory Committee, referred to them as reactionary thinkers, and this reference appeared so often in their resolutions and propaganda, that the tenants picked up on this. Consequently, affiliation to the right-wing *Nyilas* movement became an accusation that was more emphasized in the denunciations than other, potentially graver, acts of the Budapest *házmester*. The People's Court followed a rather legalistic approach in its proceedings, and was only ready to condemn the concierges if they actively took part in causing the arrest, deportation or physical abuse of the Jewish Hungarians. In a nutshell, the post-war investigations proved that Budapest building managers were active agents and not passive bystanders. If there was one aspect of on-looking related to them, it was ruing the missed opportunities: they failed to help in many situations where they potentially could have assisted the Jewish Hungarians in need. This sort of bystanding was exceptionally discussed by the post-war retribution authorities, partly as an aggravating circumstance in the most serious cases of war criminals, but also sometimes if the wives or children of building managers committed crimes. In the latter cases the male *házmester*, as the head of the family was condemned by the Justificatory Committee, for allowing these wrongdoings. This was a rare recognition of guilty inaction, but it was not at all applied for the masses of building managers, and other ordinary Hungarians, who witnessed the persecution of the Budapest Jewry.

The importance of this study is that it contextualizes the events of 1944 much more broadly than is usually done by Holocaust scholars. I explained the wartime agency of the building managers partly by their decades-long struggle for a higher salary, social appreciation and their aspiration to authority. Another factor that one has to bear in mind when trying to understand the concierges' 1944 behaviour is the tradition of tipping. A good example of ignoring these pre-war circumstances is the definition of *Righteous Among the Nations* set by Yad Vashem. One of its main criteria excluded everyone whose intention was to help persecuted Jews for payment or any other reward. The requirement of an absolute altruistic mindset seems impossible to reconcile with the supplementary payments, even though these tips were usually given already in peacetime conditions to the *házmester* of Budapest. In a similar vein, future research should investigate other long-standing issues that are less obvious explanations of the events of the Holocaust than for instance interwar anti-Jewish movements. For example, it would be worth examining the longer history of other groups of ordinary individuals, who showed greater involvement in the Holocaust, such as the employees of transport companies. More generally, my work shows the value of situating the tragic events of 1944 within a longer timeframe. As I explain, it is vital to position the role of concierges vis-à-vis the Jewish Hungarians within a broader context that includes both the pre-war and the early post-war years.

Certainly, bystanders are the least studied group within Holocaust studies. The present book has sought to explore some of the complexities of this research by following the history of the Budapest building managers. Their agency happened to influence the fate of Jewish Hungarians in various ways: they could and did treat certain Jewish Hungarian neighbours one way, and other Jewish Hungarian neighbours within the same building another way. This study hopes to serve as an explanation of their decisions, while it also brings to the fore the feelings of those Jewish Hungarians who were not helped by the *házmester*.

NOTES

1. BFL XVII/1598, Justificatory Committee Files, district V, the case of István Barko. See for example Mr György G's letter, written on 23 June 1945, or Mr Róbert S.'s letter, written on 24 July 1945.
2. Sara Bender and Pearl Weiss (eds.) *The Encyclopedia of the Righteous Among the Nations: Rescuers of Jews during the Holocaust, Europe (Part I) and other countries* (Jerusalem: Yad Vashem, 2007), p. 261.

BIBLIOGRAPHY

PRIMARY SOURCES

Budapest City Archives (hereafter: BFL) IV. 1409/c. Documents of the Mayor's Office.

BFL IV/1419/J. Census data from the 359/b counting unit.

BFL IV/1419/N. Census data from the 356/a counting unit.

BFL IV/1420R. Data surveys for the 1610/1944 M.E. decree.

BFL VII.5.c. Criminal cases of the Royal Budapest Court.

BFL IX/3354/1944. Petitions submitted to the Mayor of Budapest.

BFL XVII/1512. Municipal justificatory files: the documents of Justificatory Committee no. 271/a, building managers and assistant Building managers.

BFL XVII/1598. The files of Justificatory Committee no. 291/a of the Hungarian Building Managers and Assistant Building Managers, District I–XIV, box no. 1–31.

BFL IX/143.451/1945. Mayoral decree on the regulation of certain questions related to the service and justificatory process of the building managers.

BFL XXV.1.a. Files of the Budapest People's Court.

BFL XXV.2b-1945-9344. Criminal Files of the People's Prosecutor Office.

United Sates Holocaust Memorial Museum (hereafter: USHMM) Archive, Acc. 2000.155.

USHMM Archives, RG-39.016M, Acc. 2008.70. Documents of the Budapest Mayor's Office.

USHMM Archives, ACC. 2000.155, The dairy of Imre Patai, boxes 1–5.

Yad Vashem Archives, Collection O.3, File number 12504.

Documents from the private collections of Erzsébet Róna, Budapest, XIII.

© The Author(s) 2016   193
I.P. Adam, *Budapest Building Managers and the Holocaust in Hungary*,
The Holocaust and its Contexts, DOI 10.1007/978-3-319-33831-6

NEWSPAPERS, PERIODICALS

Belügyi Közlöny, XLVII.
Fővárosi Közlöny, vol. LVI.
Haladás, vol. 1.
Házfelügyelők Közlönye, II-XI.
Házfelügyelők Lapja, I-XXI.
Házfelügyelő, I.
Magyarország, LI.
Magyar Szó, III.
Nemzeti Házfelügyelő, I-XIII.
Népszava, LXXIII.
Pesti Hírlap, LV.
Szombat, XXIII.
Világ, I.
Virradat, IX

ORAL HISTORIES

Oral history interview with Nissan Hirschman, conducted by the author on 1 November 2010, in Budapest.

Oral history interview with László Pusztai, conducted by the author, on 19 September 2012, in Budapest.

Oral History interview with Klári Füredi, conducted by the author, on 28 October, 2012, in Haifa.

Oral history interview with Gábor Kálmán, conducted by the author, on 21 December 2012, Washington DC.

Oral history interview with Iván D., conducted by the author, on 30 April 2013, in Washington DC.

Oral history interview with Ágota Sebő, conducted by the author on 4 February 2014, in Budapest.

SECONDARY WORKS

Frank Bajohr, *Aryanization in Hamburg: The Economic Exclusion of Jews and the Confiscation of their Property in Nazi Germany* (Oxford: Berghahn Books, 2002).

Ildikó Barna and Andrea Pető, *Political Justice in Budapest after World War II* (Budapest: Central University Press, 2015).

Victoria J. Barnett, *Bystanders: Conscience and Complicity during the Holocaust* (Westport: Greenwood, 1999).

Omer Bartov, "Wartime lies and other testimonies: Jewish-Christian relations in Buczacz, 1939-1944", *East European Politics and Societies*, 25, 2011.

Zygmunt Bauman, *Modernity and the Holocaust* (Ithaca: Cornell University Press, 1989).

Sara Bender and Pearl Weiss (eds.), *The Encyclopedia of the Righteous Among the Nations: Rescuers of Jews during the Holocaust, Europe (Part I) and other countries* (Jerusalem: Yad Vashem, 2007).

Lars G. Berg, *The Book that Disappeared: What happened in Budapest* (New York: Vantage, 1990).

Wolfgang Benz, "Anti-Semitism in Europe. Traditions, Structures, Manifestations." (Uppsala: Uppsala University Press, The Hugo Valentin Lectures III, 2004).

István Bibó, *Válogatott tanulmányok* (Budapest: Magvető, 1986–1990).

Cristina Bicchieri, *The Grammar of Society: The Nature and Dynamics of Social Norms* (New York: Cambridge University Press, 2006).

Péter Bihari, *Lövészárkok a hátországban* (Budapest: Napvilág, 2008).

Jeffrey Blutinger, "An Inconvenient Past: Post-Communist Holocaust Memorialization", *Shofar*, Vol. 29, No. 1, 2010.

Randolph L. Braham, *A Magyar Holocaust* (Budapest: Gondolat, 1988).

Randolph L. Braham, *The Politics of Genocide, The Holocaust in Hungary* (New York: Columbia University Press, 1994).

Randolph L. Braham, "The Holocaust in Hungary: A Retrospective Analysis" in David Cesarani (ed.) *Genocide and Rescue: The Holocaust in Hungary 1944* (Oxford: Berg, 1997).

Randolph L. Braham, "Rescue Operation in Hungary: Myths and Realities", *Yad Vashem Studies*, Vol. 32, 2004.

Christopher R. Browning, *The Path to Genocide* (Cambridge University Press, 1992).

Christopher R. Browning, *Ordinary Men, Reserve Police Battalion 101 and the Final Solution in Poland* (New York: HarperCollins, 1998).

Christopher R. Browning, *Collected Memories. Holocaust History and Postwar Testimony* (Madison: The University of Wisconsin Press, 2003).

Ronald S. Burt, "The Social Capital of Structural Holes" in Mauro F. Guillén, Randall Collins, Paula England and Marshall Meyer (eds.) *The New Economic Sociology* (New York: Russell Sage Foundation, 2005).

Ronald S. Burt, *Brokerage and Closure: An Introduction to Social Capital* (Oxford University Press, 2013).

David Cesarani, *Eichmann élete és bűnei* (Budapest: Gold Book, 2004).

David Cesarani (ed.) *Genocide and Rescue: The Holocaust in Hungary 1944* (Oxford: Berg, 1997).

Tim Cole, "Constructing the 'Jew', Writing the Holocaust: Hungary 1920–1945", in *Patterns of Prejudice*, vol. 33, no. 3, 1999.

Tim Cole, *Selling the Holocaust* (New York: Routledge, 2000).

Tim Cole, *Holocaust City: The Making of a Jewish Ghetto* (New York: Routledge. 2003).

Tim Cole, "Writing 'Bystanders' into Holocaust History in More Active Ways: 'Non-Jewish' Engagement with Ghettoization, Hungary 1944", *Holocaust Studies*, 2, no. 1, 2005.

Tim Cole "The Return of György András M.: Writing Exceptional Stories of the Holocaust", *Journal of Jewish Identities*, 1, no. 2, 2008.

Tim Cole, *Traces of the Holocaust: Journeying in and out of the Ghettoes* (New York: Continuum, 2011).

Tim Cole and Alberto Giordano, "On Place and Space: Calculating Social and Spatial Networks in the Budapest Ghetto", *Transactions in GIS*, 15, no. 1, July 2011, pp. 143–170.

Gustavo Corni, *Hitler's Ghettos. Voices from a Beleaguered Society 1939–1944* (London: Bloomsbury, 2003).

László Csősz, *Tettesek, Szemtanúk, Áldozatok. A Vészkorszak Jász-Nagykun-Szolnok megyében* (Szeged: PhD Thesis, University of Szeged, 2010).

Szilvia Czingel, *Szakácskönyv a túlélésért* (Budapest: Corvina, 2013).

Tivadar Dános, *Háztulajdonos, Lakó, Házfelügyelő* (Budapest: Egyetemi Nyomda, 1936).

István Deák, "A Fatal Compromise? The Debate over Collaboration and Resistance in Hungary", in István Deák, Jan T. Gross and Tony Judt (eds.) *The Politics of Retribution in Europe* (Princeton University Press, 2000).

István Deák, "Political Justice in Austria and Hungary after World War II", in Jon Elster (ed.) *Retribution and Reparation in the Transition to Democracy* (Cambridge University Press, 2006).

István Deák, "The Peculiarities of Hungarian Fascism" in Randolph L. Braham and Raphael Vago (eds.), *The Holocaust in Hungary – Forty Years Later* (New York: Columbia University Press 1985).

Bület Diken and Carsten Bagge Laustsen, *The Culture of Exception: Sociology Facing the Camp* (New York: Routledge, 2005).

Charles Fenyvesi, *When the Angels Fooled the World: Rescuers of Jews in Wartime Hungary* (Madison: University of Wisconsin Press, 2003).

Zsófia Frazon and Zsolt K. Horváth, "A megsértett Magyarország: A Terror Háza mint tárgybemutatás, emlékmű és politikai rítus", *Régio. Kisebbség, Politika, Társadalom*, 2002/4.

Kinga Frojimovics and Judit Molnár, *A Világ Igazai Magyarországon a második világháború alatt* (Budapest: Balassi, 2009).

Andor Gábor, *Pesti sirámok* (Budapest: Szépirodalmi, 1958).

Ágnes Gergely, *Két szimpla a Kedvesben: Memoár* (Budapest: Európa, 2013).

Christian Gerlach and Götz Aly, *Az utolsó fejezet: A Magyar zsidók legyilkolása* (Budapest: Noran, 2005).

Jan T. Gross, *Neighbors: The Destruction of the Jewish Community in Jedwabne* (London: Arrow Books, 2003).

Gábor Gyáni, *Identity and the Urban Experience: Fin-de-Siécle Budapest* (New York: Columbia University Press, 2004).

Gábor Gyáni, "Emlékezés és felejtés", *Kritika*, September 2006.

Péter György, *Apám helyett* (Budapest: Magvető, 2011).

Jürgen Habermas, *A posztnemzeti állapot. Politikai esszék* (Budapest: L`Harmattan, 2006).

Péter Hanák, *The Garden and the Workshop* (Princeton University Press, 1998).

Péter Handi, "A ház rétegei", *Remény*, vol. 13, no. 1, 2010.

Raul Hilberg, *The Destruction of the European Jews* (Chicago: Quadrangle Books, 1961).

Raul Hilberg, "Two Thousand Years of Jewish Appeasement" in Donald L. Niewyk (ed.), *The Holocaust: Problems and Perspectives of Interpretations* (Boston: Wadsworth Cengage Learning, 2011).

Thomas E. Hill Jr., "Moral Responsibilities of Bystanders", *Journal of Social Philosophy*, vol. 41, no. 1, 2010.

Gordon J. Horwitz, *In the Shadow of the Death: Living Outside the Gates of Mauthausen* (New York: Maxwell Macmillan International, 1990).

Heléna Huhák, András Szécsényi, Erika Szívós (eds.), *Kismama sárga csillaggal* (Budapest: Jaffa, 2015).

W.A. Douglas Jackson, *The Shaping of our World: A Human and Cultural Geography* (New York: John Wiley, 1985).

Gábor Kádár and Zoltán Vági, *Aranyvonat* (Budapest: Osiris, 2001).

Gábor Kádár and Zoltán Vági, *Self-Financing Genocide: The Gold Train, the Becher Case and the Wealth of Hungarian Jews* (Budapest: Central European University Press, 2004).

László Karsai, *Vádirat a nácizmus ellen, vol. 4* (Budapest: Balassi, 2014).

László Karsai, "The People's Courts and Revolutionary Justice in Hungary, 1945-46" in István Deák, Jan T. Gross and Tony Judt (eds.) *The Politics of Retribution in Europe* (Princeton University Press, 2000).

László Karsai, "The Hungarian Holocaust as Reflected in the People's Court Trials in Budapest", *Yad Vashem Studies*, vol. 32, 2004.

László Karsai "A holokauszt utolsó fejezete", *Beszélő* vol. 10, 2005/10.

László Karsai, "The Last Chapter of the Holocaust", *Yad Vashem Studies* vol. 34, 2006.

László Karsai, "Miklós Horthy, 1868–1957, legends, myths and the reality", *Beszélő*, vol. 12, no. 3, 12 March 2007.

Jacob Katz, *From Prejudice to Destruction* (Cambridge: Harvard University Press, 1980).

Nathaniel Katzburg, *Hungary and the Jews: Policy and Legislation 1920–1943* (Jerusalem: Bar-Ilan University Press, 1981).

Dezső Kosztolányi, *Édes Anna* (Budapest: Szépirodalmi Kiadó, 1988).

Alajos Kovács, *Magyarország népe és népesedésének kérdése* (Budapest: Magyar Statisztikai Társaság, 1941).

Mária M. Kovács, "The problem of Continuity between the 1920 *Numerus Clausus* and Post-1938 Anti-Jewish Legislation in Hungary", *East European Jewish Affairs*, vol. 35, 2005/1.

Mária M. Kovács and Viktor Karády (eds.) *The Hungarian numerus clausus law and academic anti-Semitism in interwar Central Europe* (Budapest: Pasts Inc., CEU, 2011).

Hanna Krall, *The subtenant, To Outwit God* (Evanston, Ill.: Northwestern University Press, 1992).

Ferenc Laczó, "Between History, Politics and Historical Responsibility. The Legacy of the Hungarian Holocaust in Contexts", *OSTEUROPA*, 12/2011.

Ferenc Laczó, "Caught Between Historical Responsibility and the New Politics of History: on Patterns of Hungarian Holocaust Remembrance", in Simona Mitroiu (ed.) *Life Writing and Politics of Memory in Eastern Europe* (London: Palgrave, 2015).

Attila Lajos, *Raoul Wallenberg: mítosz és valóság* (Budapest: Minerva, 2007).

Béla Lázár, *Írók és művészek között* (Budapest: Pallas, 1918).

Jenő Lévai, *Fekete könyv a magyar zsidóság szenvedéseiről* (Budapest: Officina, 1946).

Jenő Lévai, *A Pesti gettó története* (Budapest: Officina, 1946).

Jenő Lévai, *Zsidósors* (Budapest: Magyar Téka, 1948).

Jenő Lévai, *Eichmann in Hungary: Documents* (Budapest: Pannonia Press, 1961).

Paul A. Levine, *Raoul Wallenberg in Budapest: myth, history and Holocaust* (London: Vallentine Mitchell, 2010).

András Lugosi, "Sztalin Főhercege Kohn báró vacsorái a Falk Miksa utcában a fajgyalázási törvény idején", *FONS*, vol. 17, no. 4, 2010.

John Lukacs, *Budapest, 1900: A város és kultúrája* (Budapest: Európa, 1991).

John Lukacs, *1945: a nulla év* (Budapest: Európa Kiadó, 1996).

Sándor Márai, *Memoir of Hungary, 1944–1948* (Budapest: Corvina, 1996).

Géza Markó, *"Marok" kereskedők és iparosok szaknévsora* (Budapest: Held, 1941).

Michael L. Marrus, *The Holocaust in History* (London: University Press of New England, 1987).

Mátyás Matolcsy, *A zsidók házvagyona Budapesten és a vidéki városokban* (Budapest: A Nyilaskeresztes part kiadványa, 1941).

Dan Michman, *The Emergence of the Jewish Ghettos during the Holocaust* (Cambridge: Cambridge University Press, 2011).

Paul Morrow, "Mass Atrocity and Manipulation of Social Norms", *Social Theory and Practice*, vol. 40, no. 2.

Éva Nádor (ed.), *Csillagos házak: Emberek, házak, sorsok* (Budapest: Nádor, 2015).

Ágnes Nagy, "Lakóközösség kontra háztulajdonos, házmegbízott kontra házfelügyelő: osztályharc a bérházban: a budapesti házfelügyelők igazolása 1945-ben", *Budapesti Negyed*, vol. 17, spring 2009.

László Németh, *A medve utcai polgári* (Budapest: Pannónia, 1988).

Donald L. Niewyk (ed.), *The Holocaust* (Boston: Wadsworth Cengage Learning, 2011).

Zsuzsanna Ozsváth, *When the Danube Ran Red* (New York: Syracuse University Press, 2010).

Laura Palosuo, *Yellow Stars and Trouser Inspections: Jewish Testimonies from Hungary, 1920–1945* (Uppsala: Uppsala Universitet, 2008).

Gunnar S. Paulsson, *Secret City: The Hidden Jews of Warsaw 1940–1945* (New Haven: Yale University Press, 2002).

Katalin Pécsi, *Salty Coffee: Untold Stories by Jewish Women* (Budapest: Novella Kiadó, 2007).

Attila Pók, "Germans, Hungarians and the Destruction of Hungarian Jewry" in David Cesarani (ed.) *Genocide and Rescue: The Holocaust in Hungary 1944* (Oxford: Berg, 1997).

Vera Ranki, *The Politics of Inclusion and Exclusion: Jews and Nationalism in Hungary* (New York: Holmes and Meier, 1999).

Sári Reuveni, "Magyar fák az Igaz Emberek erdejében", in László Karsai (ed.), *Küzdelem az igazságért: Tanulmányok Randolph Braham 80. Születésnapjára* (Budapest: Mazsihisz, 2002).

Máté Rigó, "Ordinary Women and Men: Superintendents and Jews in the Budapest Yellow-star Houses in 1944-45", *Urban History*, vol. 40, no. 1, 2013.

Robert Rozett, *Conscripted Slaves: Hungarian Jewish Forced Laborers on the Eastern Front during the Second World War* (Jerusalem: Yad Vashem, 2014).

Ágnes Ságvári, "Did They Do it on Order?" in Randolph L. Braham, Attila Pók (eds.) *The Holocaust in Hungary Fifty Years Later* (New York: Columbia University Press, 1997).

Ágnes Ságvári, *Studies on the History of Hungarian Holocaust* (Budapest: Napvilág Kiadó, 2002).

David Sibley, *Geographies of Exclusion* (New York: Routledge, 1995).

Georg Simmel, "The Bridge and the Door", *Theory, Culture and Society*, February 1994.

Bonnie G. Smith, *Confessions of a Concierge: Madame Lucie's History of Twentieth-Century France* (New Haven: Yale, 1985).

Éva Standeisky, "Erkölcsök 1945-ben", *Mozgó Világ*, vol. 31, no. 2, 2006.

Tamás Stark, "Málenkij Robot: Hungarian Forced Labourers in the Soviet Union (1944–1955)", in Győző Cholnoky (ed.), *Minorities Research: a collection of studies by Hungarian authors* (Budapest: Lucidus, 1999).

Samu Stern, *Emlékirataim: Versenyfutás az idővel* (Budapest: Bábel, 2004).

Anna Szász, *Aki zsidónak vallotta magát* (Budapest: Argumentum, 2005).

József Szekeres (ed.), *Források Budapest történetéhez* (Budapest: Budapest Főváros Levéltára, 1971).

Gyula Szekfű, *Három Nemzedék* (Budapest: Maceneas, 1989).

Ernő Szép, *The Smell of Humans, A Memoir of the Holocaust in Hungary* (Budapest: CEU-Corvina, 1994).

Tivadar Szinnai, *Sötét ablakok* (Budapest: Dante, 1947).

Szabolcs Szita, *Magyarország 1944: Üldöztetés-embermentés* (Budapest: Pro Homine, 1994).

Szabolcs Szita, *Aki egy embert megment – a világot menti meg: Mentőbizottság, Kasztner Rezső, SS-embervásár 1944–1945* (Budapest: Corvina, 2005).

Éva Teleki, *Nyilasuralom Magyarországon* (Budapest: Kossuth, 1974).

Magnus Thor Torfason, Francis J. Flynn and Daniella Kupor, "Here's a Tip: Prosocial Gratuities are Linked to Corruption", *Social Psychological & Personality Science*, vol. 4, no. 3, 2013.

Loránt Tilkovszky, "A zsidótörvények, mint a Holocaust előzményei" in Randolph L. Braham, Attila Pók (eds.), *The Holocaust in Hungary: Fifty Years Later* (New York: Columbia University Press, 1997).

Marian Turski, "Bunt skazanych", *Polityka*, no. 16, 17–23 April, 2013.

Péter Újvári (ed.), *Magyar Zsidó Lexikon* (Budapest, 1929).

Krisztián Ungváry, *Budapest ostroma* (Budapest: Corvina, 2001).

Krisztián Ungváry, "Nagy jelentőségű szociálpolitikai akció - adalékok a zsidó vagyon begyűjtéséhez és elosztásához Magyarországon" in Rainer M. János and Standeisky Éva (eds.), *Évkönyv X.* (Budapest:1956-os Intézet, 2002).

Krisztián Ungváry, *A Horthy rendszer mérlege* (Budapest: Jelenkor, 2012).

Krisztián Ungváry and Gábor Tabajdi, *Budapest a diktatúrák árnyékában* (Budapest: Jaffa, 2012).

Bela Vago, "The Hungarians and the Destruction of the Hungarian Jews", in Randolph L. Braham and Raphael Vago (eds.) *The Holocaust in Hungary: Forty Years Later* (New York: Columbia University Press 1985).

Ernesto Verdeja, "Moral Bystanders and Mass Violence" in Adam Jones (ed.), *New Directions in Genocide Research* (London: Routledge, 2012).

Miroslav Volf, *Exclusion and Embrace: A Theological Exploration of Identity, Otherness and Reconciliation* (Nashville: Abingdon, 1996).

Tibor Zinner, "Háborús bűnösök perei. Internálások, kitelepítések és igazoló eljárások 1945–1949", *Történelmi Szemle*, no.1, 1985.

INTERNET SOURCES

http://www.liberation.fr/monde/01012333757-le-gouvernement-orb-n-impose-son-revisionnisme-a-la-hongrie. Last accessed on 6 February 2012.

http://www.kormany.hu/hu/kozigazgatasi-es-igazsagugyi-miniszterium/kozigazgatasi-allamtitkarsag/hirek/aktivabb-egyuttmukodes-a-zsido-kozossegekkel. Last accessed on 21 May 2014.

http://www.yellowstarhouses.org/last. Last accessed on 27 July 2014.

http://forward.com/articles/200542/hungary-jews-recall-nazi-collaborators-role-in-hol/#ixzz35KyxfIqC. Last accessed on 7 August 2014.

http://www.yadvashem.org/yv/en/righteous/faq.asp#1. Last accessed on 22 September 2014.

http://www.kormany.hu/hu/emberi-eroforrasok-miniszteriuma/hirek/vissza-kell-utasitani-az-embereket-megalazo-gonoszsagot. Last accessed on 21 February, 2013.

INDEX

© The Author(s) 2016
I.P. Adam, *Budapest Building Managers and the Holocaust in Hungary*,
The Holocaust and its Contexts, DOI 10.1007/978-3-319-33831-6

204 INDEX

Pusztai, Gizella, 8–10, 75
Pusztai, Lajos, 8

R
Racial defilement / miscegenation, 21
Reconciliation, 140, 159
Registry book of residents, vii, 20, 21, 71, 140
Rental fees, 2, 15, 16, 42, 43, 135
Retribution, 56, 75, 147–85, 191
Reuveni, Sári, 115, 141n17
Righteous among the Nations, 75, 110, 112, 113, 115, 116, 141n17, 190, 191

S
Safeguarding / Safekeeping, 47, 48, 132, 151
Second Jewish Law, 25, 26, 150
Semmelweis utca 4, 18, 155
Simmel, Georg, 57
Social capital, 45, 51, 102, 130, 139
Social Democratic Party, 138, 157, 158
Spatial control, 3, 82, 83, 96, 97, 112
Stáhly utca 1, 20
Structural holes, 38, 110, 139
Supervisor, 51, 81, 84, 96, 136, 137, 154
Surveillance, 7, 20, 56, 170, 188
Szálasi, Ferenc, 79, 88, 89, 93, 94, 97, 113, 129, 153, 154, 162
Szent István körút 13, 54–5
Szent István körút 15, 47
Szent István körút 18, 165, 166
Szent István park 10, 26, 27, 45–6, 54, 95, 96, 100, 101, 123–5, 127
Szentmiklóssy, József, 39, 58n14
Szervita tér 5, 81
Sziget utca 43, 83

Szinnai, Tivadar, 9, 37, 48, 52, 53, 95, 118, 120, 122, 140
Szinyei Merse utca 25, 21
Szív utca 17, 93
Szondy utca 18, 47
Szondy utca 42c, 137, 162
Sztójay, Döme, 22, 37, 38

T
Tátra utca 24, 102
Tátra utca 25, 99
Tátra utca 5/c., 99
Third Jewish Law, 21
Trianon, 18, 72, 86

U
Újpest rakpart 7, 95
Urbanization, 3, 10, 104n18

V
Váci út 28, 85
Verdeja, Ernesto, 109, 110, 112, 115
Vilmos császár út 41, 102
Vilmos Császár út 19/d, 56
Visegrádi utca 60, 128–30, 132–9, 190

Y
Yad Vashem, 113–15, 117, 118, 190, 191
Yellow Star house, 2, 38, 42, 44, 46–8, 51–5, 57, 58n14, 67, 76, 79–108, 123, 124, 130, 132, 134, 140, 164, 171, 188

Z
Zoltán utca 10, 173, 174, 176